AN ARGENTINE PASSION

AN ARGENTINE PASSION

María Luisa Bemberg and her films

Edited by JOHN KING, SHEILA WHITAKER and
ROSA BOSCH

VERSO

London • New York

First published by Verso 2000
© in the collection Verso 2000
© in individual contributions the contributors 2000
All rights reserved
The moral rights of the authors have been asserted

Verso
UK: 6 Meard Street, London W1V 3HR
USA: 180 Varick Street, New York, NY 10014–4606

Verso is the imprint of New Left Books

ISBN 1–85984–788–9
ISBN 1–85984–308–5 (pbk)

British Library Catologuing in Publication Data
A catalogue record for this book is available from the British Library

Library of Congress Cataloging-in-Publication Data
A catalog record for this book is available from the Library of Congress

Typeset by The Running Head Limited, www.therunninghead.com
Printed by Biddles Ltd, Guildford and King's Lynn

CONTENTS

ILLUSTRATIONS

FILMOGRAPHY

Sheila Whitaker

SHORTS

1972 *El mundo de la mujer*
1978 *Juguetes*

FEATURES

AS SCREENWRITER

1970 *Crónica de una señora* (dir: Raúl de la Torre)
1975 *Triángulo de cuatro* (dir: Fernando Ayala)
1997 *El impostor* (dir: Alejandro Maci)

AS DIRECTOR

1980 *Momentos* (scr: María Luisa Bemberg with the participation of Marcelo Pichon Rivière; prod: Lita Stantic; phot: Miguel Rodríguez; art dir: Margarita Jusid; music: Luis María Serra. With Graciela Dufau, Miguel Angel Solá, Héctor Bidonde)
1982 *Señora de nadie* (scr: María Luisa Bemberg; ex. prod: Lita Stantic; phot: Miguel Rodríguez; art dir: Margarita Jusid; music: Luis María Serra. With Luisina Brando, Rodolfo Ranni, Julio Chávez)
1984 *Camila* (scr: María Luisa Bemberg, Beda Docampo Feijóo, Juan B.

Stagnaro; ex. prod: Lita Stantic; phot: Fernando Arribas; art dir: Miguel Rodríguez; music: Luisa María Serra. With Susú Pecoraro, Imanol Arias, Héctor Alterio)

1986   *Miss Mary* (scr: María Luisa Bemberg, Jorge Goldenberg from an idea by María Luisa Bemberg, Beda Docampo Feijóo and Juan B. Stagnaro; prod: Lita Stantic; phot: Miguel Rodríguez; art dir: Esmeralda Almonacid; musical motif, *Carolina*: Luis María Serra. With Julie Christie, Nacha Guevara, Eduardo Pavlovsky, Gerardo Romano, Luisina Brando, Donald McIntyre, Sofía Viruboff, Barbara Bunge)

1990   *Yo, la peor de todas* (scr: María Luisa Bemberg, Antonio Larreta based on *Sor Juana Inés de la Cruz o, las trampas de la fé* by Octavio Paz; prod: Lita Stantic; phot: Félix Monti; art dir: Voytek; music: Luis María Serra. With Assumpta Serna, Dominique Sanda, Héctor Alterio)

1993   *De eso no se habla* (scr: María Luisa Bemberg, Jorge Goldenberg from a story by Julio Llinás; prod: Roberto Cicutto, Vincenzo de Leo, Oscar Kramer, Raul Outeda; phot: Félix Monti; art dir: Jorge Sarudiansky; music: Nicola Piovani. With Marcello Mastroianni, Luisina Brando, Alejandra Podestá)

PREFACE

Sheila Whitaker

In 1982 I was Director of the Tyneside Cinema where we also ran the Tyneside Film Festival. This event was dedicated entirely to independent cinema which was our contribution to the promotion of those film-makers who were breaking the boundaries of subject matter, form and financing. This was also the time when the Falklands/Malvinas Islands were being cynically used by the Argentine and British governments and Britain was split between the jingoists and those who abhorred the chauvinism, not to say racism, that supported militarism in defence of the islands.

During my preparations in those early days of independent cinema, scouring the world for those gems that we hoped would help rupture studio hegemony, I stumbled (I choose the word advisedly) on an extraordinary film from Argentina. It was *Señora de nadie*, directed by María Luisa Bemberg, which immediately I determined to screen in Newcastle despite (and because of) the conflict. So it happened that we closed our festival with a packed house and an audience that was clearly delighted with the choice.

Bemberg, then unknown outside Argentina and with only two films to her credit, was to become not only one of Latin America's greatest directors but also one who could properly lay claim to be among the most accomplished, courageous, complex and adventurous of contemporary film-makers. She had international commercial success far beyond any other Latin American film-maker, particularly in the United States where

Sony Classics, through the perspicacity and support of Marcie Bloom, ensured that all her films were shown. Inevitably though, her films were screened through the so-called 'arthouse' circuit which perhaps inhibited certain audiences engaging with them. Why wasn't she better known, why weren't her films screened in the multiplexes? Why didn't her success with her next film, *Camila*, nominated for a best foreign film Oscar, ensure a wider audience? A question, of course, that brings me back to where I began: Bemberg suffered, along with so many other fine cinema artists, from being outside the system, making non-English language films and combining profound (again a word I use advisedly) themes into entertaining narratives. Such films were increasingly squeezed out of the mainstream. By combining the personal and the political, Bemberg not only travelled the lonely path of independence but also a dangerous one to which she steadfastly adhered.

When Rosa Bosch, John King and I discussed the idea of editing a book on her films, it was with two aims. The first was to publish a tribute not only to a very fine film-maker but also to an extraordinary woman who had become a much valued friend. The second was to provide a long overdue analysis of her work which would further its appreciation and understanding as well as prompt further scholarship. Much of the material included arose out of a National Film Theatre/Warwick University homage to her in October 1996. If we also succeed in bringing her work to a wider audience, we shall have paid her due tribute.

Thanks are due to many who helped with this publication, not least to the contributors drawn from Argentina, Europe and the United States. Thanks must go to María Luisa's daughter, Cristina Miguens, who substantially supported our efforts, particularly by allowing us to reproduce photographs from the María Luisa Bemberg archive, Buenos Aires, and to other members of María Luisa's family. Also special thanks must go to Guido Di Tella and the Argentine Foreign Ministry for making a contribution to the cost of this publication. We would also like to thank the British Council in Buenos Aires, Mario O'Donnell in the Argentine Ministry of Culture, the Cultural Department of the Foreign and Commonwealth Office, the Argentine Embassy in London, and the Research and Development Fund at

Warwick University for their support. The text has benefited greatly from the careful editing of Carole Drummond at The Running Head, Cambridge. My particular thanks go to Patricia Maldonado who provided unstinting patience and help during my visit to Argentina, together with Mercedes García Guevara, Patricia Barbieri and Tita Tamames. Last, but not least, thanks to Lita Stantic, Bemberg's long-time producer, who, after the screening of *Señora de nadie*, also became a good friend and supported and helped (not least in providing hospitality) in all aspects of this project.

ONE

MARÍA LUISA BEMBERG AND ARGENTINE CULTURE

John King

IN THE FAMILY

'Anything, only not divorce', answered Dolly.
(Karenin) 'But what is anything?'
'No, it is awful. She will be nobody's wife; she will be lost.'

Tolstoy, *Anna Karenina*[1]

María Luisa Bemberg was born on 14 April 1922 into one of the wealthiest and most influential families in Argentina. Her formative years illustrate the advantages and drawbacks of her genealogy.

She evoked her childhood and adolescence in a number of interviews and, most significantly, in her film *Miss Mary* which explores the tensions within an aristocratic Argentine family in the late 1930s. It is from this privileged, yet potentially stifling, background that some of Argentina's most influential female cultural figures have emerged, in particular the writers Victoria and Silvina Ocampo. Memoir accounts – especially those of Victoria Ocampo – tend to see family history in terms of the developing Argentine nation.[2] Bemberg was fascinated by her distant relative Victoria Ocampo and once even considered filming her life.[3] She remarked in more than one interview that Ocampo was one of the most important women in twentieth-century Argentina, alongside Eva Perón. Bemberg could see in the life and work of Ocampo, a precursor: a woman who created her own space (a room of her own, to paraphrase Virginia Woolf) in a male-dominated literary world and one who fought to extend woman's place in social and cultural spheres. Born in 1890, at the moment of accelerated expansion of the nation's economy and population, Ocampo would later write: 'Argentine history was the history of our families, it is only fair to recognise this.'[4] How can the Bembergs likewise be placed in this family history?

María Luisa Bemberg's most popular film, *Camila* (1984), recreates the story of Camila O'Gorman, a young woman from one of Argentina's most influential families who was executed in 1848, alongside her lover, the Catholic priest Ladislao Gutiérrez, for having eloped with him. The execution was carried out under the orders of the federal dictator, Juan Manuel

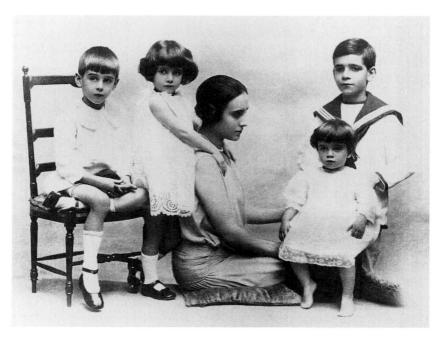

María Luisa Bemberg with her mother and siblings

de Rosas (in power from 1829 to 1852), the supreme 'father' of the nation.[5] Bemberg weaves the larger social and political forces at work in the development of post independence Argentina into her portrayal of family history and passion. Camila comes from a lineage of transgressive women. Her grandmother, Ana María Perichón de Vandeuil, 'La Perichona', was subject to continued house arrest as a punishment for her treasonable affair with the royalist viceroy, Santiago Liniers, between 1807 and 1809. The film opens with La Perichona's arrival at the family house and her subsequent incarceration by her autocratic son, Camila's father. From her early childhood, therefore, Camila has a 'forbidden' mentor, a 'mad' woman in the family attic who tells and recreates love stories with the active participation of the younger woman. Love is seen as the dominant transgressive force against patriarchal authority so the Camila of the film reads romantic fiction alongside political tracts and stories which are circulated clandestinely by Rosas's opponents, exiled 'unitarians' such as Esteban Echeverría.

Perhaps the most influential anti-Rosas essay, written in 1845, some two years before Camila's elopement, was Domingo Faustino Sarmiento's *Facundo: Civilization and Barbarism*, which was to become one of the vertebral texts of Argentine cultural history. Written at this time of cultural crisis, when Rosas was attempting to organise the province of Buenos Aires under his exclusive rule and shut it off from outside influences, *Facundo* broadly expresses the views of a sector of the Argentine elite which opposed Rosas and sought to promote a dynamic export economy linked to the expanding British Empire. The export traffic would pass through the city and port of Buenos Aires and yield a high revenue which would benefit the whole country. The central city of Buenos Aires would thus control a process which would encourage foreign investment, technology and immigration. Refracted through the Romantic prose of Sarmiento, this struggle between liberalism and autarchy was expressed in terms of a war between civilisation and barbarism. Barbarism was equated with the backward interior of the country, with the local *caudillos* or strong men and the Argentine plainsman – the *gaucho* – who were inferior social types who represented introverted nationalism. Civilisation could be found by adopting European patterns in political, social and cultural spheres. Argentina had to open its trade to the rest of the world, attract European immigrants and acquire at the same time values of sociability and respectability which would lead the country out of fragmentation caused by excessive individualism into a well organised social system. Rosas stood in the way of this imagined nation.

Rosas was overthrown in 1852, four years after he signed the death warrant for Camila O'Gorman, and with his departure the country changed rapidly. As David Rock explains: 'Politically, the country ceased to be a segmented imbroglio of *caudillo* chieftanships, and it gradually surmounted its interregional conflicts to form a nation state that gained undisputed authority throughout the republic. Economic expansion occurred on an unprecedented scale.'[6] Argentina was soon to develop into a society of immigrants and large cities, as railway networks replaced carts and horses, linking the country to the city, and steamships could offer rapid access to foreign markets and labour pools. Exports in wool, beef, hides and cereals were to become enormously profitable and attracted foreign investment. The Bembergs were to become a major part of this process. The first Bemberg to take up residence in Argentina, Otto Pedro, arrived in Buenos Aires in around 1850, the final period of the Rosas regime. He set up a commercial house which specialised in imports/exports following the liberalisation of trade in the 1850s: importing cloth and linseed and exporting hides, wool and cereals.[7] He married into the heart of the *criollo* Argentine aristocracy in 1852, taking as his bride Luisa de Ocampo y Rigueira. The family business expanded, moving significantly into beer production with the establishment of the Quilmes beer company in 1869. (Bemberg had experience of the German beer industry in Hanover.) By the time the fourth generation of the family had lived in Argentina (María Luisa's generation), the Bembergs were firmly established through marriage and through a diversified fortune. Their interests included tea production, milk, beer production at all stages – from growing hops and corn, to processing and bottling plants – rural and city land ownership and a wide portfolio of investments in other companies. Even though the patronym had immigrant origins, the Bembergs became part of the creole elite which, up until the late 1910s at least, controlled commerce and politics as an oligarchy.[8]

This elite had firm ideas about the education of children. This is what Victoria Ocampo says of her upbringing at the turn of the century: 'The education given to women was by definition, and deliberately, incomplete, deficient. "If she'd been a boy, she would have had a career", my father said of me, in a voice probably tinged with sadness.'[9] Lessons for girls were given at home by a series of private teachers, governesses and nannies. They stressed facility in languages, especially French and English, reading and reciting 'appropriate' literature in these languages, music and other refinements. At the heart of this endeavour stood the British governess. The writer and political activist, María Rosa Oliver, a close friend of Victoria Ocampo, has written with affection in her memoirs about her Scottish nanny, Lizzie Caldwell, and paints a picture of a whole community of

A typical society photography of María Luisa Bemberg (left) and her sister Magdalena Bemberg

British women working as nannies, meeting in their employers' houses or in the parks and squares of downtown Buenos Aires, where the elite had their town houses. Victoria Ocampo also wrote with relish about notable battles with her governess, the redoubtable Miss Ellis.[10] Little changed in the intervening years up to 1922, the date of María Luisa's birth. A traveller in Argentina in 1919, Katherine Dreier, remarked that a girl from the elite could look for a brilliant match in society and, to that end, could be refined but never educated.[11]

The Argentine *Who's Who* for 1947 has the following entry for María Luisa's father: Bemberg, Otto Eduardo, industrial engineer. Born: Buenos Aires, 23 June 1887. Parents: Otto Sebastián Bemberg and Josefina Elortondo. Wife: Sofía Elena Bengolea. Children: Otto, Eduardo, Josefina B. de

María Luisa Bemberg on
her wedding day

Quirno Lavalle, María Luisa and Magdalena. Education: Arceuil and the Institut Tannenberg, France, and Weihenstephan, Germany. Current posts: President of the 'Cervecería Argentina Quilmes', of 'Santa Rosa Estancias Ltda' and of the 'Crédito Industrial y Comercial Argentino', as well as a member of numerous companies and public bodies. His clubs include the Círculo de Armas, the Jockey Club, the Argentine Yacht Club, The French Yacht Club and the Polo Club de Bagatelle. Even a home address is given: Talcahuano 1234 and a phone number at home: 44–2356.[12] Here, in brief presentation, is the map of a life: an international education, a society marriage, vast holdings in industry, in land and in credit and commerce, political connections, and leisure activities in the most distinguished clubs in the land. And a dynasty of two boys and three girls. María Luisa has talked little about her family and childhood – she made movies rather than write memoirs – but references scattered through numerous press interviews have been usefully collected and put in biographical and thematic format in a forthcoming book by Julianne Burton.[13]

Of her father she has said that, as a child, 'I detested him. He seemed a sinister being, the incarnation of everything I hated. Later, I understood that he had noble qualities and that he had been forced, by his birth, to live an existence that he did not like. The Bemberg fortune had made him a prisoner. As he grew older, he became softer. He liked to draw . . . I had gone from hating him to affection and I went to visit him every afternoon, even when I was filming. I read to him. I had promised myself that when I saw him dead, I would have nothing to reproach myself for.'[14] Her mother, Sofía Elena Bengolea, a renowned beauty in her day, similarly offered little warmth or stability: Bemberg has talked of her as a victim who busied herself shaping future victims, unable to break with her surroundings or to encourage her children into independence. She only saw her parents for a few minutes each day. Her partly autobiographical *Miss Mary* offers a number of scenes of family life which she declares in a letter to be 'true': 'which I remember from my own childhood, although not from my own experience'. After listing some seven scenes, she concludes in English, 'It's all there: horrid memories of a terrible world.'[15] Her upbringing was in the hands of governesses. In an interview given in English to Sheila Whitaker soon after the release of *Miss Mary*, Bemberg spoke of filming:

> a tribute to those dear old ladies of whom I knew so many as a child myself and with whom one had a love/hate relationship. Even as a child of eleven or twelve, I was very much aware of the craziness of the lives of these women, what sad, wasted lives, looking after other people's children, in other people's houses, far away from home, as if very rich but not having a penny, just as alien from the kitchen as they were from the living room, because the servants thought they were traitors. They were in-between. They all seemed to be carrying their world in their trunk, under the bed, and they all seemed to mix one into the other, all spinsters, probably all virgins. All drank a little at night, I guess because they were lonely and depressed. They raved about their little princesses. They were very conservative, very Victorian, very repressed sexually, but usually with a sense of humour and tenderness. I was brought up by these English – or rather Irish – women. My mother preferred them Irish because she wanted to be sure that they were Catholics . . . I wanted to show through this English governess the influence of the English commercially and culturally on the Argentine upper classes.[16]

Some 23 governesses – numbers vary according to different interviews – covered the span of María Luisa's childhood and adolescence, some stayed years, some for just a few days. No formal syllabus was taught, no school certificate obtained: dance, piano and languages were the bulk of the teaching on offer. Her two eldest brothers, by contrast, went away to school, first to Switzerland and later to the United States, where they obtained doctorates at Harvard. The girls would follow their parents on long business and cultural trips abroad. The 'voyage to Europe' had been part of the elite education process since the 1880s, and María Luisa followed this route, though without the same flamboyance as earlier generations of Argentines who flocked to Paris at the turn of the century, taking over apartments and hotels in the most fashionable areas: Neuilly, Passy and L'Étoile. It was then that the phrase *'riche comme un argentin'* begins to appear in French usage. Victoria Ocampo, for example, describes the travels of her youth as a kind of biblical exodus, the family embarking with a host of servants and tutors, as well as chickens and cows to provide

Julie Christie (Miss Mary) and Barbara Bunge (Terry) watch Sofía Viruboff (Carolina) in
Miss Mary

food and milk for the long boat journey and the subsequent stay: not trust-
ing, perhaps prophetically, in the health and taste of non-Argentine live-
stock.[17] But it was on these trips, through first-hand contact with works
of art in galleries and museums, that María Luisa could develop her very
strong visual and aesthetic sense which is a hallmark of all her films.

From after the First World War, the United States was also an increasingly important destination for business as well as cultural trips for, unlike
Britain, Argentina's traditional trading partner, the United States, could
provide the consumer goods and the most up-to-date machinery and technology of the second industrial revolution. It became increasingly the
norm for Argentine men, like María Luisa's brothers, to study for post-
graduate degrees in the United States. By contrast, the women of María
Luisa's class – such as the lively Carolina in *Miss Mary*, who, as a young

María Luisa Bemberg
in her early days

girl, always asked 'why?' – remained at home, cultivating their imagination, but with little hope of any independent career. María Luisa's move from the family home came when she changed from being *Señorita* Bemberg to *Señora de* Miguens with her marriage, on 17 October 1945, to Carlos Miguens, an architecture student.

This date, of course, is one of the key dates in recent Argentine history, with pride of place in Peronist mythology. It was the day when the increasingly ambitious and popular army man, Juan Domingo Perón – who had been dismissed some days previously from his different government posts and put under house arrest – was released following a mass demonstration of thousands of workers who came up from the working class neighbourhoods and converged on the Plaza de Mayo, the main square, in front of Government House, the Casa Rosada. From this moment, Perón's election campaign gathered unstoppable momentum and he became president in 1946. The film *Miss Mary* also uses this date symbolically, taking 16 October, the eve of the mass demonstrations, as the moment when the younger daughter is married, and the dawn of 17 October as the time when the governess Miss Mary returns to England. It suggests that an era is ending for this aristocratic family and, by extension, for Argentina.

In many ways, the thesis of the film is accurate for, in the time span covered by the film (the army coup led by General Uriburu in 1930 up to 16 October 1945), Argentine politics changed dramatically and irreversibly. The 1930s have been dubbed the 'Infamous Decade' of Argentine history when a small group of conservatives – represented by the Martínez-Bordagain family in *Miss Mary* – maintained power through falsifying elections and banning other political parties. This ruling group also initiated economic reform that allowed Argentina to recover quickly from the Great Slump. Yet, as David Rock points out, 'after 1939, new political forces took shape, forces the conservatives were unable to control and which finally overwhelmed them. In June 1943, they too were overthrown by a military *coup d'état*. During the *de facto* regimes of Generals Ramirez and Farrell, the next two and a half years brought political change arguably greater in scope than any since the early 1860s. Its outcome was the election of Perón to the presidency in February 1946. Backed by a new movement whose base was the trade unions and the urban working class, the *peronistas* swept into power brandishing a programme of radical social reform and industrialisation.'[18]

There is still widespread debate about the true nature of the Peronist regime. For the purposes of this survey, it is sufficient to say that the ten-year period of the first *peronato* can be seen as a deliberate assault on aristocratic, liberal, European values. Peronism claimed for itself a new synthesis of democracy, nationalism, anti-imperialism and industrial development and railed against the undemocratic, dependent Argentine oligarchy. Whilst Perón's aggression remained at the level of rhetoric – he stopped short of class confrontation – his use of symbolism and mythology was deliberately populist. The image of Evita, the studiously cultivated resemblance of Perón to the legendary tango singer Carlos Gardel, the *descamisado* and the *cabecita negra* (terms used to describe Perón's working class supporters), the rhetorical manipulation of Perón's speeches and his use of radio and the press, all made up a new style that was anathema to liberal groups. He also embarked on disputes with certain members of the older order: one notorious dispute was with María Luisa's father. It concerned inheritance and the family control of businesses and financial services following the death of Otto Sebastián Bemberg and his wife in the 1930s. The legal battle was long and drawn out, but the Peronists became closely involved, favouring an aristocratic scapegoat whom they could accuse of tax avoidance and financial impropriety. In 1949, the government seized certain assets of the Bemberg financial group and imprisoned some members of different companies. Restitution would only be made following Perón's downfall in 1955.[19] María Luisa's mother and father spent most of the Peronist years outside Argentina in France and in Spain and the young Miguens family, now with three children, joined them in 1953 and lived abroad for two years. María Luisa's youngest child was born in Spain.

Although her views on Eva Perón would mature, later seeing her as a contradictory force – a woman who had helped women to win the vote, yet at the same time who constantly declared that no woman could achieve greatness without espousing a great man – it seems clear that in the late 1940s and 1950s, María Luisa would have shared a Manichean anti-Peronism that was the currency among many liberal intellectual groups. Indeed, one of her co-scriptwriters, Jorge Goldenberg, remarks in this book that her thinking on politics was not nuanced until she came to

María Luisa Bemberg and her husband, Carlos Miguens

study a particular topic in depth. Victoria Ocampo, who was briefly imprisoned by Perón, brought out a celebratory issue of her magazine *Sur* when
Perón was overthrown. It was called 'Towards national reconstruction' (*Sur*,
No. 237, November–December 1955). In it, Agentina's greatest writer,
Jorge Luis Borges, expressed his hatred of Perón: Peronism was literally bad
art, a substandard music hall act: 'There were thus two stories: one of a
criminal variety, made up of prisons, torture, prostitution, robbery and
fires; the other, more theatrical, made up of ridiculous events and plots for
the consumption of louts.' In the same vein, Victor Massuh affirmed that
the values of Peronism were 'suburban and their expression never reached
the quality of literature'.[20] By this time, Bemberg had returned once again
to Argentina, with four children and with a marriage that was breaking up.
After ten years of marriage, she separated from her husband and began a

complex legal battle – with his support – to have her family name restored; from *Señora de Miguens* she became *Señora de nadie*.

TOWARDS FILM-MAKING

> What is certain is that hitherto woman's possibilities have been suppressed and lost to humanity, and that it is high time she be permitted to take her chances in her own interest and in the interest of all.
>
> Simone de Beauvoir, *The Second Sex*[21]

It would be almost another decade before Bemberg felt that her children were independent and established and that she could pursue her interests in the cultural field. In direct contrast to her own lack of educational opportunities, both her daughters became university-trained professionals: one an engineer, the other an architect. By this time, the 1960s were in full swing in Argentina and Buenos Aires was an interesting and exciting place to live. After the cultural cloistering of Perón, when Argentina was largely cut off from scientific and artistic development taking place in other parts of the world, the 'winds of change' blew through Argentina. There was, of course, a volatile political situation, with Peronism banned, a sequence of weak civilian governments and the constant threat of military intervention, but this did not for a time affect the pace of cultural change and innovation. These were 'boom' years in Argentina. Just as the sale of refrigerators and washing machines increased and considerable sums were spent on advertising, so visits to the psychoanalyst became an integral part of middle class life, people flocked to the films of Ingmar Bergman and the French and Italian 'new wave' directors and began to buy the works of the boom novelists such as Julio Cortázar in tens of thousands, whereas before a traditional print run had been between two to three thousand.

The key book of the early 1960s was Cortázar's *Rayuela* (*Hopscotch*) (1963). Mario Vargas Llosa explains why: 'The effect of *Hopscotch* when it appeared in 1963 in the Spanish speaking world was explosive. It shook to the foundations the convictions or prejudices that writers and readers had about the means and the ends of the art of narration and extended the frontiers of the genre to previously unthinkable limits. Thanks to *Hop-scotch*, we learned that to write was a wonderful way of having fun . . .'[22] *Hopscotch* was effortlessly modern, cosmopolitan, intellectually sophisti-cated, heralding a sexual revolution: it became every young person's bible as he or she sat in the downtown cafés or browsed in bookshops such as Galatea, which was stocked with the latest intellectual movements from France, from structuralism, to structural Marxism (Althusser) to Lacan. A new newsweekly magazine, *Primera Plana*, was founded in 1963, which both reflected and directed this sense of cultural modernity. Publishing houses expanded, Argentine artists experimented with local versions of 'art informel' and pop art and theatre workshops expanded, encouraging local dramatists such as Griselda Gambaro, and translating and performing the works of North American and European independent playwrights. The hub of this activity was the Di Tella Arts Centres, which exhibited art shows from home and abroad, awarded art prizes, presented experimental theatre and had a training school for Latin American composers.[23] It was into this world that Bemberg made her first tentative steps, first design-ing costumes for the well known actress Mecha Ortiz in a production of Durenmatt's *The Visit*, in association with Marcelo de Ridder. The press reviews, which praised the costumes, were a great source of encouragement to her, in face of strong family opposition. As a child she had wanted to be an actress, but knew that this would be an impossible career for a member of her class. Even as a mature woman in her 40s, with four chil-dren, she faced initial family disapproval, a mistrust of the artistic milieu. This early involvement in the world of theatre would lead her later to found, with Catalina Wolff, the Teatro del Globo where, as she explained in an interview given in 1982, she became increasingly drawn to the front of the house: 'But instead of staying in the small room upstairs, where we had to talk about numbers, the size we were going to make the posters, what we could afford to spend on publicity, I was down below, alongside the director, seeing how a work was staged, how the lights were arranged, watching the set designer at work.'[24] After the five-year contract for the theatre elapsed, Bemberg decided to give up theatre promotion and tried to write. This was in the late 1960s. She sent in a play to a competition organised by the newspaper *La Nación*, a work that would be the basis of her first film script, *Crónica de una señora*.

Her initial entry into the film world was by chance: through her son, she met Raúl de la Torre, an up and coming director, who asked her to develop a script for him. How can we describe the world of Argentine film making in the late 1960s? Firstly, it was a world almost entirely bereft of women as directors or producers. One has to scour the archives to find names of women directors: there are fleeting references to Emilia Saleny and María V. de Celestini as silent film directors and short movies by Vlasta Lah in the early 1960s. There are more examples of women as script-writers; perhaps the most relevant for Bemberg was the novelist Beatriz Guido who collaborated with her husband, the director Leopoldo Torre Nilsson, on his film projects. This world of male film-making in the 1960s can be divided, loosely, into three tendencies: mainstream commercial cinema, often comedies, represented by the work of the successful production company, Aries; 'new wave' films with independent directors, often heavily influenced by their French or Italian counterparts, and an increasingly influential political cinema, as exemplified by the work of Fernando Birri and Fernando Solanas.[25] Solanas's *The Hour of the Furnaces* had been showing in clandestine fashion since 1968 because, after 1966, a military coup had brought into power an economically modernising but culturally stultifying regime under General Onganía. Onganía could not stem the flow of creativity in Argentina, but he certainly produced conditions – through intervention in the university, censorship and police harassment – of increased politicisation, where the dream of revolution and the return of Perón from exile as a radical leader, were becoming less of a chimera and more of a possibility. In these conditions, Bemberg's script about an affluent woman struggling against an indifferent husband and his all consuming business deals, whose life comes into crisis with the suicide of a friend, was frowned upon by the censors as being detrimental to family values, but it could still be made in 1970 (and it was premiered in 1971).

Perhaps the defining moment for Bemberg was the dissatisfaction that she felt with the direction of Raúl de la Torre. In her view, he felt no sympathy for the woman protagonist, Fina, and her existential emptiness. She remarked on this to the director of photography, Juan Carlos Desanzo, who replied: '"Why don't you direct yourself?" My reaction was . . . me? . . . a woman? I know nothing about the technical side. Desanzo argued that all one needed was to know the basics and count on a good assistant director, a lighting technician and an editor. He was right, as Françoise Pasturier has said, *it's time for us women to dare to dare*. And I dared.'[26]

THE FILM-MAKER

In *Crónica*, the character Fina is seen reading or examining two key works of early feminism: Simone de Beauvoir's, *The Second Sex* (1949), in the original French edition and Betty Friedan's *The Feminine Mystique* (1963). When interviewed about her script by the press, she declared herself to be a feminist. The history of feminism in Argentina from the late 1960s has received scant attention, unlike the many studies of 'second wave' feminism in Britain or the United States.[27] In general, at this historical moment, most intellectuals and young people were drawn more to theories of social revolution than to sexual revolution. The military regime was crumbling and talks were beginning that would bring Perón back to Argentina and to power in 1973.[28] Armed guerrilla groups, the Montoneros and the ERP – the Ejército Revolucionario del Pueblo (People's Revolutionary Army) – had started operating, whose myth was that of the heroic (male) guerrilla fighter, even though they claimed, in chants, Evita Perón as a revolutionary figure: 'Si Evita viviera, sería montonera' ('If Evita were alive she'd be a Montonero').[29] The appropriation of Evita was that of a proto-revolutionary rather than a proto-feminist. The spiritual leader of the diverse movements for social change, the ageing Perón, was hardly a feminist icon: he had married again in Madrid one of his couriers, María Estela Martínez de Perón, 'Isabelita', whom he used as a political expedient to mask divisions in the Peronist movement. She was not the stuff of Evita and she was strongly influenced by another of Perón's entourage in Madrid, the right wing José López Rega whom, it was widely believed, dabbled in the occult.

It was a very male world in the early 1970s: a government controlled by men in uniform, the political alternative an old, ex-army man, in exile, a militant union movement riven by factions between older, conservative, men and younger, more militant, men, a youth movement, of both women and men, who believed that liberation could be achieved through fighting in the street and guerrilla movements which had already taken up arms. The journals and publications of the day are full of Marxist theory (especially Althusser), discussions of Mao, of Vietnam, of Cuba. The slogan was 'Todo es política' ('Everything is politics'). There was little discussion of women, few signs of the debates that were current, for example, in the United States. It was a very different political culture.

In this world of male-directed effervescence, Bemberg and a group of friends initially set up a consciousness-raising group to talk about their condition as women. This grew into an organisation entitled the Unión Feminista Argentina (the Argentine Feminist Union), whose acronym, UFA, is a way of saying, 'I've had enough'. In the second year of its foundation, the distinguished Argentine feminist, Leonor Calvera, joined the organisation and María Luisa became a close friend of hers. Calvera would later write the major study on Argentine feminism, *Mujeres y feminismo en la Argentina*.[30] The group disbanded when the political situation grew more volatile. It was an initiative still against the tide: not many people were listening, especially after Perón returned in 1973, ruled for a few months and then died, leaving the reins of government in the hands of a woman, his wife Isabelita, who made a mockery of Evita's legacy and the whole political process. From late 1974 until the military coup of March 1976 there was guerrilla activity, right wing death squads acting with impunity, struggles for power in the union movement and inflation spiralling out of control.

Perón's return was still a year away when Bemberg made her first documentary short in 16 mm: *El mundo de la mujer* (*Woman's World*) (1972, 17 minutes). She took her camera to the Femimundo exhibition in Buenos Aires, a fair packed with consumer goods for women. The beauty items on display reinforced the 'ideal' image of women set out by the marketing men. She continued her writing, preparing a script *Triángulo de cuatro* (*Four-sided Triangle*) for the well known director, Fernando Ayala, which was shot in 1974, at a time of brief optimism for the film industry, with Perón's return, and premiered on 10 April 1975 at the Atlas cinema. This comedy drama of infidelity and sexual intrigue among wealthy couples had a glamorous cast, including Graciela Borges and Federico Luppi. It had commercial success, but still failed to satisy Bemberg, who once again saw a gap between her intentions and the final outcome. It was the final confirmation that, if she wanted to project her own vision and ideas through film, then she would have to direct herself.

This realisation, however, in her mid-50s came at the blackest moment for Argentine society and, by extension, for Argentine culture. By 1975, a number of film directors and actors who had received death threats from the Triple A right wing death squads, linked to the federal police – Solanas, Getino, Vallejo, Murúa, Norma Aleandro, Héctor Alterio – were heading into exile. This situation was exacerbated by the military coup of March 1976, which brought to power a junta intent on finally extirpating Peronism from the country through a systematic campaign of banning political parties, executions, 'disappearances', torture, censorship and generalised state terror.

Under these conditions of terror, censorship and increasing self-censorship, cinema in Argentina declined rapidly. Production fell and a diet of inoffensive comedies and musicals became the norm. There was blatant censorship which banned certain foreign films or mutilated others, rendering them incomprehensible. All scripts of prospective Argentine features had to be passed by the censors (military men or military appointees). Bemberg's third script, which she now intended to film herself, *Señora de nadie* (*Nobody's Wife*) was turned down by the censors on the grounds that it set a bad example to housewives, since it was to be filmed by a woman, it dealt with adultery and also included a homosexual character. The colonel in charge of script censorship remarked that he would rather have a son with cancer than one who was a homosexual.[31]

She was, however, able to make another documentary short, *Juguetes* (*Toys*) (1978, 12 minutes), shot at another trade fair in La Rural de Palermo, which explores explicit gender differences in the toys made for girls and boys: the girls' toys reinforce traditional gender passivism, the boys' toys, by contrast, stimulate adventure and imagination. In this 'empty' moment of Argentine artistic production, when survival was that of a 'catacomb culture' certain producers and directors tried to make decent and thoughtful films, using indirect modes to escape censorship. One such film was *La isla* (*The Island*) (1978) by Alejandro Doria, produced by Lita Stantic, who was later to form a long partnership with María Luisa. Lita Stantic was very important in facilitating Bemberg's entry into the film world. Even though the intellectual field was now fractured, the dominant discourse of the 1970s had been populist and revolutionary, offering a blanket critique of the Argentine 'oligarchy', to which Bemberg was seen to belong. She was also an aristocratic *woman*, trying to find space in a man's world. Eliseo Subiela, one of Argentina's most prolific and engaging directors of recent years, sums up the reaction of many at the time: 'At the beginning, I was on the defensive with her. She was a woman, a feminist and an "oligarch". Too much for a little "neighbourhood macho" who was still full of ideological prejudices.'[32] Lita Stantic had worked with the 'revolutionary' film-makers of the 1960s, had direct experience of the military repression that she would later explore in her movie *El muro de silencio* (*The Wall of Silence*) (1993)[33] and was very well regarded as a producer. Together they formed a partnership and a production company, GEA Cinematográfica, and would work together until 1992.

In 1980, Bemberg began to develop another script, in conjunction with Marcelo Pichon Rivière, a writer from a family of very well known Argentine psychoanalysts.[34] The references to psychoanalysis in this early work, later to be titled *Momentos* (*Moments*) (1980), were in themselves contrary to the dominant military discourse which had labelled many practitioners as subversives.[35] As a preparation for her first major directing project, to overcome what she often referred to in interviews as a paralysing nervousness, Bemberg went into analysis herself with the distinguished Gestalt therapist, Miguel Bayo. She also went to New York to study acting on a three-month course at the academy run by Lee Strasberg. She had her own money to invest in her film project, but this was the first and last time that she ever had to use her own financial resources in a film. Almost uniquely in Latin America, all her films were successful and profits could fund the next movie (in conjunction, increasingly, with co-production money).

In *Momentos* Bemberg explored marriage and adultery in a moderate way – analysed in this book by Catherine Grant – in order to escape censorship. Yet in 1981, at its first screening, it still caused offence. Bemberg has written of some of the extreme reactions to certain scenes: 'On a TV programme, I was denounced as the "feminist Armando Bo", for having Miguel Angel Solá naked in the breakfast scene. That they should compare that most respectful sequence with the use and abuse of the body of Isabel Sarli in all the films of Armando Bo speaks volumes . . . Another gentleman came out of the cinema enraged, shouting, "I'd have given her more than rice". (How old fashioned.)'[36] The film did very well at the box office, with a nine-week run and some 500,000 spectators. It also won the prize for opera prima at the Cartagena film festival in Colombia. Her career and her reputation were thus firmly launched.

In the early 1980s, the grip of the military had begun to slacken and film critics and film-makers grew in confidence. María Luisa was able finally to get approval for *Señora de nadie* which premiered, ironically, on the day of the Falklands/Malvinas invasion. But even then, being filmed and edited in 1981 and 1982, Bemberg felt it necessary to offer two endings. The first has the protagonist in bed with the gay man who has proved to be her constant friend and support, laughing at their misfortunes (he has just been beaten up and she finds him bleeding on the stairs of their shared apartment). This gives the film the symmetry of beginning with sex without love and ending with love without sex. The second ending has the protagonist going back to her children which, for Bemberg, was excessively ideological, an enforced 'closure' on what was a fluid but uncertain future.[37]

The film's release on the day of the Falklands/Malvinas occupation affected the box office in the short term – although figures were still a very respectable 500,000 – since it was a time when people remained glued to their television screens as the conflict in the South Atlantic unfolded. In the long term, however, the war and the subsequent defeat of the military government hastened the movement towards redemocratisation. The film sparked a lively debate in the press and was the butt of cartoons in several major daily papers, all variations on the cowering, hen-pecked husband. In one cartoon, a large lady is screaming, 'Machista, machista, a thousand times machista', while a puzzled little man asks, 'who brought this on me? María Luisa Bemberg?' In another, two women are talking while a tiny husband clings to his wife's hand, 'Ay Mechita, I don't know if it is because my husband, poor thing, is so insignificant, so useless, that I felt so iden- tified with *Señora de nadie*.' A third has a large lady exclaiming, 'Now, right now, you moron, you're taking me to see *Señora de nadie*', while her minis- cule husband replies, 'whatever you like, my dearest'.[38] At a time when the military version of the nation as family was entering a final crisis – as the recruits, '*los chicos de la guerra*' (the boys of the war) were sent out to the Malvinas with fanfares and returned in silence[39] – Bemberg was offering another view about honesty and openness in marriage.

In the period of increased liberalisation, which eventually led to the election of the Radical party candidate Raúl Alfonsín in December 1983,

Luisina Brando as
Leonor meets her
gay friend's lover in
Señora de nadie

Bemberg prepared her next film project – *Camila*. This, as Lita Stantic points out in this book, could only be released under a democratic regime owing to the sensitive nature of the topic: the love, in an earlier dictatorial regime, of Camila O'Gorman for a Catholic priest. In this climate of guarded optimism but still uncertainty about the political situation, GEA Cinematográfica arranged a co production package with Spain. Apart from guaranteeing human resources for what was conceived of as an ambitious historical reconstruction, co-production with Spain at least secured a release for the film in Spain. It was a topic that the church hierarchy in Argentina saw as threatening its authority. Bemberg was refused permission to film in any of the churches in Buenos Aires. She eventually found a priest in the small town of Pilar who was willing to let her film interiors in his church, but this man was later severely rebuked by his bishops. The film's subsequent release led to a number of direct and indirect attacks from church figures. The English language daily, *The Buenos Aires Herald*, to take one instance, reported on the deliberations of the Standing Committee of the Episcopal Conference in March 1985. 'Msgr. Carlos Galán, the secretary-general of the Conference, said some bishops expressed concern at the treatment given by some Argentine films to subjects which irritate the church and mislead the faithful. Observers believe this was a reference to the film *Camila*, a candidate for an Oscar as the best foreign film.'[40]

Shooting began days after the election of Alfonsín and *Camila* became the first and biggest box office success of the new regime. Over two million people saw *Camila* in Argentina, the largest audience ever for a national film. Such was the impact on the popular consciousness that, in the months following its release, one girl in every six born in that period was named Camila.[41] Of the many reasons for its success, one important aspect was that it was read by many as an allegory of the recent political terror, and that the viewing experience acted as both an individual and a collective catharsis. Such a reading was encouraged by at least one of the posters for the film which showed the final execution scene, the two blindfolded young lovers strapped to execution posts. Above them a banner headline read 'Nunca más' ('Never again'). This was a reference to the Truth Commission that had

Héctor Alterio and Susú Pecoraro as father and daughter in *Camila*

been set up in Argentina to investigate cases of human rights abuses by the military. The report of these proceedings was entitled *Nunca más*.[42]

Camila gave Bemberg – and by extension Argentine cinema – an international profile. It opened in 30 countries abroad. It was nominated for an Oscar for best foreign film but lost to the Swiss feature *Dangerous Acts*. This exposure doubtless helped to create the preconditions for the award of the Oscar the following year to Luis Puenzo's *La historia oficial* (*The Official Version*) and was a major part of Argentina's post-democracy internationalist strategy in film-making, led by Manuel Antín, the director of the National Film Institute, which offered credits for film making. The trade paper *Variety* noted this trend: 'Argentine films currently are one of the darlings of the festival circuit. You see them at festivals from New Delhi to Montreal, from London to San Sebastián. So invites no longer make headlines, since Argentine films have been winning awards at a dizzying rate . . . Never before has there been such a mass of tangible approval as in the years since democratic rule returned at the end of 1983.'[43] Success also gave Bemberg's production company easier access to international co-production funding.

Co-production is now seen by many critics as the 'fate' of Latin American cinema, the only way of funding projects and thus competing in an era of increasing globalisation. The case of María Luisa Bemberg adds a necessary complexity to what is often a Manichean debate. Bemberg was the first director in Latin America to make systematic use of non-Spanish speaking 'stars' in her next three features: Julie Christie in *Miss Mary*, Dominique Sanda in *Yo, la peor de todas* (*I, the Worst of All*) and Marcello Mastroianni in *De eso no se habla* (*We Don't Want to Talk About It*). Such figures obviously increase the possiblity of a film entering international markets. Yet they are not used as luminous 'extras', a situation parodied in Jean-Luc Godard's *Week-end* (1967) in which a group of Italian actors hang around the film set not knowing what they are doing, chanting, 'we're the Italians of the co-production'. Instead, they are the protagonists, with an essential narrative function that can both use and reassess their 'star' status.[44]

The film *Miss Mary* – the next project after *Camila* – was not written as a star vehicle, as co-scriptwriter Jorge Goldenberg argues below. It had its origins in the autobiographical memories of the director herself. A film about the education of young women of the Argentine aristocracy would be, of necessity, bilingual, for these were the cultural codes of that class in that era, not a concession to the English language market for cinema. A governess would have to be played by a British or a North American actress. The choice and acceptance of Julie Christie then adds interesting levels: an actress chosen for her considerable acting abilities, but one who is asked to act against her image of the 'darling' or the 'Lara' of the 1960s or her role in key films of British 'heritage cinema', by playing an English governess in a very different Argentine 'heritage' film.[45] Also, to have such a significant British actress working for months in Argentina at a time when Britain and Argentina were still officially 'at war' was a bold act of cultural diplomacy by both Bemberg and Christie.

In her outlook of looking to open spaces for her own work, Bemberg would surely have agreed with the remark by Argentina's most famous man of letters that to be Argentine was to be open to the heterodox, to the universal:

> We must believe that the universe is our birthright and try out every subject; we cannot confine ourselves to what is Argentine in order to be Argentine, because either it is our inevitable destiny to be Argentine, in which we will be Argentine whatever we do, or being Argentine is a mere affectation, a mask. I believe that if we lose ourselves in the voluntary dream called artistic creation, we will be Argentine and we will be, as well, good or adequate writers.[46]

The most important phrase here is the surrender to the 'voluntary dream'. After *Camila*, Bemberg knew that melodrama was a successful narrative mode, but in *Miss Mary* she chose a topic and a style that was much cooler and more distant. In the event, the film was distributed in 35 countries abroad and was the first of her films to be distributed in the English language video market.

Her choice to bring to the screen the life and work of the remarkable seventeenth century poet and scholar, Sor Juana Inés de la Cruz, presented new problems. In terms of her abiding interest in women and creativity and the ways in which creativity can be stifled, Sor Juana was an exemplary case. Here was a woman who, many centuries before Virginia Woolf had pointed out the need for women to have 'a room of their own', had joined a convent to escape the life of marriage and the court and to dedicate herself to science, philosophy and poetry. Her 'free' space was, however, confined also by the confessional and the sermon, bastions of male authority. Filming the life of Sor Juana, based on the biography by Octavio Paz, had its own potential entrapments. There was first the interest of a Hollywood production company, a negotiation that fell through partly on Bemberg's insistence on having her own, and not a studio's, control over the final cut. Then there was an interest from Mexico where Sor Juana is seen as a national patrimonial figure. This would, however, have meant filming on location in Mexico with Mexican crews and with a particular 'star', Ofelia Medina. But Bemberg felt confined in this instance by having to focus on another historical reconstruction, another costume drama. She came up with a solution that was more abstract. As Denise Miller argues below, she decided to 'de nun' the setting, moving it out of real cloisters into abstract sets filmed entirely in an Argentine studio. It allowed her to explore painterly, chromatic features in a series of tableaux that drew their inspiration from baroque painting.

Her following feature, *De eso no se habla* (*We Don't Want to Talk About It*) (1993), was based on a short story by the Argentine surrealist Julio Llinás. It was an opportunity to explore a different genre, a fable, through comedy. It was also a high risk endeavour, since to make a film about an ageing man of the world who falls in love with a dwarf from a provincial Argentine town was to court unfavourable comparisons with Buñuel or Fellini (especially since the leading actor was Mastroianni). There was also the need to avoid the temptations of the grotesque and the *sainete* (the farce), both of which have a long tradition in Argentine theatre.[47] In the event, the acting of the three main protagonists, Luisina Brando (Bemberg's preferred actress), Alejandra Podestá and Marcello Mastroianni, achieved the transparent 'simplicity' of the fable, whilst at the same time the film offered a political reading of a society in which 'not talking about' and trying to suppress difference had become tragic features of recent history.

A diagnosis of cancer in September 1994 found Bemberg at work on another literary adaptation, a short story by Silvina Ocampo, once again set, like *Miss Mary* and *De eso no se habla*, in Argentina in the 1930s. As film-makers Mercedes García Guevara and Alejandro Maci detail below in their moving accounts of her final months, this was a project that she worked on right up to her death. Hers was a deeply rooted Argentine passion, which brought a new inflection to international film-making as later chapters in this book argue. This ability to innovate from the 'periphery' was what Borges argued to be the distinct contribution of the best of Argentine culture:

A later study of
María Luisa Bemberg

What is Argentine tradition? I believe that this question poses no problems and can easily be answered. I believe that our tradition is the whole of western culture, and I also believe that we have a right to this tradition, a greater right than that which the inhabitants of one western nation or another may have . . . [w]e can take on all the European subjects, take them on without superstition and with an irreverence that can have, and already has had, fortunate consequences.[48]

NOTES

1   L. N. Tolstoy, *Anna Karenina*, Penguin, London, 1980, p. 419.
2   Victoria Ocampo was the most influential and the most notorious woman of letters and cultural patron in twentieth-century Argentina. Her important legacy was the literary periodical *Sur* which she financed and edited full time from 1931 to 1970 and irregularly up to her death in 1979. Her literary output was vast: she wrote a six-volume autobiography, ten volumes of *Testimonios* and a number of critical works on literary figures. She was a first-rate

translator. Her friendships covered the globe: she travelled incessantly, part literary ambassador, part cultural bridge-builder, part cultural head-hunter. She was a proto-feminist and, in her own life, she transgressed the rules of her class, pursuing 'forbidden' passions of literature and extra-marital love. For her own analysis of the transgressive nature of literature and love, see the most explicit volume of *Autobiografía Vol. III, La rama de Salzburgo*, Sur, Buenos Aires, 1981.

3 A film was eventually made of Victoria Ocampo in the early 1990s, *Cuarto caras para Victoria* (*Four Faces for Victoria*) directed by Oscar Barney Finn, 1992.

4 'La historia argentina, que era la de nuestras familias, justo es recordarlo.' Victoria Ocampo, *Testimonios* (*quinta serie*), Sur, Buenos Aires, 1957, p. 28.

5 For an account of the Rosas period, see John Lynch, *Argentine dictator: Juan Manuel de Rosas, 1829–1852*, Oxford University Press, Oxford, 1981. On families and children, see Mark D. Szuchman, 'A challenge to the patriarchs: love among the youth in nineteenth-century Argentina', in Mark D. Szuchman (ed.), *The Middle Period in Latin America: Values and Attitudes in the 18th–19th Centuries*, Lynne Rienner Publishers, Boulder, 1989, pp. 141–65.

6 David Rock, *Argentina, 1516–1982*, I. B. Tauris, London, 1986, p. 118.

7 See *Todo es historia*, March 1982, for a discussion on the development of the Bemberg economic interests.

8 For an analysis of the fortune of German immigrants in Argentina, see Ronald Newton, *German Buenos Aires, 1900–1933, Social Change and Cultural Crisis*, University of Texas Press, Austin, 1977.

9 Victoria Ocampo, *Autobiografía Vol. II: el imperio insular*, Sur, Buenos Aires, 1980, p. 16. This translation is by Sylvia Molloy in her book, *At Face Value: Autobiographical Writing in South America*, Cambridge University Press, Cambridge and New York, 1991, p. 57.

10 María Rosa Oliver, *Mundo, mi casa*, Sudamericana, Buenos Aires, 1965; Victoria Ocampo, *Autobiografía Vol. I: El archipiélago*, Sur, Buenos Aires, 1979.

11 Katherine Dreier, *Five Months in the Argentine from a Woman's Point of View: 1918–1919*, New York, 1920, quoted in Beatriz Sarlo's essay on Victoria Ocampo in B. Sarlo, *La máquina cultural: maestras, traductores y vanguardistas*, Ariel, Buenos Aires, 1998, p. 121.

12 *Quien es quien en la Argentina: biografías contemporáneas*, Kraft, Buenos Aires, 1947.

13 Julianne Burton, *Three Lives in Film: the Improbable Careers of Latin America's Foremost Women Filmmakers*, University of Texas Press, Austin (forthcoming).

14 'Yo lo detestaba. Me parecía un ser siniestro, encarnaba todo lo que yo odiaba. Más tarde comprendí que era un hombre noble que había sido obligado por su nacimiento a vivir una existencia que no le gustaba. La fortuna de los Bemberg había hecho de él un prisionero. A medida que envejeció se fue dulcificando. Le agradaba dibujar . . . Yo había pasado del odio al cariño y lo iba a visitar todas las tardes, aun cuando filmaba. Le leía. Me había prometido que cuando lo viera muerto, no tendría nada que reprocharme.' Quoted in María Esther de Miguel (ed.), *Mujeres argentinas: el lado feminino de nuestra historia*, Alfaguara, Buenos Aires, 1998, pp. 162–3.

15 'Muchas de las escenas *son verídicas y* que recuerdo de mi propia juventud, aunque no de mi propia experiencia'. María Luisa Bemberg in a letter to John King, 11 August 1992.

16 Interview with Sheila Whitaker in J. King and Nissa Torrents (eds.), *The Garden of Forking Paths: Argentine Cinema*, British Film Institute, London, 1988, p. 118.

17 Victoria Ocampo, op. cit.

18 David Rock, op. cit., p. 214.

19 For a robust defence of Bemberg, published during Perón's regime, see José Manuel Saravia, *El caso Bemberg en Córdoba*, Buenos Aires, 1953.

20 'Hubo así dos historias: una, de índole criminal, hecha de cárceles, torturas, prostituciones, robos, muertos e incendios; otra, de carácter escénico, hecha de necedades y fábulas para consumo de patanes.' Jorge Luis Borges, 'L'illusion comique', *Sur*, no. 237, November–December 1955, p. 9; 'Eran suburbanos y su expresión no alcanzó a ser literatura.' Victor Massuh, 'Restitución de la verdad', *Sur*, no. 237, p. 107.

21 Simone de Beauvoir, *The Second Sex*, Penguin, London, 1972, p. 724.

22 Mario Vargas Llosa, *Making Waves*, Faber and Faber, London, 1996, p. 248.

23 For an analysis of the Di Tella Art Centres and 1960s culture in Argentina, see J. King, *El Di Tella y la cultura argentina en la década del sesenta*, Gaglianone, Buenos Aires, 1985. On the intellectual climate, see Oscar *Terán, Nuestros años sesentas*, Puntosur, Buenos Aires, 1991 and Silvia Sigal, *Intelectuales y poder en la década del sesenta*, Puntosur, Buenos Aires, 1991.

24 'Pero en vez de quedarme en el cuartito de arriba, donde había de hablar de números, del tamaño que le íbamos a dar al cartel, de lo que podíamos gastar

en publicidad, yo estaba abajo, al lado del director, viendo cómo ponía la obra, viendo cómo se instalaban las luces, mirando trabajar al escenógrafo.' Quoted in 'La vida de María Luisa Bemberg', *Revista La Semana*, 14 February 1982, p. 57.

25 For a more detailed account of Argentine cinema in the 1960s and 1970s, see J. King, *Magical Reels: A History of Cinema in Latin America*, expanded edition, Verso, London, 2000.

26 'El me contestó que por qué no la dirigía yo. Mi primer reacción fue, ¿cómo yo, mujer, iba a dirigir una película? Yo que no sabía nada de técnica. Desanzo me dijo . . . [que] sólo necesitan conocer lo elemental y contar con un buen asistente, un iluminador y un compaginador. Desanzo tenía razón. Como dijo Françoise Pasturier, es hora de que las mujeres nos atrevamos a atrevernos. Me atreví . . .' Quoted in *Revista La Semana*, op. cit., p. 56.

27 For further reading, see E. Bergmann et al., *Women, Culture and Politics in Latin America*, University of California Press, Berkeley, 1990.

28 For an analysis of political activity in the early 1970s, see Miguel Bonasso, *El presidente que no fue*, Planeta, Buenos Aires, 1997.

29 There has been a recent account of women who were involved in armed struggle in the 1970s: Marta Diana, *Mujeres guerrilleras: la militancia de los setenta en el testimonio de sus protagonistas femeninas*, Planeta, Buenos Aires, 1996.

30 Leonor Calvera, *Mujeres y feminismo en la Argentina*, Grupo Editor Latinoamericano, Buenos Aires, 1990.

31 Interview with Sheila Whitaker, op. cit., p. 116.

32 'Al principio yo estaba a la defensiva con ella: era mujer, feminista y oligarca. Demasiado para un "machito de barrio" que todavía arrastraba prejuicios ideológicos.' Eliseo Subiela, *Clarín*, 9 May 1995.

33 See J. King, 'Breaching the walls of silence: Lita Stantic's *Un muro de silencio*', *Revista Canadiense de Estudios Hispánicos*, vol. XX, 1, Otoño, 1995, pp. 43–53.

34 For a history of analysis in Argentina, see Jorge Balán, *Cuéntame tu vida*, Planeta, Buenos Aires, 1994.

35 See Andrés Avellaneda, *Censura, autoritarismo y cultura: Argentina 1960–1983*, two volumes, Centro Editor, Buenos Aires, 1986.

36 'On a TV programme, I was denounced as "la Armando Bo feminista" porque había puesto desnudo a Miguel Angel Solá en la escena del desayuno! Que se compare esa respectuosa secuencia con el uso y abuso que se hizo del cuerpo de Isabel Sarli en todas las películas de Armando Bo me parece harto elocuente.

A la salida de una proyección . . . un señor salió muy enojado, gritando "otro que arroz le iba a dar yo!" (i qué antiguedad, nó!) María Luisa to John King, op. cit.

37 Ibid.

38 'Machista, machista, y mil veces machista.' '¿A ésta quién me la mandó? ¿María Luisa Bemberg?' Clemente, *Clarín*, 13 April 1982. 'Ay Mechita,! Yo no sé si será porque mi marido, pobre, es tan intrascendente, tan poca cosa, que me sentí tan identificada con *Señora de nadie*.' Fontanarrosa, *Clarín*, 19 April 1982. 'Ahora mismo estúpido, me llevas al cine a ver *Señora de nadie*.' 'Como quieras queridita.' Landrú, *La Razón*, 28 April 1982.

39 Accounts of the Argentine conscripts and regular soldiers who fought in the Malvinas can be found in Daniel Kon, *Los chicos de la guerra,* New English Library, London, 1983; and in Graciela Speranza and Fernando Cittadini, *Partes de guerra: Malvinas 1982,* Norma, Buenos Aires, 1997.

40 'Patria potestas has the bishops worried', *Buenos Aires Herald*, 27 March 1985.

41 María Luisa Bemberg to John King, op. cit.

42 *Nunca Más*, Faber and Faber, Index on Censorship, London, 1985.

43 *Variety*, 25 March 1987, p. 85.

44 See Richard Dyer, *Stars*, revised edition, with an additional chapter by Paul McDonald, British Film Institute, London, 1998.

45 For heritage cinema in a European context, see Ginette Vincendeau (ed.), *The Encyclopedia of European Cinema*, British Film Institute/Cassell, 1995.

46 Jorge Luis Borges, 'The Argentine writer and tradition', *The Total Library, Non Fiction, 1922–1986*, Penguin, London, 1999, p. 427. This text dates from 1951.

47 On these traditions of Argentine theatre, see Adam Versényi, *Theatre in Latin America*, Cambridge University Press, Cambridge and New York, 1993.

48 Jorge Luis Borges, op. cit., p. 426.

TWO

WORKING WITH MARÍA
LUISA BEMBERG

LITA STANTIC

Lita Stantic set up GEA Cinematográfica, a production company, jointly with María Luisa Bemberg and produced her first five films.

It's 2.30 in the morning and I'm with María Luisa, the actors and the crew having dinner in El Tropezón. *Señora de nadie* has just had its first night release and, in the midst of the celebrations, the head of production, Marta Parga, offers to go and get the papers so that, according to custom, the reviews can be read out loud. Marta goes off and comes back a few minutes later with the papers under her arm. In banner headlines all the papers proclaim: 'Argentina has invaded the Malvinas'. General consternation. We read the news on the front page very carefully before going to the review of the film we'd just premiered.

We did not know that at this precise moment the right conditions were being created for María Luisa's third film, *Camila*. This is because almost all the critics agreed that in María Luisa's films to date (*Momentos* and *Señora de nadie*), there was no belief in the possibility of love. This machista interpretation of María Luisa's female characters led me, a few days later, to throw down the big challenge: now you have to do a love story. You have to tell the story of Camila O'Gorman.

The recovery of the Malvinas by the military government and the sub-sequent declaration of war were also, paradoxically, a window that opened the possibility of a return to democracy; and the story of Camila could only be released under a democracy. Between 1930 and 1982, Argentina suffered constant military coups. There were brief democratic intervals. Even during the nine years of the government of Perón, a military man elected by the people at the polls, when César Amadori tried to film the story of Camila O'Gorman, Perón advised him against the project, for fear of the reaction of the church.

The defeat in the Malvinas certainly speeded up the fall of the military government. María Luisa Bemberg and her co-scriptwriters, Beda Docampo Feijóo and Juan Bautista Stagnaro, wrote seven drafts of *Camila* before the final version between August 1982 and July 1983. The first day of filming was after President Alfonsín came to power on 10 December 1983. The script for *Camila* was therefore written under the dictatorship. We made the film in co-production with Spain since we were aware that we might not be able to release it in Argentina. Spain would offer an alternative if we could not manage to get permission to show it in Argentina.

What was it like to work with María Luisa? The first thing I can say is that she accepted every challenge. She was a fundamentally brave woman – brave enough to leave a comfortable world and to set herself new chal-lenges constantly. At a time of life when most woman retire from activ-ity, María Luisa began another life – the one she had dreamed about since she was a child. This same courage led her to take on the story of Camila because María Luisa filmed a Camila O'Gorman who was coherent with her distinct point of view.

The six female characters in her films are transgressive, as she was when she decided to change her destiny. Her work is without doubt one of the most coherent in the history of my country's cinema and her characters are the best portrait there is of her.

To work with María Luisa was to enter a world in which one had to live for the film that was being made. Life was cinema and everything else took second place. She saw herself as rigorous, with a very strong sense of dis-

María Luisa Bemberg talks to producer Lita Stantic on the set of *Yo, la peor de todas*

cipline. She said that she could not waste time, that she had begun late and that each one of her films might be her last.

She defined artistic creation as a plunge into the depths of the unconscious, where dreams and fantasies reside, as well as nightmares and phantoms. She did not enjoy filming. It was only when she was seated in front of the moviola that she could relax and take pleasure in her work. She would often become ill during filming, but she would never allow herself to stop. She always said, 'I have very bad good health.' She meant that I am not feeling well, but I can go on.

During the filming of *Camila* she had a constant fever, but she stoically kept to the shooting plan with such discipline that she finished a week early. She kept so tightly to the timetable that her films, much to the delight of the production team, never went into overtime. She had great powers of concentration, even in her 'moments of vagueness'. I remember one story from the time *Miss Mary* was in pre-production when, ensconced in her office, she spent half an hour explaining with drawings the hair-styles that she wanted for her characters to a bemused extra whom she had called in thinking that he was the film's hairdresser.

She liked to surround herself with an excellent technical team and she knew how to get the best out of each member of it. She learned about cinema by watching films, reading books and making movies. She listened to the technical staff and she relied heavily on her cinematographers: Miguel Rodríguez (*Momentos*, *Señora de nadie* and *Miss Mary*) and Félix Monti (*Yo, la peor de todas* and *De eso no se habla*). In *Camila* the Spanish co-production arrangement made her employ a Spanish director of photo-graphy, Fernando Arribas. She wanted to keep Miguel Rodríguez with her and asked him to be art director. But art direction was María Luisa's strong point. She had a wide-ranging aesthetic background and she took com-plete charge of the set design, the décor and the wardrobe. Technical matters intimidated her but she was still able to transmit with absolute precision what light she needed for the scene that she was filming and she kept a close control of the sound track. She loved editing – this was her moment of sheer pleasure. Alongside her editor she spent long days eagerly marking each cut.

The pre-production stage of her films was long enough to have all the locations prepared and written into the shooting scripts. María Luisa always came with a very well developed shooting script. She shot with very little film. *Camila* and *Miss Mary* were filmed with 15,000 metres of neg-ative. *Camila* had a very long preparation time. It was filmed completely in natural locations. Since there are very few locations in Buenos Aires that date from the 1850s and we did not build any sets, the team had to travel to the five different locations we chose within a radius of 120 kilometres from the capital. Despite this inconvenience, filming was completed in nine weeks.

When we were distributing a film, we spent many hours talking and coming up with new challenges. Together we invented different ways of promoting her films which contributed to their box office success. When a film opened, María Luisa went along with me to check the box offices in cinemas in the suburbs. It was very amusing to see the look of amazement on the faces of the ticket office staff and the usherettes because it is not usual for directors in Argentina to take such an assiduous interest in their films.

In Argentina, the role of the producer becomes very blurred owing to a kind of 'director system', which has, in recent years, turned directors into omnipotent beings who do not take kindly to having a producer with opinions working with them. Paradoxically, the most 'auteurist' of our directors understood more clearly than anyone else the role of a producer. With her, I could be the person who, from the outside, could approve or correct the path along which her imagination was leading her. I helped her to tell the stories that are approximations of her life and I learned a great deal in the 12 years that I worked with her. She quoted Kipling who said that success and failures are impostors. The success of *Camila* did not change her, rather it imposed on her a responsibility to delve deeper into herself and to come up with her most personal and committed work: *Miss Mary*.

The idea for *Miss Mary* came when *Camila* was in post-production. María Luisa had decided to draw on memories from her infancy and adolescence and to put them together in a story that would once again feature her as a character, this time as Carolina, the adolescent who always asks 'why?' Every one of her female characters has something of María Luisa in them, but Carolina is unquestionably the most autobiographical of them all. When we were savouring the extraordinary success of *Camila*, María Luisa handed me some sheets of paper on which she had jotted down certain incidents that she and her brothers and sisters had experienced with one or other of their governesses. María Luisa had seen her British nannies come and go throughout her childhood and she said that each change was a profound wrench. *Miss Mary* was to be an evocation of, and a homage to, these women who spent more time with her than her parents. Her strict education had meant that she spent only a few minutes a day with her mother and father. With her special sense of humour, she sometimes called me nanny number 23.

I wondered whether this sketch of small anecdotes could be the starting point for a film and I felt that it could. I had already been working
with her for five years and she had often told me of the very special circumstances of her childhood which were for me both fascinating and
utterly remote. There was no one better placed than María Luisa to capture
the world of an upper class Argentine family in the 1930s and 1940s.
Before meeting her co-scriptwriter, Jorge Goldenberg, she tried to write
the script with her scriptwriters from *Camila*, Beda Docampo Feijóo and
Juan Bautista Stagnaro. This first attempt did not work and Jorge Goldenberg was asked to collaborate. He was able to structure these memories
and place them in the political and social context of an era of fundamental change in the history of our country.

With the matter of the script resolved, we needed to sign up an English
actress. I remember in particular the day when Julie Christie, after having
read the script, rang from London to tell María Luisa that she accepted the
part of the governess. Sheila Whitaker helped a great deal in this decision
because, in the post Malvinas period, when the wounds of the war were
still open, she had asked us for a copy of *Señora de nadie*, María Luisa's
second film – which was premiered on 2 April 1982 – so that she could
screen it in Great Britain. In this way, she became the first English friend
that we had gained after losing the islands once again. *Miss Mary* initially
had the working title of *Miss Maggie* but as soon as she arrived Julie asked
us to change it. She said that, in Britain, *Miss Maggie* would be read as an
allusion to Mrs Thatcher.

I remember also that on the day I went with María Luisa to pick up
Julie, María Luisa told me that we should not return by the motorway
since this route would give Julie an initial bad impression of the city. The
non-motorway road was much more visually pleasing, but also consider-
ably longer. On the way back, I was driving and I began to complain in
Spanish to María Luisa that it was ridiculous to waste all this time since,
during her stay, Julie was going to see a lot of Buenos Aires, the good and
the bad. At the end of our argument, we realised that Julie understood
Spanish and was amused that María Luisa thought she had to give her a
first good impression of the country where she was going to work. Despite

the fact that she soon got to know the horrible motorway, Julie spent four and a half months in Argentina after the filming and the dubbing of the scenes that were not filmed in direct sound. She became very fond of our country just as we became very fond of her.

Casting the protagonist for *Miss Mary* took us some time, as it had with *Camila*. With regard to the character of Camila, although María Luisa knew Susú Pecoraro, she had initially not considered her, since she wanted to have a younger Camila. It was only after a year's search that she tested her and gave her the part. But the rest of the casting for *Miss Mary* was settled very quickly. Sofía Viruboff had been suggested and eventually discounted two years previously for the role of Camila. María Luisa called her once again to test for the part of Carolina and gave it to her immediately. María Luisa chose her actors and actresses for their acting ability, but she was fundamentally interested in their photogenic qualities. It was important that they were handsome or beautiful and her sense of ugliness, or of what was not acceptable, was very stringent. She could never have worked with actors or actresses who did not have her aesthetic approval. She looked for harmonious features. Lack of harmony in a face or in a body upset her, in the same way that she got annoyed at a wrinkled tablecloth, a picture hanging crooked or a discordant note when she was listening to music.

When she saw her films after they had been released, she became irritated at scenes that she considered imperfect or that she thought could have been improved. When she was very ill, a homage to her work had been organised and I sat with her in her room watching the clips from her films that an editor had prepared for screening at that event. She had very little strength, but she was upset by the choice of the clips and the way they were edited. She asked me to take note of her observations. She marked the cuts between each take with anger and desperation: something was escaping her control. The following morning I got together with the editor and came up with an idea that saved the day: they could show the trailers that María Luisa had made for each of her films. I called her and this idea calmed her. The homage took place without her, although right up to the last minute she had insisted on being taken to it. She rang me to thank me for the words that I had spoken at the event. That was the last conversation I had with her. She died a few days later.

For me, *Miss Mary* is María Luisa's best picture, fundamentally because of its truth and because some of the scenes have a beauty and sensibility that can only be transmitted by someone who can evoke a beautiful lost world, but with sufficient distance to question the lack of social sensibility of her class. I can state that María Luisa always approved of a large percentage of the scenes in *Miss Mary* which was the film that irritated her least in subsequent viewings. In other words, it was the film she loved the best.

JORGE GOLDENBERG

Jorge Goldenberg is one of the major screenwriters in Argentina and Latin America. He worked with María Luisa on Miss Mary, Yo, la peor de todas, De eso no se habla *and* El impostor.

I have not kept the notes that I took when I was working with María Luisa on the scripts for *Miss Mary* and *De eso no se habla*. I regret this. Not because these notes referred to anything more than the work itself – ideas for new scenes, outlines of dialogue, changes, doubts and the like – but because they would perhaps have allowed me to give a somewhat less conjectural overview of the ups and downs and nuances of that experience. As we all know, the registers of memory do not stay the same and the emotional colours of the present tend to shade them at the very point of remembering. And, at this present moment, the death of María Luisa has coloured me and my memory, with intense emotion. So these lines must be seen in this context and should perhaps be taken as the account of a memory rather than as a true testimonial.

Let me tell the story then: it was just before *Camila* was about to be shot. María Luisa had wanted to exchange a few ideas on the script she had in hand and called me to ask for my opinion.[1] Her call came as a surprise. We had had no previous contact, we came from utterly different (if not opposed) social and political backgrounds and the issues that her films

María Luisa Bemberg
sets up a shot

dealt with explicitly had little to do with the issues that I had tried to explore up to that time. But it would be unfaithful if this account were only to include my feeling of surprise. The surname Bemberg resonated and still resonates in the established social imagination as a synonym for the upper classes and of enormous wealth, which has as its fateful corollary, the idea of tacit or explicit complicity with political power. As a left wing Jew, the son of immigrants, I could not be immune to these resonances. However much my conscience correctly told me to reject any preconceptions, I could not avoid approaching the meeting with ambiguous feelings, a mixture of prejudice, pride, social revenge and boyish curiosity. On the strictly cinematographic level, I feel that I was more serene, that I had opinions rather than prejudices. In the first place, though, I thought and still think that María Luisa's first films were excessively explicit and almost naively didactic in the illustration of her militant feminism.[2] I saw in the films the stamp of a personal tone and a sensibility that went beyond the manifest. Secondly, I rejected the way in which certain self-regarding progressives criticised her films (she makes movies because she has money to spare, was the imbecilic charge).

From that first meeting, I can hazard that we both, albeit urbanely, kept our guard up. María Luisa outlined her feminist creed . . . and I put forward my creed, which was an all-encompassing way of understanding and describing human conflict (in particular social conflicts). Then, as if the fact of establishing our respective non-negotiable areas had put us more at ease, the conversation became more nuanced and, much to my surprise, more amusing. I had not remotely expected María Luisa's humour, her lack of solemnity and, as I would discover later, her theatricality. Now I venture to think that it was at this moment that most of my prejudices began to fade and that the possibility of true collaboration in the future became tangible.

However, when some time later she proposed that I work on *Miss Mary*, a slight hesitancy delayed my reply. The nature of the project in question could generate additional problems to those which naturally arise in any joint collaboration. María Luisa outlined for me much of the subject matter with which we would be working: the main characters, some anecdotes and some situations. Although I cannot say that these were strictly auto-biographical, they were close, even very close to her life. From the outset it was clear that she was looking to deal once more with the situation of women across a spectrum that would cover different generations. Apart from the British governess (whose Christian name would provide the title for the film), almost all the main characters would be members of the same oligarchic family. Put in these terms, the project interested me and, in any event, only by working on it would I know if I could contribute appropriately. But, although politics proper would not occupy the centre of the story, the fact that the action would revolve around an aristocratic family between 1930 and 1945 made a political reading of the period inevitable, and I presumed that María Luisa's reading of it would not coincide with mine. Which was how it was – but not quite. In the end I accepted, still with a certain apprehension.

The beginning of our collaboration was like the first round of a boxing match, when the opponents are sizing each other up: time to take in the strategy of the other, a time in which one is a bit hesitant, imprecise and suspicious. But in the second round, María Luisa came out punching, very forceful and assertive, as if she had no doubt about any aspect of the project. This attitude disconcerted and even irritated me . . . until I realised that this was a spontaneous strategy, a way of testing out her ideas and starting up a frank discussion. Then our fight really became intense.

We did not follow a method laid out in advance, but rather dealt with problems as they emerged. So we worked by trial and error or, put more elegantly, by intuition and criticism. A tacit agreement slowly began to emerge during the course of our almost daily meetings: that we would present our ideas, images or intuitions just as they had occurred to us, without any reticence, even at the risk of seeming absurd or ridiculous. It was as if we were giving a vote of confidence to the productive nature of discussion and our exchange of ideas. Just as I cannot say this about myself, I cannot say that María Luisa never showed any signs of vanity, blind obstinacy or sheer cussedness, but I must emphasise that she never defended her ideas out of mere narcissism. Her intellectual and artistic honesty would not have allowed it. If some criticism or suggestion on an aspect of the work seemed to her really convincing, she accepted that the material should be deleted or modified, even if she had proposed it in the first place and had originally fiercely defended its appropriateness or quality.

I first saw this attitude in action when we came to discuss the question of the film's point of view. At first, it was not agreed that the point of view – as would later occur – would be that of the governess, baptised Miss Mary.[3] In fact, the possiblity of the narration having an explicit point of view had not even been considered. I cannot remember exactly when I suggested this alternative treatment, but I do know that, on a conscious level, my ideas were based on somewhat technical reasons to do with the treatment of time. After considering other possibilities, María Luisa agreed. Today, at the risk of over-interpretation, I venture to suggest that the deep motives for her agreement lay elsewhere and were much more significant. Either after reflection or through intuition (I could not know which), María Luisa preferred to 'transfer' the property of the memory or, in any event, filter it through the perspective of a foreign woman who did not belong to the family nucleus. It was a way for her to keep her distance, to exorcise the danger that the raw material on which the script would be based would remain attached to the circumstances and sensations of the moment in which they were registered and that, as a consequence, their verisimilitude would depend on their being lived experiences. The images and memories of María Luisa had to be transformed into the images and memories of Miss Mary. If we remained faithful to the process, this metamorphosis would ensure that the material would shed any association that might lead to resistance, awkwardness or reticence. Put another way, the gaze of the interpreter would be the means by which the characters and situations would become free of affective references to a place of origin and would develop – as I believed happened – in complete dramatic autonomy.

Returning to my a priori doubts and fears, the perspective that time gives has made me recognise a paradox that I did not perceive at the time. The most heated discussions that I had with María Luisa came about when our criteria for aesthetic appreciation differed, not when we disagreed over the political events that the film would have to touch on. I think that I did not appreciate this at the time because the way the work developed seemed to confirm my apprehensions. When it came to the passions and emotional conflicts of the characters, María Luisa dealt with them with subtle sensibility and with a particular feel for nuance. When, by contrast, the action demanded a political dimension, her proposals really irritated me, since they expressed the prejudiced simplifications with which the dominant classes in Argentina had constructed a conception of the country and of the world.

'This is going to end in a break up', I suppose I must have thought at some moment. And although I recognised that she had indeed moved beyond many conventions and clichés, both in her private life and in her work, I considered that these breaks were almost exclusively related to the situation of women. Even though in *Camila*, the socio-political environment of the age occupied a certain space, the analysis did not go beyond a generic defence of freedom and a denunciation of the crimes that are committed in the name of the state. *Miss Mary* required a much more precise and nuanced political focus since the story began precisely in 1930, with the military coup of the philo-fascist General Uriburu and ended with the irruption of Peronism, two fundamental moments in twentieth-century Argentine development. Of course María Luisa was aware of this. Furthermore, she was particularly interested in setting the story in this period. But it was evident to me that, apart from a few scattered readings, she also considered the political dimension from her own life experience, which in no way allowed for a consistent political analysis. As a result, her interpretation rarely moved beyond a Manichean frame and, in my opinion, merely expressed the tissue of loyalties, exclusions and prejudices that formed the stunted imaginary of the most primitive sectors of the oligarchy.

Put in these terms, the mechanism for an abrupt end to our joint work was in place and any discussion would have triggered it. But although there were skirmishes and even open combat, the abrupt end never came about and, as I said above, this area did not generate the most difficult discussions. I am sure that this was due first and foremost to María Luisa's intellectual honesty (an aspect of her personality that I am pleased to reiterate). Secondly, it was also due to the decision to use the point of view of the governess which was more than a technical decision. Miss Mary's gaze made us explore, now on the level of political interpretation, those primary images that generated the film project. What would Miss Mary see? What country? What human landscape? María Luisa worked hard on these questions, which led almost naturally to the questioning of all her schema (and many of my own). She was thus prepared to revise, for example, her views about social stratification in the countryside.[4]

I can guess that this revision would have caused her a considerable effort and perhaps even a painful wrenching. But conjecture aside, it is certain that her attitude was not an opportunistic concession to the democratic mood that seemed to grip Argentina after the dictatorship, but rather a demonstration of her commitment as a film-maker. This was shown to such an extent that, during the work, María Luisa was never bothered by the eventual reactions that her critical gaze might cause in her own social environment (a preoccupation that, paradoxically, she would show much later during the writing of *De eso no se habla*, which had little to do with any social class in particular).[5] For that reason, I was not surprised, some five years after the film was released, to read in the Santa Fé newspaper *El*

Litoral a declaration by María Luisa that '*Miss Mary* was not a betrayal of the social class to which I belong, since everything I say there is true.' Perhaps this should be read as a clever manoeuvre, an intelligent way of putting the onus of proof on to others (to use a sporting metaphor, to put the ball in the opponent's court). I prefer a more literal interpretation. María Luisa's words expressed her conviction – it matters little whether it was naïve or well thought out – that moral prescriptions are irrelevant in the face of an emerging truth and that the true loyalty of an artist belongs in this domain.

Before ending this account, I would like to make an observation that, in María Luisa's case, is not a platitude: her death really was premature. This is not a generic protest against the bitter fate of mortals, or an easy way of expressing the affection that I felt for her. It is an accurate opinion: I think that María Luisa was at the height of her creative powers. An examination of her filmography illustrates this clearly: from one film to the next she was refining the use of her expressive media and taking ever more aesthetic risks. The fact that until the last minute she was working on adapting for screen *The impostor*, a beautiful but extremely complex short story by Silvina Ocampo, is a clear proof of this.

FÉLIX MONTI

Félix Monti is one of Argentina's and Latin America's most distinguished cinematographers who worked with María Luisa on Yo, la peor de todas *and* De eso no se habla.

Some memories:

1987 A sunny afternoon in Mexico. The patio of the house I am in has the protective shade of trees. It's the house of Gabriel Figueroa [Mexico's and Latin America's most distinguished cinematographer]. We talk about cinema, not only about photography, but also about our work alongside the director.

A director is his gaze, which is beautiful, strange, secret.

With a director we must cut through the mist that shrouds that image, a search that is sometimes easy and sometimes difficult.

We speak of our director, he is like those old troubadours who went from town to town singing stories, and we are like his guide, his eyes.

What a strange pair we make.

'Come in, I want to show you my light exposure prints.' We go into his studio. Figueroa begins placing his print strips on the emeried glass, the faces of Pedro Armendáriz, María Félix, Dolores del Río appear.

In these print strips, which go from overexposure to the other extreme, the face of the actor gradually appears frame by frame until it reaches its light, as if emerging from a fog. This is almost a metaphor of what is created day by day in our work.

'Do you know María Luisa Bemberg?'

The question surprises me.

'Yes, of course.'

'She's going to film here in Querétaro, the story of Sor Juana, my daughter's going to work with her.'

'Will you do the cinematography?'

'No, María Luisa is working with a great friend of mine, Miguel Rodríguez. Perhaps María Luisa and Miguel have reached that union of two in one that we were talking about.'

1990 María Luisa has on her desk the designs by Voytek. On the walls are photos of actors. Today, we're going to do screen tests.

We work in the studio, the screen tests are there to explore the characters, to view the clothes and make-up. But for me it is also an exploration of María Luisa, to see in her face, whilst the lights are, one by one, working on the actors, the smallest, most intimate reaction; María Luisa speaks to me with her face.

During the weeks of preparation, the world of Sor Juana was our world, so Mexican, so Spanish. With Voytek, we explored hard light, and the struggle between light and shadow that one finds in metaphysical paintings.

María Luisa listens to us, she considers our proposal. She does not want the light to be too defined.

'Read her poems. I'm thinking about the world of the baroque', she tells us.

The first day of filming and the first day that I'm going to work with María Luisa. We are sitting in the patio of the Convent of Sor Juana. The studio doors are still open and the lights are already working on the set.

'Félix, remember Zurbarán's light', she tells me.

The great doors of the gallery are closing and they call María Luisa to go and see Assumpta.

I stay alone in the studio with her lights in my hands.

1999 I cannot speak of María Luisa in the past.

When Figueroa spoke to me about Sor Juana, without knowing then that I would be working with María Luisa, our conversation was about that sensation of working and feeling with a director, sharing the same quest.

Working with María Luisa has the same feeling as making chamber music.

María Luisa makes us part of her world, takes us along with her in her quest.

She does not shout or act like some diva, she controls us with her slight gestures and her soft voice.

JULIE CHRISTIE IN CONVERSATION WITH ROSA BOSCH AND SHEILA WHITAKER

In 1986 Julie Christie went to Argentina to film Miss Mary, *the story of an Argentine oligarchic family and its English nanny.*

María Luisa Bemberg wanted to see me in England about a film. I had seen *Camila* which I liked a lot. I liked the intelligence and the political and feminist mind behind it, so I knew that this was an interesting woman. At the time I was very keen on working in non-English speaking films or films made in non-English speaking countries so I met María Luisa.

One of her main qualities was that although she wasn't young she had a gift for youthful bonding, which is very appealing, so that you feel ooh, we can be girlfriends. I liked the things she talked about, I liked her politics. I asked her why she chose me and she rather horrified me by saying 'Because I think you're so English dear.'

María Luisa's presence was like that of a big sister who was never awesome or frightening, who respected you and wasn't patronising so it was like working in tandem rather than under someone's authority or tutelage. I liked watching her because she was learning on that film, and she very much put herself in the hands of her cameraman. When I say that she respected her co-workers I mean that she let them get on with it and it was almost as if she was learning from them as well which, as a very latecomer to film, was probably what helped her progress so very quickly, which she did from one film to the next. She made big leaps of style and moved ahead in possibility and imagination from one film to another quite startlingly.

María Luisa broke new ground – she did this with every film and you don't find that very often. Most people repeat themselves and grow over a slow period whereas María Luisa grew with each film. She didn't make us do a lot of takes. This was partly a financial consideration but also, I felt, evidence of the confidence that she had in her more experienced actors. Some directors, like Joseph Losey, have it all planned beforehand so you're working within a pre-conceived vision. Of course, Joe was a great director and out of that comes wonderful things. Every director is so different. In María Luisa's case she seemed to perceive each take as a new world, a new set of challenges, manifesting themselves in the real objects to be dealt with on the set as well as the actors and lighting. I'm thinking particularly of a scene where blood was found on the sheets of the little girl as she had obviously just menstruated for the first time. Because the sheets had light through them they presented all sorts of possibilities and she worked out those possibilities when she got to the presence of the sheets and the blood. Their actual presence dictated how she shot the scene no matter how she'd visualised it beforehand. María Luisa allowed herself to be very spontaneous because she had the humility to know that she didn't know everything. She learned and created on the spot.

She became my buddy and it's always wonderful to work with a buddy, especially when it's a woman buddy. It's the same as when I was working with Sally Potter, there's a shared complicity which is not only to do with the work, it's to do with one's understanding of life and power and who holds it. One's talking and sharing of knowledge on the surface may not seem connected to the film but it creates harmony. María Luisa and I bonded because we shared many views in common and when you're on set this gives you confidence, makes you feel secure and more relaxed. It's not necessarily going to turn out to be a better performance – there's just no way of knowing how it's going to turn out – sometimes a more demanding, contrary method of directing might produce a better performance, I don't know. I didn't think of María Luisa as demanding but other actors and crew might. As I've said, she didn't have that particular obsession with insisting on take after take which I think is a sign of insecurity in a director. She trusted her actors and didn't seem consistently to want something else, which is a kind of not letting go, not giving in to your actors.

As an actor, you realise that you can be giving a terrific performance but if the camera's in the wrong place the heart of what you are doing will not be caught because it's too far away or too close or whatever. Getting the camera in the right place for the performance and for the editing, and indeed in order to disguise things when perhaps you're not doing things so well, that's what makes a good director. There's no question that María Luisa knew exactly what she was doing, it was an instinct that she had. She understood the language of cinema which was quite evident from her first film, *Momentos*.

Miss Mary is a dense and complex film, full of ideas as all her films are. I loved the way the film was shot, the intelligence with which it was imbued and the way she streamlined her message without losing it – her themes of sexual repression, oligarchy, imperialism, class, and the disempowered person who in fact was in some ways the most powerful person – powerful because she was from the imperial power, disempowered because of her role as a servant more or less. I liked the way she brought these aspects out in various different scenes. Nothing was lost, if anything they were magnified and clarified in the film and I liked the way that she worked with the other actors, what she got out of them. It was almost as if, when I say that she wasn't demanding, I mean that each of us had a statement to make and she was almost secretly making that statement through us and we didn't know it.

She broke ground with each new film which is not to say that one film was necessarily better than another. The thing that was quite startling is that she, instead of, as it were, climbing a mountain in a series of ascents, each one that much higher than the other, getting nearer and nearer to the peak, was making sideways ascents all the time, she was moving up but in such a non-linear ascent that I think of each film (ascent) as a genre. That's what was really interesting, she seemed to think 'OK, I'll make a film in this genre now.' She did this very stark, almost actionless, beautifully photographed and unrealistically lit film *Yo, la peor de todas*, which was more like a series of beautiful stills and then she'd do a magic realist film – which was *De eso no se habla*, another kind of film-making and she did it beautifully. That was what was so impressive – she had that range. Her potential was far greater than anything she finally accomplished, sadly, because she died too young. Who knows what other genres she would have startled us with? – I know that she wanted to make a film, possibly contemporary, about a group of sexy middle-aged ladies who come across boys on an outing and the sexual pranks that they got up to – that would have been another genre altogether. One can't guess how much more she would have done but we have that small body of films which are startlingly different, each one from the other I think.

She was a vital, fascinating and fun person whose main areas of interests were feminism, sex and class interspersed with a not inconsiderable pleasure in things utterly frivolous. *La vie quotidienne* was not María Luisa's concern at all. She was completely focused on her work and on making as many films as she could knowing that she had limited time as a result of starting her film career so late. What an incredibly brave thing to do! It's a shining example of how you can start late and create a magnificent body of work in a relatively short time – a fantastic example because our world is not geared up to starting new powerful careers later in life. Of course not many people are capable of beginning a major new artistic career of this sort when they are no longer young. It's not a solo activity like painting. For her, deciding to make films was like deciding to be a general at a late age when you have never been in the army. It's tied up with her fearlessness in breaking into that male world in which she was aware that she was regarded as the enemy, entering what most Latin American males perceived as their territory (and not only Latin American males!). She probably had to deal with a lot of scepticism and that very powerful male capacity to humiliate and ridicule but she was strong and clear enough to see it for what it was, basically male fear. Being utterly committed it failed to daunt her. She didn't let her vulnerability in this respect get the better of her commitment despite the fact that she didn't really know what she was capable of and that she was venturing into the unknown. This is true of every first-time film-maker but with her the problems were magnified. In a way it's like having children late in life (I'm thinking of men here because, of course, women don't have that opportunity – yet) everything is focused on those children because the time is limited and it stops people being distracted by everyday banalities and the world at large which get in the way of absolute concentration.

GABRIELA MASSUH

Gabriela Massuh is Cultural Director at the Goethe Institute in Buenos Aires. She is also a well known critic. Here, in a paper given at Warwick University in October 1996, she describes the film world in which María Luisa Bemberg worked.

In Spanish there is a common proverb 'Nadie es profeta en su tierra', which can be translated as 'No one is a prophet in one's own land'. Sadly, it is often applied to artists whose works are first recognised abroad and who later become famous in their own country. Such was the case with Jorge Luis Borges, who was valued in Argentina only after having had considerable success among the French *nouvelles critiques* of the 1950s. There are many such examples in Argentina, the most striking probably being that of María Luisa Bemberg.

With *Camila*, her third film, María Luisa received international recognition which included enthusiastic letters from directors like Frank Capra and Lindsay Anderson. In Germany by 1986 she was already recognised as a very important exponent of Latin American film-making, along with Fernando Solanas or Tomás Gutiérrez Alea.

To the present day in Argentina and indeed in Latin America (with the probable exception of Cuba) María Luisa has not gained the recognition that her films merit. The way in which her films were accepted and evaluated by her colleagues (directors, producers, film critics, cinema fans – all those who we usually call *gente de cine*, film intellectuals) was in inverse proportion to her big success with the public.

María Luisa was very popular and her films had a very large audience. Not only did she have an audience, she created her own audience – that is to say, those people who went to see her films because she had directed them. I cannot give you the exact box office figures, certainly I know that each of Bemberg's films earned enough to allow the next film to be made. This is quite unusual in Argentina's recent film history.

So, let us return to María Luisa's relationship with the so called 'movie people' or film intellectuals – those who judge a film only in terms of its formal innovation (people who idolise Godard, for example). They (and, above all, the film critics) always had the feeling that María Luisa was somehow a maker of inferior or even minor films. On the one hand she had success – this is always suspicious – and on the other she made 'films for women', a label which in Argentina always implies something derogatory.

Let me remind you that I am speaking about film critics and intellectuals who are, after all, the ones who write the history of film. Even today, I'm afraid, there is not a single intellectual in Argentina who would dare to state openly that he or she admires her films.

Let us think about some of the reasons for this denial of due recognition by Argentine intellectuals. María Luisa was one of the first women in

Argentina who dared to admit her unconditional feminism in public. By the end of the 1960s, during the military dictatorship, being a feminist did not necessarily mean political damnation but it certainly meant public damnation. At that time, feminism was – and may still be – a demonic, taboo concept, something like the Erinyes in Aeschylus' *Oresteia*. Being a feminist was like being insane, irrational, man-hating and – even worse – lesbian.

That an aristocratic, rich, cultivated and beautiful woman from the *haute bourgeoisie* should claim affiliation to the feminist movement was absolutely shocking. And feminism did not only exasperate people from the high bourgeoisie, it also – and mostly – upset and angered the intellectuals. (Intellectuals are often Marxist, never feminist.)

The first fiction film made by María Luisa, *Momentos*, somehow appeased those who expected the horror of a feminist manifesto. Even though it deals with the process of a woman's liberation, the film also contains an un-expected aesthetic and visual subtlety. Furnishings, clothes, photography and actors are 'noble' enough so that the substance, the topic of the film, can remain on a secondary level, in the background.

At the same time the plot of the film belongs to the tradition that in literature is called 'Bovarism'. That means a woman who, following on from her husband's rejection, looks for redemption through the fiction of a love affair with a young man. This is traditionally a topic of the so-called women's magazines such as those one may read at the hairdresser's. Perhaps this was the secret of the success of the film, but the intellectual class announced it disdainfully as 'a film for women'. This label confined María Luisa Bemberg's films to those genres which are popular but do not make history.

You all may know that María Luisa Bemberg was the first woman direc-tor in Argentinian film-making. Until then this vocation had been reserved for a caste of striving, persevering, adventurous and strongly nar-cissistic males. The appearance of a woman here was unexpected, and many claim that her success was a product of sheer chance or, at best, because she only made films for women. From then on, nobody has ever taken the trouble to analyse to what extent María Luisa was developing her own film language.

In box office terms *Camila* was, not only in Argentina but in all of Latin America, one of the most successful films in the history of our movie industry. Enter the envy factor. You may consider it as a rather crude (or primitive) explanation for a phenomenon which is quite complex, but it is indeed an important factor in a young country with a limited market.

Those of you who have seen *Miss Mary* and are aware that it is her most autobiographical film may know that María Luisa belonged to a class – or rather to a 'family' – who owned, and still do, one of the largest fortunes in Latin America. The Bembergs were wealthy landowners with property all over the country, and their various companies are closely associated with transnational capital. They have embodied the myth of the Argentine brought up to be part of European high society, the sort of people who know how to lodge in great hotels but haven't any idea which bus to take from home to downtown. María Luisa was one of such people, so imagine this refined lady landing among the mafia of film directors. This was a novelty.

(I once overheard a woman, who was far from poor, say that 'Bemberg can make movies because she has a lot of money.' My surprise quickly turned to anger. In due course I got used to the idea that this woman had expressed the feeling that many people had.)

In spite of a good education María Luisa could not be considered as a highly cultured person. She probably did not have the time to be one. Be that as it may, she was not an intellectual either. (Had she been one, her films would perhaps not have been so good.) But she did have a great aesthetic sense, an enormous narrative intuition, a strong will and a rare capacity to use common sense at the right time. On top of that she was a wealthy lady who did not invest a single dollar of her own in any of her films. And those films were shown at the best international festivals. All of this was unbearable. And she was never forgiven.

Probably time will prove me wrong. I really hope so.

MERCEDES GARCÍA GUEVARA

Mercedes García Guevara worked as an assistant on De eso no se habla. *She directed her own first film,* Rio escondido, *in 1999.*

> There are moving images with sound and light that never leave the projectors of the soul . . .
>
> Ingmar Bergman, *Magic Lantern*

Those of us who knew María Luisa well rarely agreed; she was obsessive with her work, intelligent, stubborn, at once impulsive and meticulous, sincere, sharp, generous . . . always attentive to the needs of those around her, in cinema and in life. She appreciated efficiency, hated wasting time. But she could spend a long Sunday afternoon reading newspapers or seeing three films one after the other.

I gave up trying to understand her. She was complex, unfathomable, sometimes adorable and sometimes disturbing. Approximations aside, María Luisa is sorely missed.

We first met in 1981. At that time her younger son, Diego, with a group of friends and myself, was going round the world in a yacht. María Luisa visited us in Polynesia. She stayed for only four days, long enough to reassure her that Diego and the rest of the crew were well. And she left as she had arrived, asking questions about our life on board, interested in everything that she did not know about, slightly preoccupied: had she been a nuisance to us? Some time later, in mid-voyage, Diego and I got married. Then María Luisa, who scarcely knew me, wrote me a warm letter welcoming me to the family. Six months later, when we reached the port of Buenos Aires, she greeted me with a hug. My marriage to Diego ended five years later. But that initial embrace, which was then extended to our daughter Luna, lasted for almost 14 years until the evening of 7 May 1995 when she died.

Most of the articles that have been written about María Luisa discuss her history, her feminism and her career as a film director. But she was not an easy person to interview, still less to know; she did not talk to the press about her private life or about other people. She disliked endless banal chatter about any topic under the sun and did not feel happy talking about issues that she did not understand well. She thought that cinema was the only aspect of her that could interest people. And she was so rigorous in this that she was thought of as an inflexible woman. She had been educated to value austerity and efficiency, two precepts that determined her career.

However, alongside this disciplined person was the intuitive, sensitive artist; María Luisa expressed herself in her films and continually revised her certainties. She had the curiosity of a 15-year-old girl. She often became very enthusiastic when she came across an original view on some topic that interested her and it was impossible to distract her. She was, indeed, unpredictable. I thought that I knew her well. However, I never imagined what she would be capable of: gravely ill and with an integrity that could only have come from her passion for cinema, María Luisa prepared before us, with the utmost care, what would be her final act. This is the story of those months in which she transformed the suffering of a long illness into a period of intense creativity.

In September 1994 it was discovered that María Luisa had terminal cancer. A few months earlier, she had begun to work on a film script, adapting Silvina Ocampo's story, *El impostor (The Impostor)*. The plot, which is set in the 1930s, tells the story of Sebastián, a strange young man who lives in seclusion in a country house, and his relation with Juan, another young man of the same age who is sent by Sebastián's family to investigate the reasons for this disturbing isolation. María Luisa had been fascinated by the link that develops between them in an unreal atmosphere dominated by the vastness of the plains and the mysterious noises of the night.

She was entering a new stage in her career; she wanted to make a film that was different to her six previous ones. Taken by the project, she had begun to meet her co-scriptwriter, Alejandro Maci, almost on a daily basis. Now all she had to do was to deal with this irritating operation that was hanging over her and get well as soon as possible so that she could get back to her work routine.

At that time, I was preparing my first work as a film director, a short that María Luisa was financing because, as she said, 'If one day you want to film a feature, you must first have done a short, which will be your letter of introduction.' She knew the importance of encouraging those just starting out. She had made her first short, *El mundo de la mujer* (*Woman's World*) full of doubts and fears at the age of 50. Now she was helping me to take that fearsome first step.

To our initial surprise and subsequent dismay, the operation was not a success. And although there was the possibility of treatment, the situation was not hopeful. María Luisa spent those days in hospital without really knowing the truth of her condition: the important thing was for her to recover quickly so as to be able to face up to what would come next. I visited her daily, almost always just for a few minutes, so as not to tire her. She slowly got her strength back, she could sit up and, later, get out of bed. One afternoon I went to visit her. She was sitting in front of the window, with a blanket over her legs, staring at the blue sky. I sat beside her and told her that I had come to ask for her help. She turned to me. I then explained that I had brought along the photos of three possible leads for my short and I needed her opinion. She looked at me affectionately, but apologised: 'I am very tired, I just want to sleep.' Without giving it much thought, I opened the folder with the photos and said that she had encouraged me to make the short and that she could not abandon me now, that I only needed ten minutes of her time and after that she could sleep all day. Without much strength to argue and, rather reluctantly, she put on her glasses and made herself more comfortable. She began to look closely at the first photo, then at the second and the third. She asked me which one I preferred; what was I looking for exactly? I explained to her what I wanted and why the first was my choice. She listened to me carefully, but she preferred the second, she had a more interesting look . . . and the third really did seem characterless . . . although you should try testing them . . . I stole a glance at her. Her tiredness and apathy had disappeared. The ten minutes became 20, then 30 . . . at the end of which time, I had things much clearer and María Luisa asked me about the rest of the cast. I told her that I'd bring along more material the next day, grabbed my things, kissed her and said goodbye. She smiled at me again and closed her eyes. That night, about ten, my phone rang at home. It was María Luisa. I was very surprised that she was calling me from the hospital. She told me that she'd had a good day and added, 'I want to thank you.' I didn't know what to say. 'Me? Why?' There was a very short pause and then she answered, 'because you didn't let me sleep, and I know that if I sleep, I'm not going to recover.'

SEVEN MONTHS OF WORK

Her words in some way confirmed what I had intuited: María Luisa needed a project. Obviously at that moment it was not possible for her to work, the doctors would not have allowed it. But I had seen her transformation: a few minutes of work had produced an energy that even she did not know she had. The next step was to talk to Alejandro: I told him what I thought and I suggested that on his next visit, he should start talking to her about the script that they had begun to write together a short while ago. The idea was that slowly, without any strain, they should take up the story at the point that they had left it. That is what they did: ten minutes one afternoon, 15 minutes the next day, they just spoke about the script as if it were any other topic. Nothing suggested that these quiet conversations were about work. When María Luisa was strong enough to leave the hospital, her children and the doctors explained to her the outcome of the operation; for the time being she had to suspend all her activities and begin a treatment in a New York clinic. That same day I went to see her. I found her upset, discontented. This was not part of her plans with all there was to do! To some degree her ill humour reassured me, it was clear that she was not going to give up. Soon after, she left for New York.

In the meantime, the time for filming my short was approaching. The night before the shoot, she phoned me, told me to keep calm, to concentrate on the actors during the filming and that everything would turn out well. Three days later, when I finished the shoot, I sent her a long fax giving her all the details. I learned later that on that night she had been feeling very bad but had asked for the fax to be read to her and, while she was listening, with her eyes closed, she'd said, 'excellent . . . excellent'.

A month later she returned to Buenos Aires. She was a little weaker and tired of so much doctoring. She had felt very homesick and, on the way back to her house from the airport, she asked me if the jacarandas had flowered. She wanted to see them from her balcony.

She immediately took up the script of *El impostor* again. At the beginning, when there were more hours during which she felt well, she could work, be with her family and receive callers. But her health worsened. Then she had to find a balance: gradually, as if she were editing the film of her own life, she began to cut what she did not consider essential. And she reserved her few hours of health for her children and the script. She worked every day, for one, two or three hours. In these moments it was impossible to interrupt her: on more than one occasion I left without seeing her. But I was not worried since I knew what was happening almost every day: when Alejandro arrived, María Luisa, who was almost always reclining in a chair, with a blanket around her, greeted him with a faint voice. He sat beside her and began to read the scenes from the previous day that he had typed up. She listened in silence, in the same position until a word or a piece of dialogue struck her. Then she sat up, threw the blanket to one side and stopped the reading in a tone of voice that was now not so weak. As the minutes passed and they both got into the story, María Luisa, as if she had drunk a magic potion, recovered her strength and even her appetite. On many occasions the afternoon sun caught them having tea with biscuits, surrounded by papers, discussing changes and imagining new scenes. Day after day, week after week, isolated from the world, one could hear them inventing situations and conflicts which, for those hours, were more real than the illness.

At the beginning of January 1995, María Luisa thought that she could shortly make a plan for the shoot. She was already thinking about the setting and the costumes and the possible actors for the leading roles. But this hope faded at the end of the month when the doctors announced that the treatment that she had received had not been successful.

EL IMPOSTOR

My short was finished. María Luisa was the first to see it and to point out to me my beginner's good points and mistakes. Hearing her speak, I remembered all the times that she had replied to my queries, at any hour of the day and night, and how much she had been with me and helped me. I then felt what she termed 'the most lonely of lonelinesses', that moment at which nobody counts, the moment of facing up to creation: from here on, I would have to work and make decisions on my own. The problem was that I did not know if I was ready. María Luisa gave me the answer much later, without knowing it, through a book that she had lent me: *Hitchcock* by François Truffaut which I read slowly each night, pausing to read the countless marks and notes that I always found in María Luisa's books.

At the beginning of April, her friend Taco Larreta came especially from Montevideo for a reading of the first version of the script. It was a meeting of friends and colleagues in the film world, but, more particularly, it was a work meeting. María Luisa had expressly asked us to come with pen and paper to note down our impressions. Once the reading was over, we all made different suggestions. María Luisa listened carefully to us and thanked us for our comments. But she had been watching us all the time, had heard our silences and our noted our reactions and she concluded that the script still had several weak points and would need correcting. Her work routine continued as before, although now there were no more sunny afternoons in the living room because María Luisa spent most of the time in bed. It was now clear that she would not be able to direct the film. But it was not necessary to tell her: she herself accepted that reality. But what nobody expected was her subsequent reaction: her wish that *El impostor* should be filmed with or without her. On 25 April, in a smaller meeting, the second version of the script was read out. María Luisa, who was now very weak, was not present, but she asked that the meeting take place in her house so that from her bedroom she could hear the sounds of the reading and sense the atmosphere generated by the scenes and the dialogues. The following day she asked me to call. I went into her darkened room, sat down beside her and she opened her eyes. I got close to her so that she could hear me clearly and told her that the script had improved a great deal and that everyone had liked the changes. Without speaking, she indicated that she wanted more details. I told her how the meeting had been, who had said what, and how much we had missed her. Then she closed her eyes and I stayed with her, in silence. A few minutes passed, María Luisa was breathing softly, as if she were asleep. Suddenly, with her eyes closed, almost inaudibly, she said one word. I got closer still and asked her to repeat it. She took a breath and said, 'frogs'. I then replied in her ear, 'Yes, in the scenes in the country, do you want to see them or hear them?' She took a second and replied 'both'. A few days later, in her house, surrounded by her children and those of us who loved her best, María Luisa died.

On my dressing table was the book that I had not returned to her. One night I began to read it again. Suddenly, when I began a new chapter, I saw that there were no more marks or notes. Somewhat put out, I flicked the pages that remained: there were more than a hundred left that had not been touched. I put the book down. María Luisa was telling me: 'I've helped you this far, from now on the marks will be yours.' It was clear: she was telling me that I was ready. And I believed her, what else could I do?

I picked up a pencil and began reading: page 215, 216, 217 . . . I was now completely focused on the text when, hidden on a page, I found the tiniest mark, the last one. I smiled. She had often done this sort of thing to me.

December 1996

ALEJANDRO MACI

Alejandro Maci worked as an assistant on Yo, la peor de todas *and* De eso no se habla. *He also assisted with the script of* El impostor *which he directed after María Luisa Bemberg's death.*

> *The Swans*
> Si los riesgos del mar considerara
> Ninguno se embarcara,
> Si antes viera bien su peligro
> Ninguno se atreviera,
> Ni al bravo toro osado provocara.
>
>   Sor Juana Inés de la Cruz

The first time I saw María Luisa Bemberg she was working at her desk. The press had led me to believe her to be a rather cold person so I was surprised to find her radiant. I wanted to see her because I knew she was working on a new project about the life and work of Sor Juana Inés de la Cruz based on an essay by Octavio Paz. I was trying to start my career in cinema and I was interested in the possibility of watching the process of filming to see exactly how the set works.

'That's no good', she spat out brusquely. From then on her smile disappeared and she carried on talking in a strained tone. 'You should work as a runner. That's the only way to learn cinema in Argentina. Anything else is a waste of time.' She then proceeded to explain to me the nature of the job: a sort of internship for the period of filming. I was caught off guard. On the one hand I had not expected this much. On the other, given the tone the conversation had taken on, it did not sound as though she was proposing anything concrete. She added 'but I've already got about ten people who want that job and they were all here before you'. I did not know what to say. My initial enthusiasm evaporated totally. I wanted to leave as this person disorientated me. But then something strange happened. After she had announced the worst, some liberating mechanism was triggered off in her and she relaxed. She smiled again and it seemed as though we could now talk without restraint. It was as though any ties that we had made were broken.

Entrenched in her own distance, María Luisa shone once more. I told her that I had recently finished my degree in philosophy and of my endless theatre studies. I told her that although cinema was what I most desired it was the last thing on my way. This led the conversation to her own story and how she found cinema late in her life and how she put things off. She talked about time, the acting course she took with Strasberg in New York, of her concern with always giving her fiction a feminine subtext and how that made her choices harder and more of a challenge. Then she talked about Sor Juana and her poems. The conversation went on for a while, at least a quarter of an hour or longer. In the end, smiling once more, María Luisa made it clear that my time was up. Almost as a way of tying things up she informed me that she would let me know when she took the decision about an assistant. I thanked her for her time and was about to leave.

As I started to gather together my things María Luisa asked me whether I had seen anything in the cinema that had attracted my attention recently. I did not hesitate to reply *Betrayal*, the filmed version of Pinter's play by the same name. My choice seemed to intrigue her and she asked me why. I told her about my predilection for Pinter's work, the plays I had been most drawn to and the particular narrative interest that *Betrayal* held for me, told 'backwards', in that sort of inversion of a tale where the end works as the beginning. The conversation started again and she asked me to sit down once more. She talked about Pinter, whose plays she knew well. We had a common interest in his dialogues, his estranged nature, the way in which he introduces the existential void into the characters' everyday routine. María Luisa lit a cigarette. Somehow the fragile quality of the interview dissipated and the meeting took on a more solid dimension.

The conversation took off again. Half an hour later we were laughing about the difficult paths Pinter had led us down. I was still wearing my jacket and holding my bag. María Luisa seemed like a different person, freed from an examining attitude. Later I would learn that this was her way of protecting herself from strangers.

María Luisa was someone who lacked that social grace of pretending to be interested when she was not. But when something genuinely interested her a primary and childlike phenomenon took her over. Her whole body lost its bearing, her look became transparent and she let herself be invaded by an endless capacity for surprise. Something hidden became visible in her: perhaps it was her very fragility, which she always tried to hide, as this was something she disliked in people and was her sore point. Any sign of fragility in herself or others irritated María Luisa.

A fortnight after our meeting, Julia Vergara – who had obtained the interview for me, informed me that María Luisa had chosen me. After that, and because of the many delays to the project about Sor Juana, I had the opportunity to get to know her better. It did not take us long to become good friends. During the period between filming on location in Mexico and filming in the studio, María Luisa was extremely generous towards me. We often spoke of the cinema, of Rufino Tamayo's paintings (whose colours reminded her of baroque Mexico), of her preferred maestro Bresson's clean use of the camera, of Juana's Phaethon sonnet, of the complex relationship between Juana and the vicereine, of the book about the plague which Gabriel García Márquez lent her with engravings which inspired several scenes in the film and of her search for the actress for the role of the nun-poet.

In one way, this period of reviewing the project became a unique period of insight which let me see close up just how María Luisa, who always had an eye for the artistic, could put a pictorial composition into the framework of a cinematographical creation and see exactly how non-fiction (Octavio Paz's essay) could become fiction and could become cinema.

I have often thought how in some sense my connection with María Luisa is thanks to the fortuitous mention of Harold Pinter's name. That April day, when the interview was at an end, one comment made the conversation last for several years more. Destiny only intervened to seal a pact: briefly and eternally. It is curious how much later, on starting a new project, this time based on one of Bioy Casares's detective stories, I put forward Pinter's name to adapt the story. At the time it seemed like a remote and harebrained possibility. Chance would have it that around then we had to travel to England as the film *De eso no se habla* was being shown in the London Film Festival. Inspired by the possibility and with the help of Julie Christie and Sheila Whitaker, we managed to get an interview with Harold Pinter himself. The meeting was unforgettable: lunch at the old restaurant Amy's. We gave him a translation of the story in question and a few days later we met up again at his studio in Chelsea. He had found the story intriguing, and was interested in the ironic tone which Bioy used to characterise the intervention of destiny. The possibility was left open: Pinter had the time to write the first rough copy. Unfortunately problems arose with the author's rights to the story and discussions with Bioy Casares's agent were never ending and the project petered out – 'I can't hang about waiting, I'm not a young woman any more', María Luisa pronounced. Soon afterwards an equally interesting story came into her hands – *El impostor*, the story of an adolescent in full existential crisis who cuts himself off on a farm and fantasises of death.

Although the plot was fascinating it was not easy to adapt for the screen as it was based on a series of Chinese boxes (stories within stories) which led to the denouement. María Luisa suggested that we work on the script together. At that time she also started to make frequent visits to the doctor because of a series of digestive complaints.

In a few months we managed a first script that convinced us of everything. When we were just about to start another one, María Luisa had to postpone our meetings to make a short visit to New York to participate in the Latin Cinema Festival, which she returned from in a very concerned state of mind. With a heavy heart she told me that her discomfort had increased and that her doctor had recommended exploratory surgery. Inevitably our work would have to be interrupted for a while. She thought it would be no longer than a couple of weeks.

The operation, which was supposed to last only a couple of hours, took twice that. I recall that when I went to visit her soon after the surgery, she was extremely weak. She was temporarily in an intensive care ward where a voile screen separated each patient. When I came in she had just woken up from the anaesthetic. As soon as she saw me she beckoned to me to come closer and in the faintest voice she told me that in the bed next to hers there had been a teenager who had suffered head injuries after a car accident. 'The doctor was asking him exactly the same questions Juan asks Sebastián [the main characters of *El impostor*] when he falls off the horse', she told me. With that a nurse came in and told me off for making a sick person talk and asked me to leave. As I left, María Luisa whispered with an air of secret complicity 'I'll tell you later.'

Outside in the corridor I heard that the doctor's diagnosis was not good. The operation had been much more extensive than previously thought and recovery, if it were possible at all, would at best be very slow.

A few days later, cowed by the doctor's news, María Luisa told me that she had been thinking of temporarily stopping the progress of the script until she could recover from her extremely weak state. She was still unaware just how painful and uncertain the therapeutic process she had to go through would be. During that period we saw each other regularly, first in the clinic, then at her home. With an almost tacit agreement of silence we stopped talking about work. She had just learnt that she would have to spend a month in the United States undergoing chemotherapy. One afternoon, in that unusual way she had of facing her destiny, as soon as I came in she said, 'I've got cancer. The doctor says I have a 50:50 chance of making it. I am afraid I may never film again.'

The treatment was very hard on her and when she got back to Buenos Aires we met at her home again. Something of her eternal youth had been lost on that journey. Her skin had a grey hue and her eyes were masked. 'I am tired', she repeated. 'I am not sure if I shall be able to work again.' To distract her a little from talking about the hospital in New York and the chemotherapy, doctors' opinions and so on we started to chat about Sebastián Heredia, the character in *The Impostor* who cuts himself off in his parents' farm. Discussing his existential angst was a round about way of talking about our own. Both Sebastián and María Luisa had their lives under threat – their lives, not their ghosts.

These daily conversations started to become a vitally important part of our meetings and were totally different from those we had had when working on adapting the story. Now the conversations became an obsessive distraction from that other ever-more demanding question, the illness. That is how, for motives at a tangent from our work, both Sebastián Heredia and Juan Medina, the other character in the story, became people intimately known to us. So often, tempted to talk uselessly of supposed pros and cons of diagnosis and treatments, we stuck to our characters like life savers. We often had lively discussions about aspects of their lives. We grew to know them intimately. Little by little we found out about Juan Medina's betrayal and the strange way Sebastián Heredia locks himself in to write obsessively before he kills himself.

María Luisa's weak health had entered into a holding pattern. Everything now hung on the doubtful effect of the treatment. By then, the treatment in the hospital in New York had been so hard on her that she decided to continue the next chemotherapy course in Buenos Aires.

We began to meet almost every day. She had a temporary respite from the illness. Our conversations about *El impostor* became more frequent. Sebastián Heredia and Juan Medina were always a topic of our meetings. Speaking about the characters' deaths had a cathartic effect on us. But as work on the script had not been resumed, our approach to the biographical aspects of the characters was similar to the way one talks about one's relatives or friends: sometimes friendly, sometimes scathing, nearly always critical. It is curious that even before they were fully invented we knew these characters intimately. So the task of scriptwriting was practically an extraction from the fiction of our daily conversations.

I started to notice that every time María Luisa took up the conversation where we had considered it wise to abandon it, her spirit revived. We used to discuss the characters with vehemence, pushed perhaps by our own rage at the injustice of life. We got back to work very quickly and were only interrupted by the periods when María Luisa had to be given her medicine. 'My blood is being inoculated with platinum', she would say with childlike ferocity.

In fits and starts our script started to take shape in a direct inverse parallel to María Luisa's health which deteriorated more and more. Paradoxically, the weaker and more precarious her state became, the more intense and purposeful were our meetings. Our very relationship changed. We had been friends for years, but what held us together now was of a very different nature. Now we were challenging death. We were pushing it away, putting it off. We were fighting a battle against time. On the one hand, we worked as hard as possible to finish the script but on the other, what would happen afterwards? Every now and then María Luisa would confess that she did not want to finish the task. 'I want to finish and not to finish', she would say.

Although her health was deteriorating day by day, she definitely improved when she was working. Often at the beginning of the session she would be pale and wan, hardly able to speak. But after a few minutes it was remarkable how she would be involved in a heated discussion about the characters in the story. We began to meet every day.

One afternoon, between four and six o'clock was the best time for her, María Luisa greeted me circumspectly. After closing the doors to the dining room which shut us off from the rest of the house she announced sadly to me: 'I am dying. The treatment is not working.' There was a long silence. Hearing her pronounce these words filled me with an infinite silence because she enjoyed life. She loved life. Above all she wanted to carry on making films. 'I would like to leave ten films behind me', she told me once.

The change that cinema made in her life was so deep that even though it had happened several years earlier, one could still see that she was a person who was always adapting. She always felt guilty because her work forced her to leave aside other demands. 'I am a hopeless grandmother'. she used to say. I am ignorant of whether she was or not but she was a very busy grandmother. She was a person to whom life had become abruptly intense and presumptuously short. María Luisa was a passionate woman. And, as in all passion, she was not without her share of ferocity: 'I've got no time for love affairs', she would say, 'I have films to make.'

That summer afternoon María Luisa repeated: 'Nothing can be done about it. I'm going to die. There's no way out.' *The Impostor*'s manuscripts spread out messily on the dark wooden table took on a look of banality. There are no words for death. Death is mute. María Luisa looked at me sadly. I always found something of a little fighting girl in her ('my old little girl' Julie Christie once said to her). That afternoon I saw a desolate girl who stared at me, searching for an answer that life had already given her. Not really knowing what to do I told her that the script was not finished yet and we embraced for a long time.

The next day we took up our work as though nothing had changed, but from now on not in the dining room but in the bedroom. María Luisa had become very weak and could hardly get out of bed. We were on the final versions of the script. The work sessions had, of necessity become very brief. It was difficult to get on. We decided to split the working day into two parts. We would work for a little before midday and then for another period around four o'clock in the afternoon. In spite of her condition María Luisa would get enthusiastic about the progress of the work and fantasised about getting better and filming again. 'I shall need long breaks between the shoots. I'm not the person I used to be', she would say. She was dying.

One day, before reading what I had prepared at home, she told me a dream of hers. On a deserted beach a very small girl was crying beside the sea. Then some people dressed in black came closer and looked at her accusingly. Afterwards they disappeared and left the girl alone again. I asked her if she was the girl. María Luisa gave me a long look. She did not speak. The script was finished.

It was April, and soon it would be her birthday. I thought she would be pleased to have the new finished version of the script. So I got a copy bound and put it in a large gift-wrapped box. That afternoon was the first time in many months when I was not able to visit her. A sudden fever had accentuated her weakness. Some friends and family stayed almost in silence in her living room, all ready for a celebration that was not to be. The next day I went to visit her. She was still in bed. A nurse looked after her constantly. When she saw it was me she asked to be taken into the living room as she wanted to speak to me alone. The intensity of her gaze was the same: 'I shall not be directing again. My health is not good enough.' She spoke in a voice barely above a whisper. As the months went by the deterioration in her health was unfortunately evident. She, who had so stalwartly resisted accepting that reality, was now forced to assume it because of the inevitability of the facts.

I recall that a short time before then, at some moment I had seen that she was particularly frightened as though facing something completely unknown to her. María Luisa did not want to die. Sometimes she fantasised that the process of her illness was as inevitable as it was slow – an infinite path towards death with no exact end. But that April afternoon she said to me abruptly 'Do you want to direct this film? I trust you.' That very same day she communicated her decision to the family and immediately arranged a meeting with Oscar Kramer the producer for her last film, *De eso no se habla* and, together with her son Carlos Miguens, delegated to us the task of working together to finish the project. She was quite exhausted. Very much against her nature, she almost wanted to give up.

Over the next few days our meetings were practically silent. María Luisa slept most of the time. Sometimes, to keep her up to date, I would take out the script and read her passages from it. I proposed corrections, trying to provoke her. She would hardly ever answer. Once, as I read a sequence aloud, she took my hand.

The next evening I went to see her. She was lying on a sofa in her room with her eyes closed. I greeted her. She did not reply but she did start to move her hands, murmuring something unintelligible. I do not think she was aware of my presence. I sat down beside her and stayed quietly waiting. I said her name out loud but she did not hear me. She just whispered feverishly. I put my ear to her lips and heard, like an almost inaudible faraway rumour what she was saying. 'The swans, the swans . . .' It was the name of the ranch where Sebastián Heredia cut himself off from his family forever. She was there too, trapped in a dream. She was not coming back. I left. It was a clear night. Autumn was beginning.

The next day I was informed of María Luisa's death. One year later I started to shoot *The Impostor*, my first full-length film.

Not long ago I dreamt of her. I could see her silent, thinking in the garden of the house in Chivilcoy where the film is set. She was watching the shooting peacefully from her wheelchair. If things do happen as Borges liked to think, with parallel times that are written continuously and independently, perhaps today María Luisa is there, on a sunny afternoon, visiting an endless filming at The Swans ranch.

The contributions by Lita Stantic, Jorge Goldenberg, Félix Monti and Mercedes García Guevara have been translated from Spanish by John King.

NOTES

1 Almost certainly at the request of the producer and director, Lita Stantic, María Luisa's business partner, who had been a friend of mine since the 1960s.
2 I remember a scene in *Señora de nadie* in which the protagonist (a very pretty, very elegant and very upper middle class woman), in the middle of her process of becoming aware of the condition of women in general, says to her maid something like 'At least they pay you', while the maid is ironing clothes that she could never buy with her meagre wages.
3 Originally the project was called *Miss Maggie*, but these were times when another Maggie, called Thatcher, seemed, with the halo of her cruel successes, to cast a shadow on anything named Maggie in public.
4 In this regard, I remember one discussion. I proposed that during the wedding sequence there should be a background shot of carts carrying temporary labourers, the lowest level of social stratification in the countryside. These were

whole families who travelled the country from north to south, following the harvests: cotton in the Chaco (the north east), wheat and maize in Santa Fé and Córdoba (the centre) . . . ending with apple picking in the Río Negro valley (the south). These were the poorest people, the most abandoned. My idea seemed incomperhensible to María Luisa. She did not recognise the existence of these temporary labourers because she could not remember having ever seen them, they formed no part of her store of images. According to these images, before Perón, the social situation in the countryside was harmonious, there was no poverty and, at worst, the land-owning sectors were somewhat paternalistic towards the workers. However, after a long discussion, she began to research the issue and once she had verified the truth of the matter, she was quite happy to include the image in the film.

5 She often voiced her concerns about how her world would react to the fact that the story revolved around a dwarf woman. She was concerned in two ways: on the one hand she was worried that this choice would be interpreted as an expression of perversity; on the other hand, she did not want to be accused of having violated the social norms in her milieu concerning good or bad taste. As we saw later, her second fear was not groundless: some people from her world thought that it was indeed in bad taste to have worked with a dwarf.

THREE

INTIMISTA TRANSFORMATIONS: MARÍA LUISA BEMBERG'S FIRST FEATURE FILMS

Catherine Grant

Few studies of María Luisa Bemberg's films have discussed in any detail *Momentos* (*Moments*) (1980) and *Señora de nadie* (*Nobody's Wife*) (1982), the first two feature-length films she wrote and directed. Even fewer have mentioned the two early films she scripted. To date, nearly all the writers who have referred to these movies have tended to gloss over them, occasionally remarking that they present stories of similar kinds of female transgression as her later films, while being of little note in other respects. I would argue that it is only when the contexts of these films are considered, and when the films themselves are examined more fully *as films*, rather than simply as 'plots' to be abstracted, that the achievement they represent can begin to come into focus, along with their continuities with, and differences from, Bemberg's subsequent work. This, then, is the aim of much of what follows.

A PROFESSION OF HER OWN

In Buenos Aires in 1971, Victoria Ocampo published the first issue of her internationally renowned cultural periodical *Sur* after it had ceased to be a regular publication. The volume was devoted to a wide-ranging discussion of the state of womanhood in the world with particular reference to the 'second-wave' feminist movements which were gaining some ground, and much publicity, at the time. This special issue, entitled *La mujer* (*Woman*), is of interest here because it contains one of the earliest published interventions by María Luisa Bemberg on the subject of feminism that I have been able to trace. Bemberg was one of 50 female luminaries from a variety of different professions and backgrounds in Argentina to whom Ocampo sent questionnaires soliciting opinions on matters such as women's rights, divorce, sex education, birth control and abortion.[1] Bemberg's answers are notable for the rather different note they strike compared with the fairly straightforward Utopianism of many of the other pro-feminist contributions to the poll. Above all they point to her belief that the biggest obstacle to real and lasting feminist change was women's complicity in their own oppression under patriarchy, a belief based on her own experience but one which was thoroughly informed by the work of feminist writers like Simone de Beauvoir, whose words she quotes. This is shown most strikingly, perhaps, in her response to Ocampo's question about divorce, the legality of which had been annulled in Argentina by the military leaders who had deposed Juan Perón in a coup in 1955, the year after Bemberg's own divorce:

> While matrimony continues to be the best 'career' for a woman, the best solution to her emotional and economic problems, while she feels insecure, defence-less, dependent on her husband, living only by his proxy, I think that divorce will be harmful to her. Let her first become autonomous, stand on her own feet. Then and only then will divorce properly legislated for render her, if she so desires, a free woman and not a victim.[2]

More than half of those polled for *Sur* worked in the cultural field, including writers Marta Lynch, Alejandra Pizarnik, Silvina Bullrich and Beatriz Guido, actress Norma Aleandro and painter Norah Borges, with a much smaller number of contributors coming from journalism, science and education. Interestingly, Bemberg was one of only three women out of the 50 who declared no profession or activity alongside their names. This is a significant omission since by the time Bemberg (then a 49-year-old mother and grandmother) gave her responses to *Sur* she had not only helped to found the Unión Feminista Argentina in the late 1960s,[3] but she had also been involved in professional theatre throughout that decade, working first in design and administration, before going on to set up the Teatro del Globo (Globe Theatre) with Catalina Wolff.[4] She had also seen her first script turned into a successful film, *Crónica de una señora* (*Chronicle of a Lady*) (1970). Yet the non-declaration of a profession is understandable if it is considered in the light of her answer to the poll question enquiring if she had been impeded in her career on the grounds of her female gender. Bemberg replied that she was brought up exclusively to be a wife and mother, and when she realised through her own experience that 'procreation is not the same as creation', she felt at first frustrated by her lack of professional training, her repressive family climate (*clima castrante*) and her own insecurity.[5]

Crónica de una señora came about because Bemberg had passed on a copy of a one-act feminist play she had written, entitled *La margarita es una flor* (*The Daisy is a Flower*), to a friend who in turn had passed it on to a relatively new film director, Raúl de la Torre, who took it on as a project, commissioning a full-length script from Bemberg.[6] De la Torre set up his own production company and financed his first films with money he had made in the advertising industry in the 1960s. As Nissa Torrents wrote, his successful early movies (including *Crónica . . .*) presented a version of the upper class for middle and lower class consumption and were predominantly 'about women for women, [though] they remained under the firm male control of a director with a good eye for a pretty photograph and a pretty actress'.[7] The film was a domestic success and, in addition, Graciela Borges won the best actress prize for her role as the protagonist when *Crónica* was shown at the San Sebastián film festival. In an interview published in 1994, María Luisa Bemberg recounted an anecdote about one significant reaction to the movie: 'I remember having tea with Victoria Ocampo not long before she died and she liked very much [the finished film]. She saw it four times.'[8]

Crónica de una señora tells the story of Fina (the 'lady' of the title, played by Borges), the idle bourgeois wife of a wealthy businessman (Lautaro Murúa), who cannot make sense of her best friend Cecilia's suicide. The film, a well made melodrama, traces Fina's attempts to understand why someone just like her, bored, lonely, though engaged in occasional adulterous affairs, might tire of her life to such an extent that she decides to end it. It is Fina's gradual insight that her own situation is exactly symmetrical to that of her friend which provides the 'open' ending to the film. Fina finally seems more 'liberated' than at any other point in the film and, while there are hints that she might be about to discover she is pregnant, she is enjoying a new lifestyle which embraces the counter-cultural ideology of the time. Despite her happiness and her belief that she 'will not end up like Cecilia', Fina is nonetheless dismayed to discover that her current lover, a bohemian artist, was also her friend's lover just before her death. Her reaction to this news is captured in a freeze frame, one of the film's numerous stylistic allusions to certain films of the French *nouvelle vague*, although here Fina's image is frozen in long shot rather than in the medium close-up preferred by Truffaut and Godard, and others. The choice of camera position here then potentially distances the film's audience from the protagonist and her plight. The movie ends with a fade, nearly to black, which is also frozen, and a sudden burst of dissonant music immediately after this stilled image of Fina, emphasising her entrapment in a situation or 'condition' which cannot be altered, it seems, simply by having more fulfilling adulterous affairs.

Interestingly, there are some explicit references to the feminist movement made in *Crónica de una señora*.[9] About 30 minutes into the film, Fina is shown studying Beauvoir's *Le deuxième sexe*, a perfectly 'acceptable' example of elite French culture, on the surface at least, to which someone of Fina's educational background might be exposed.[10] She is repeatedly interrupted from her reading, though, by unimportant telephone calls from friends, one of the film's most frequent motifs of feminine frivolity and purposelessness. Unable to concentrate, Fina indulges instead in taking some guilty sips from a silver hip flask kept in her bedside drawer. The other named book Fina is shown examining is a translation of Betty Friedan's *The Feminine Mystique*. Some 40 minutes into the film, Fina wanders into a bookstore in downtown Buenos Aires and notices this book. The bookseller explains that the picture on its cover of a woman trapped in an ornamental birdcage is more or less the synthesis of Friedan's argument. He also informs her that this bestselling book is based on a poll of housewives in North America and deals with women's conflicting responsibilities to their husbands, their children and the home, as well as to themselves. Fina says that she will carry on looking, and after further scrutiny of the picture on the cover under the intense gaze of the bookseller, she puts the book down and walks away. The film cuts away with a dissolve to the next shot of a slightly drunk Fina dancing to American rock music in the nightclub where she will meet a new, sexually liberated lover (played by Federico Luppi) who will help her forget her troubles for a short while, until he leaves her on the grounds of her lack of independence.

Friedan's analysis in *The Feminine Mystique,* not only of middle class women's material reality but also, more importantly, of their state of mind, appears to provide the film with its psychological and philosophical frameworks: unable, or unwilling to read the books that would help her, Fina (along with Cecilia) seems to be suffering from the 'problem that has no name' described in the first chapter title of Friedan's book.[11] While Clara Fontana notes that the discourse of *Crónica de una señora* is in many ways 'doctrinaire', with its lack of conciliatory alternatives,[12] I would argue that the engagement, on various levels in this film, of Bemberg's female protagonist with matters of 'symbolic death' (the meditation on her 'double's' suicide, her own hopeless entrapment and finally her utter stasis) dramatises at once subtly and starkly the kind of radical change referred to in the screenwriter's reply to *Sur*'s 1971 survey question about the most pressing political priority for women: 'Women must take consciousness of their "feminine condition", in other words their state of political, social and economic dependency. The first step in achieving change is to desire it.'[13]

FEMININE OPTICS

In 1972, María Luisa Bemberg produced and directed a film for the first time: the 16mm documentary short, *El mundo de la mujer (Woman's World),* filmed on location at the Exposición Femimundo, a trade fair of 'everything which interests women, fashion, beauty, hairstyles, articles for the home'.[14] As Clara Fontana points out in her generally admiring discussion of this film: 'Bemberg confronts the spectator, and above all the female spectator, with a reality which is normally covered up by social practices: the so-called "world of the woman" is not "of the woman". It is a world of things, objects, merchandise.'[15] Fontana is much less positive, however, about the 1974 feature film based on Bemberg's second full-length script, written while she was filming *El mundo de la mujer*. Comparing this film, *Triángulo de cuatro* (*Four-sided Triangle*) with *Crónica de una señora* she writes:

> Once more the protagonist, this time played by Thelma Biral, seeks refuge in infidelity, like Fina in *Crónica*. . . . The plot is not very convincing and is over-audacious. It lacks the conceptual dimension which in some cases, and *Crónica de una señora* is one of them, can turn a minor story into a relevant archetype of individual and social conflict. *Triángulo de cuatro* is a commonplace drama set among frivolous people and a few critical touches are not able to rescue it from triviality.[16]

The plot, especially when crudely summarised in a few words as it is here in Fontana's only paragraph on this film, certainly lacks a 'conceptual dimension' and is only as 'convincing' as that of many romantic melodramas. But well scripted films are much more than the sum of their plots and *Triángulo de cuatro* is a much less dated film, viewed today, than *Crónica*, perhaps because of its very ambition leading to a greater variety of tone and setting as well as because of the excellent performances of its actors. A bigger budget film than *Crónica*, *Triángulo* was taken on as a project by well established director Fernando Ayala, produced by his partner Héctor Olivera and financed by their production company, the renowned Aries Cinematográfica, SA. Bemberg's film-script for *Triángulo* was awarded the ARGENTORES first prize.[17]

Laura (played by Thelma Biral) is surely not the film's only protagonist. While *Triángulo* seems to begin and certainly ends with her story and her concerns, it divides its narration reasonably equally between three characters: Laura, her husband Felipe (another very sympathetic performance from Federico Luppi) and Felipe's mistress, the model Teresa Prado (Graciela Borges once again), with the stage name and public alter ego of 'Sandra'. The film has a further important character, the fourth side of the amorous 'triangle', Laura's lover Martín, but events are rarely, if ever, seen from his perspective as they are with the other three.

The beginning of the film subtly contrasts two 'fishing' scenes: shots of a luxury villa in Uruguay's luxury resort, Punta del Este, and then of Felipe concentratedly fishing in the sea are intercut with shots of Martín fishing for the attention of a bored and lonely Laura, his Buenos Aires neighbour, by dangling in front of her first a red plastic toy from his own fishing rod and then a microphone from a sound boom. After these establishing shots, Felipe will always be associated with more serious leisure activities in the film while, by contrast, idle game-playing will mark the development of Laura's frivolous and superficial sexual relationship with Martín (connecting her explicitly to Fina in *Crónica* who is frequently shown playing games in the early part of that film). Felipe falls much more seriously in love in his affair than his wife does in hers. Initially, though, he falls for Sandra, a model hired by his advertising company, for all the 'wrong' reasons according to the film's ideological framework (her glamorous appearance, for instance). But when Sandra takes off her costume, wig and make-up at the end of their first date, she makes a more desirable appearance as 'herself': Teresa, the 'liberated' proto-feminist, who will even go on to feel terrible guilt at the prospect of hurting Laura who, despite her own affair, still seems to love her husband.

One of the film's most interesting aspects is its setting among the trappings of mediatised modernity. Most of these sequences, and all of those associated specifically with the world of advertising, are linked to the character of Sandra/Teresa. There is one sequence in particular, some 35 minutes into the film, which is set up in a manner reminiscent of Federico Fellini's film work (for example, the 'miracle sequence' in *La dolce vita*, 1960, and many parts of *Otto e mezzo*/8½, 1962).[18] In this sequence, a fake wedding starring Sandra as the blushing bride is staged by a ridiculous master of ceremonies for an advertising shoot. The next sequence shows, to humorous effect, a conversation between Teresa and her mother in which the latter realises that her daughter will not in fact marry her new partner Felipe because of his existing married status. Yet, perhaps more interestingly, the wedding scene is preceded by a short montage sequence which intercuts shots of Sandra having her photograph taken in a number of glamorous advertising poses, with ones of Teresa behind the photographic camera, framing the world and the people around her.[19] All of these sequences reveal that *Triángulo* handles some similar themes and places in the frame many of the same spaces and objects which characterise modern women's lives, as Bemberg's earlier short film, *El mundo de la mujer*. In both films, the patriarchal 'world of women' is shown up to be the normative world of the reified, the commodified and the 'looked at' precisely by dint of contrast with the highly unusual presence of a woman behind the camera.

It should not surprise us, then, that Bemberg's script for *Triángulo de cuatro* appears to valorise above all the female character in whose hands it places a camera. This character, Teresa, active and defiant in all the right places, but who is also seen to suffer, when necessary (for all the right feminist reasons), is the most unequivocally likeable female 'identification' figure, at least according to the film's overt ideological framework. Yet *Triángulo*'s affective and epistemic structures are more complicated, or confused, than they might at first seem, and there is a 'feminist' price to pay for the particular connotative connections facilitated by the completed movie. The film seems increasingly to set up Laura, Teresa's rival for Felipe's affections, as a character with whom spectators may at times be aligned, but for whom, potentially at least, they do not feel much sympathetic allegiance.[20] When Laura finds out about her husband's affair, she sees Teresa at a public function (and we also see her through Laura's optical point of view, after establishing shots which show Teresa watching Laura arrive). Thus Teresa appears to Laura in her Sandra persona. Since Laura never has any other visual access to Teresa, we are never aligned directly against Teresa. Even when we are confronted by Laura's (semi-) righteous indignation about her husband's affair, her (and, potentially, the spectators') ire is directed against the figure of Sandra. This splitting of Teresa's persona seems to have yet another related function in addition to the protective 'distancing' of that character: Sandra and Laura look alike, with quite similar hairstyles and much the same taste in glamorous make-up and evening gowns. So the more superficial, least likeable aspects of Sandra serve to remind the viewer, not of the 'liberated', more 'authentic' Teresa, but of Laura's own manifest superficiality throughout the film.

While an awareness of these subtleties of filmic point of view is absent from the brief assessments of this film that have been published, there is a sense in which some of the critical unease about *Triángulo* might emanate from them, that is to say, from the complex way in which, as I have begun to indicate above, the film organises moment by moment, cognitive and affective access to its particular array of characters. I would argue that the film, perhaps inadvertently, privileges an ironic reading of its narration, thus playing a potentially confusing game with 'good' and 'bad' femininities, in which Laura is the most prominent loser, if only in moral terms. Teresa's positively valorised creativity appears to have been at least temporarily stifled when Felipe finally returns to his wife at the end of the film. She destroys a photo of herself and Felipe taken during their last meeting together, by turning on the lights in her dark room: it isn't allowed to develop. Nonetheless, she is finally seen gazing at a split portrait of herself, simultaneously represented as both Teresa and Sandra; she blocks out the Sandra half with her hand and contemplates the remaining image.

The film concludes, by contrast, that Laura's morally suspect game-playing triumphs, albeit ironically, in the end. When she suspects, correctly, that her husband is about to leave her definitively for Teresa, she stages a half-hearted suicide attempt. Felipe comes at once to her side, leaving his mistress for good. Even though Laura's sexist doctor tells him that his wife's behaviour was simply attention-seeking, 'like lots of women', he decides to stay with her, and allows her to engineer a trip for the two of them to the villa in Punta del Este. The final sequence of the film places us back where it began: Felipe is alone, fishing from the rocks, near the villa, this time with a sunset (or sunrise?) in the background. Like *Crónica de una señora*, *Triángulo de cuatro* ends on an uncertain note: this time a dissonant phrase from its musical theme repeats itself over and over again, perhaps on this occasion signalling the entrapment of its male protagonist but also, possibly, the pyrrhic victory of Laura who is, notably, nowhere to be seen.

It is interesting that, in many interviews, María Luisa Bemberg often expressed her own dissatisfaction with the experiences she had scripting these two films for other directors. Summing up on this period, she has declared, 'these two films were enough for me to realise, and what I say does not imply a value judgement of those movies, that no one was ever going to be able to interpret as I could what I myself had written.'[21]

This kind of 'dramatisation' of her decision to stop writing scripts for other film directors is echoed by numerous other retellings of the 'story of her career' in published interviews:[22]

> I started by writing a screenplay which I was fortunate enough to have produced and it did very well. I was able to work on the film and I was absolutely caught by the magic of that world. That was in 1970, and then I immediately started writing my second script which was also taken, and again I worked on the set. But it was then that I realised that if I wanted the stories really to reflect what I was trying to say, I would have to go behind the camera myself.[23]

> Ten years ago, people in my country were so incredibly conservative concerning the women's movement that if I was too outspoken or outrageous with the characters [in the scripted films of the 1970s], I would have scared the audience away. So strategically speaking, it had to be very mild feminism. These were successful films but not what I had intended, which is why I decided to direct myself.[24]

> I think that one's first film is created on the typewriter. When one writes, for example, 'daybreak, the silhouette of a figure appears in the background, and advances towards the camera', I'm really already filming it, already framing it. I concluded then that if I wanted my film really to reflect what I had visualized then I had to begin to direct myself.[25]

In the last interview from which I have quoted, the very next question Luis Trelles Plazaola asks Bemberg is whether or not she had prepared her first two feature scripts with technical directions (*indicaciones técnicas*). She replies that she had, but that neither of the two directors had taken any notice of these: 'The film belongs to the director not to the script-writer.'[26]

What is clear from all of the above replies to interviewers' questions about this transitional period in her film-making career is that Bemberg consistently justified her decision to turn to direction as one emanating from a desire to tell her stories as only she could, in order to realise her own original visualisation of them. Some commentators on her work have also suggested, often very indirectly, that the implied inability of de la Torre and Ayala to interpret her ideas is intrinsically a question of their gender. While Fontana skirts around such assertions, she does talk of films 'which could only be conceived by women, and dare I say by women who sublimated their unhappiness in creativity'.[27] In the following quotation about Bemberg's first scripted film, hints about the very gendered origins (and object) of a certain antipathy are also quite prominent:

> A scene was being filmed in which Fina agonises over the reality of her empty existence. According to Bemberg, who always attended shooting, as the author of the scene she thought that in order to lend it some conviction a very special close-up was required. She couldn't convince de la Torre, who felt some anti-pathy towards Fina, that character whom Bemberg considered a victim of circumstances. In order to console herself she made some comments to the lighting technician who happened to be Juan Carlos Desanzo [who, in the 1970s, went on to work as a technician with at least one other Argentine woman film director, Eva Landeck]. Desanzo replied, 'Why don't you direct?' 'My reaction', commented Bemberg, 'was . . . me, direct? I know nothing about the technical side'. 'Desanzo encouraged me.'[28]

It is interesting that in this last quotation, some of these insinuations about gender, blame and victimhood are linked, all too briefly, to specific questions of filmic point of view and spatio-temporal access to film characters. I hope that I have managed to establish so far that such fleeting insights are potentially too useful in assessments of Bemberg's turn to film direction to be left at the level of anecdote: a more rigorous approach to film aesthetics is required, but also to film *context*. It is to explorations of context that I will increasingly turn in my discussion of *Momentos*, the first feature-length film that Bemberg directed in 1980, and also in my briefer treatment of her 1982 movie *Señora de nadie*.

'EL ADULTERIO "DESPENALIZADO"'[29]

All four of the first feature films with which Bemberg was associated, first as writer, and then as writer, director and co-producer with Lita Stantic, tell stories of female and male adultery. Cultural historians have typically associated this kind of story with periods when texts have chosen to confront, as Tony Tanner writes in his study of the adultery genre in literature 'not only the provisionality of social laws and rules and structures, but the provisionality of [their] own procedures and assumptions'.[30]

The adultery genre was born of the social and cultural changes associated, in the nineteenth century, '[w]ith the decline in the importance of land in the production processes of industrial capitalism, [when] the problem of the control and ownership [of women as reproducers of men] shifted to the capitalist family where industrial wealth was inherited through the male line'.[31] As Bryan Turner continues, although western men in this period 'enjoyed the benefits of a double standard, the importance of traditional sexual mores in the household was emphasised because of their crucial relationship to the inheritance of wealth. These familial and economic systems explain the importance of virginity, fidelity and sexual purity in this period'[32] and hence also explain the dramatic cultural potential of these same elements. Turner adds that following the erosion of these systems in the twentieth-century shift towards a post-industrial society, characterised by advanced capitalist consumption and the manipulation of communications through public relations industries, the traditional relationships 'between property, sexuality and the body' have largely disappeared.[33] This remarkable 'transformation of intimacy', to use Anthony Giddens's phrase, can clearly be seen in many of the forms and themes of cinema after the Second World War. In the late 1950s and 1960s, against a backdrop of demographic changes, and new laws concerning marriage, property, contraception and divorce,[34] prominent European art film directors (Visconti, Antonioni, Fellini, Bergman, Truffaut,

Godard, et al.), appropriated the traditional adultery plot to explore the changing religious and secular conceptions of personal and sexual conduct in new modernist cinematic forms which favoured open endings and gave space to other stylistic experiments.

Despite the fact that, in the same period, Argentina was *not* enjoying a similar liberalisation of marital, divorce or contraceptive laws, or of social policy in general (after 1955, if anything, the reverse was true), dramas of adultery also became associated there with a nascent *cine de autor*. Both de la Torre and Ayala, for example, the two directors who had turned Bemberg's scripts into films, allied themselves from time to time with an art-cinema inflected, *intimista* tendency most ably represented in the late 1950s and 1960s, perhaps, by some of the *Kammerspiele* influenced films of Leopoldo Torre Nilsson (son of Leopoldo Torre Ríos, who had made much more traditional adultery dramas in his directing career in the 1940s).[35]

María Luisa Bemberg was not the only woman film-maker interested in adapting for feminist purposes the 'modernist' concerns of sexual anxiety, identity and alienation which are typical of the post-war adultery drama. This was a common focus of much western 'new women's cinema', to use Annette Kuhn's term for a cluster of US and European films which appeared in the 1970s and 1980s.[36] Nor, significantly, was Bemberg interested in disavowing the stylistic influence on her film-making of certain foreign, male, art-cinema precursors.[37] Yet, in various ways, her films (and promotional interviews) do assert difference and dissent from the masculinist values of many modernist explorations of adultery in their association with the forms and concerns of the 'women's picture'. Certain critics, too, have supported these assertions. As Fontana writes, in a reference to *Momentos*, Bemberg 'reinvents [earlier adultery films by male directors] by removing all moralising connotations. No one transgresses anything. The conflict is about feelings, and not about morality.'[38] Bemberg's 'feminine perspective' in this film results in a rendering of female adultery which, for the first time, rids the adulteress of all blame. *Momentos* is the first Argentine film with a 'clear consciousness of . . . feminine gender'.[39] For Fontana, it thus contrasts sharply with the supposed lack of achievement of *Triángulo de cuatro*. Much of the marketing of *Momentos* (for example, the film's original poster and the video cassette sleeve) also focused on this angle: the publicity tagline read 'One woman's adultery as seen by another woman.'[40]

In *Momentos*, a skilfully scripted and very well made film, Lucía (played by Graciela Dufau), a landscape gardener widowed in her first marriage, is married for the second time, comfortably but passionlessly, to an older man, Mauricio (Héctor Bidonde), a psychoanalyst (she was his patient after her bereavement). Through her work, Lucía meets Nicolás (Miguel Angel Solá), a wealthy young car salesman who is married to Mónica (Cunny Vera), the daughter of his boss. Nicolás falls for the more sophisticated Lucía and, though she resists the advances of the younger man initially, they begin an affair and Lucía leaves her husband. The two lovers go to a hotel in the resort of Mar del Plata. Tedium sets in, however, and after Lucía tells emotionally of how her first husband was killed in a car accident and how she lost their child, the relationship between these very different people begins seriously to unravel. On the spur of the moment, Lucía leaves and returns to her husband.

Unlike the two scripted films, which only allude to art-cinema topics and devices, all the while opting for a fairly classical narrational style typical of much 'quality' commercial cinema in Argentina at the time, *Momentos*'s narration subtly signals its greater art-cinema modality from the outset: its opening sequence, which follows the protagonists on their river-boat trip up the Tigre Delta to their weekend house, strikingly places them, and us, in Bergmanesque territory, here inflected by a somewhat warmer, 'women's film' sensibility.[41] Like some of Bergman's work, Bemberg's film is slow paced, on the whole, preferring longer shots and long takes while occasionally breaking up its segments with stylish montage sequences, and scenes in which diegetic sound is replaced (either with non-diegetic music or with point of audition, *'trompe l'oreille'* effects) to allow for the distanced contemplation of action or conversations. It also deploys devices which disrupt the linear presentation of chronological time such as ellipses and fleeting flashbacks. In these ways and in others, the film self-consciously points up its weightiness and its languorous feel.

From the beginning, too, *Momentos* is carefully constructed around a series of highly suggestive motifs, which perform much of its work of characterisation and thematic expression: for example, motifs of autumn, and then of the beginning of winter (leafless trees, white skies), emptiness (empty chairs, deserted beaches), confined spaces (small rooms, closed-off thresholds) and especially figurations of coldness and hunger, to express the emotional and physical state, and needs, of its protagonists, especially Lucía.

Momentos's moral framework emerges subtly from this imbrication of the physical and the psychical. The respective infidelity of Lucía and Nicolás is 'justified' by the film's emphasis of the context of their involuntary attraction. Theirs is not shown to be a transgression in which they are carried off by 'authentic' passion (as in several of Bemberg's period dramas: for example, the 1983 *Camila*). Instead, through the way the film organises epistemic access in general (its protagonists discuss their romantic history on a number of occasions) and, more specifically, through Mauricio's hint about Lucía's first husband Sebastián, during an uncharacteristic outburst against his wife, *Momentos* suggests that Lucía and Nicolás are both 'acting out', in psychoanalytic parlance, compelled to repeat stifled first loves (for him, his cousin Tita; for her, Sebastián).[42] Additional justification for their affair is provided by Mauricio's implied inability to cater for all of his younger wife's needs (reading in bed, while she looks on; his infertility rendering her childless), despite the fact that the film frequently shows him, and his point of view, in a sympathetic light, patiently, and non-judgementally, trying to understand Lucía. The film is rather less kind to Nicolás's wife. In the sequence in which Lucía is finally shown succumbing to the young man's seduction, just inside the front door of his house, the two lovers wordlessly and tentatively begin to touch one another, while Mónica's voice is heard being recorded on the answering machine. It is not possible to follow exactly what she is saying, but the reedy vocal tone and the rambling nature of her message with its unimportant, domestic concerns leave us in no doubt that Nicolás is 'justified' in his desire for the older, more sophisticated Lucía.

Graciela Dufau and Miguel Angel Solá in *Momentos*

I would argue, on the whole, that Fontana is correct when she argues that *Momentos* portrays adultery in a 'decriminalised' way, from the female protagonist's point of view. The film completely lacks an explicitly expressed ideological framework for the adultery in a traditional sense: there is no Catholic or other religious guilt on show; there are no moralising or overly judgemental characters and no obvious punishment of the lover's transgression. Instead, I believe that the film's crucial focus on the 'needs' of the body and the psyche points to its implicit concerns with much newer patterns of personal expressivity which presume a significant degree of sexual equality. In *Momentos*, sexual relations are clearly shown to be based on expectations about personal satisfaction through intimacy, such as those argued for by Anthony Giddens when he writes that, in the late part of the twentieth-century, '[p]ersonal life has become an open project, creating new demands and anxieties. Our interpersonal existence is being thoroughly transfigured, involving us all in [. . .] *everyday social experiments*, with which wider social changes [to do with marriage, the family and sexuality] more or less oblige us to engage.'[43]

It is worth discussing *Momentos*'s ending in detail since the *dénouement* lasts more than 20 minutes in a film of 97 minutes' duration. Lucía's decision to leave Nicolás, which she tries to explain by reminding him of the lyrics to the *bolero*, *Nosotros* (*The Two of Us*), is not based simply on a desire to return home to Mauricio. The song's lyrics give no other explanation than the wish to leave things as they are, for the good of her lover, and in the name of their love.[44] In a scene near the end, as their relationship is shown to be on the wane, riven by their differences and by her growing fear (provoked by an episode of Nicolás's violent temper, which will be repeated in a slightly later sequence) that it will all finish badly, Lucía fantasises Nicolás's suicide by drowning. It seems clear that she consciously decides the best way of avoiding harm to them both is to terminate their relationship. Her final, spur-of-the-moment decision to return to her husband, after she runs to catch a train, is one which seems devoid of the usual rationale of the 'returning adulteress': that of wifely self-sacrifice and guilt, or the favouring of marital responsibilities (as in *Brief Encounter*, UK, 1946, David Lean, a film to which *Momentos* alludes many times). The film presents the choice as much more basic than this: Lucía appears to return because once she has left Nicolás at the railway station in Mar del Plata, she can literally do nothing else. She has no proper coat, no luggage, not enough money to buy food on the train. She arrives home, cold and starving, to find a wordless Mauricio in the middle of his supper. She simply states her need for food, explaining nothing else; he eventually clears a plate for her and gives her a spoon. As he silently watches her stuff food into her mouth, the camera pans away, tracks back down their hallway, and, in the final frame of the film, fixes on a window, obscured by a curtain.

Momentos's final sequences do stage Mauricio's somewhat grudging acceptance of Lucía back in his life and also his continued desire to help provide for at least one of her basic needs. But it certainly does not feel like a 'positive ending'.[45] I indicated above that the film's lack of an overtly moralising framework cedes space for new structures of belief based on expectations about personal satisfaction through intimacy. But the mere existence of such expectations does not mean that they can be fulfilled. As

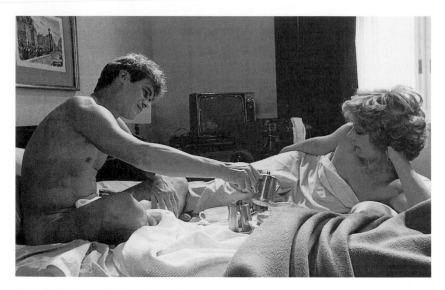

Graciela Dufau and Miguel Angel Solá in *Momentos*

he concludes his study of the bourgeois novel of adultery, Tony Tanner writes that 'adultery is [. . .] a leap into limitlessness, with the result that the whole ambiguous problematics of limits are brought out into the open.'[46] While *Momentos* may not be about blame or judgemental attitudes towards women's sexuality, it is nonetheless a film which constantly points to limits, as its final frame, its many other shots of thresholds and barriers, and its figuration of the physical and psychical 'confinement' of its characters through the ever-present leitmotif of claustrophobia, should remind us.[47]

'THE BEST JAIL'[48]

In the same way that *Momentos* appears to have no pre-existing judgemental framework (other than the conceptual one provided by psychoanalysis, interestingly),[49] it does not seem one of Bemberg's most overtly feminist-concerned films. Although an act of female transgression is staged, none of the characters is interested in feminism and no obvious feminist discourses are articulated in dialogue, unlike in the two scripted movies. There is one possible and very fleeting exception to this which has gone unremarked by critics: near the beginning of the film, Mauricio is shown listening to the tape of one of his sessions with a patient, Margarita Acosta, who alludes to her history of frustrated suicide attempts and who describes her anguished frustration with her life in the following terms: 'It was as if I was shouting from inside a bell jar.' ('Como si gritara dentro de una campana de vidrio.') This possible reference to the title, story and central motif of Sylvia Plath's well known 1963 feminist novel aside, the seeming lack of explicit radical feminist discourses has led some critics, such as José Agustín Mahieu, to assert that in Bemberg's first directed films 'a tenuous feminism is introduced, appropriate only for conversations at high tea'.[50]

I would argue, on the other hand, that the apparent absence of these discourses from the first directed film is much more usefully considered as an interpretative 'blindspot' encouraged by *Momentos*'s narration and increased when the movie is viewed outside its particular production context. After all, at the end of the film, Lucía returns to her marital home just as she might return to a prison cell.[51] *Momentos* might seem to suggest at its conclusion, therefore, that there is no *realistic* possibility of her living 'outside' of her marriage, without the 'protection' afforded by a legal and proprietorial relationship with a male spouse. While many critics have been keen to read Bemberg's later films as allegories which clearly link the personal and the political (and have seen in them various representations of female entrapment), there seems to have been no desire to perform an equivalent reading of her first two directed films. It is possible to argue that period dramas are more likely to be interpreted historically and allegorically than films set in their contemporary moment, as both of the first two films directed by Bemberg were. In addition to this, there may well be conventions which have grown up around the intimate film drama which equally might discourage such readings. Nonetheless, at this point it is worth remembering, briefly, the immediate production context of this film.

Momentos was made at the end of 1980, in the middle of the brutal period of military dictatorship in Argentina between 1976 and 1983, known by the first junta's own euphemism as the 'Process (*Proceso*) of national reorganisation'. It was not the first feature film project Bemberg had wanted to direct. In the late 1970s, she had written another screenplay entitled *Señora de nadie* for the film she would go on to make after *Momentos*. The military censors of the time did not give their approval for this project initially, with its overtly feminist story and greater range of characters, including several sexually 'promiscuous' women, and an openly gay man. As Bemberg has declared:

> it was a huge disappointment because I had got all ready to go off and make [*Señora de nadie*] and then they told me I couldn't. They gave me three reasons: first, that it was a terrible example for Argentine mothers; second, that there was a queer in it – 'I, Madam, would prefer to have a son with cancer than one who is queer'; and third, that a woman was to direct.[52]

While this anecdote about *Señora de nadie* is well rehearsed, it is important to remember that *Momentos* is a film produced under the very *same* repressive censorship regulations, the same 'regimes of truth',[53] that disallowed the earlier script. As Sarah Radcliffe writes of this period:

> The gender politics of the military regime installed in 1976 emphasized a mythical return to the family as the 'basic cell of society' where all other associative links would be broken [. . .]. Within this model of society, women were to retain order by overseeing children's behaviour while their domestic roles as wives and mothers were romanticized. [. . .] Their official identity was that of a negated political subject, the purest safe apolitical community, embedded within the dangerous(ly) political public world.[54]

While Radcliffe goes on to write of the many women who bravely and publicly resisted these particular military regime dictates (for example, the Mothers of the Plaza de Mayo), other writers and historians have described a differently inflected, even more 'intimate' form of gendered repression and censorship during the *Proceso*. For instance, Mary-Beth Tierney-Tello writes:

The authoritarian practices of the state attempted to police specific desires and imaginings. Sexuality and sexual politics, for example, were at the forefront of the struggle to cleanse the Argentine national spirit of extraneous and 'dangerous' influences [. . .]. Such 'dangers' included, of course, cultural productions that depict sexuality outside of the marital/familial relationship. Furthermore, the 'dangers' in terms of gender and sexuality also included anything that might question the traditional roles for men and women. So, policing the realms of sexuality and desire, attempting to construct and impose a single, homogenized idea of 'Argentine' sexuality, was one of the explicit goals of authoritarian practices.[55]

What were the effects of this 'regime of truth' on *Momentos*, given that, despite the censorship of the time, the film *does* manage to represent explicitly a number of these 'dangers'? Bemberg has said that she filmed both her first two movies with the censors looking over her shoulder, but that 'there is nothing worse than self-censorship. I was constantly thinking that I couldn't do this, I couldn't do that; possibly, if there had been no censorship, I would have made the erotic scenes more audacious.'[56] There is certainly very little female nudity in this film; but, instead, Bemberg's camera inverts some of the conventional gendered 'looking-relations' of the intimist drama of its period by preferring to contemplate at length the naked arms, shoulders, torso and legs of its attractive young male protagonist, played by Miguel Angel Solá. These 'productive' effects of the film's specific context could have been interpreted politically, but, according to published criticism at the time, or since, it appears that they weren't.[57] Nor has anyone remarked as such on the film's other 'signs' of its political context; for example, its use of a conceptual framework – that of psychoanalysis – which was, to say the least, regarded by the military regime as being suspiciously linked to other 'undesirable' elements (Jewishness, communism). And, as María Sáenz Quesada writes of these years:

The tendency to spend, to travel, to escape, was perhaps a collective necessity following on from the great fear which characterized the period '70/78. This anguished, privatized solitude turned in on itself, and in the absence of a public life found an escape route, a sort of compensation offered by [the Junta's early] economic policy [in the late 1970s: the so-called 'easy money' policies under the stewardship of the economy minister, Martínez de Hoz].[58]

Momentos's glamorous *mise-en-scène* is filled with the evidence of many kinds of historically contemporaneous escapist fantasies, all of which, as in the two earlier films, are found severely wanting: sexual liaisons to escape the tedium of bourgeois life, especially that of marriage; lavish parties where the film's *nouvelle bourgeoisie* can wear their expensive clothes, drink fancy cocktails and dance to local versions of North American disco music (*Oh crazy man, come on love me!*); the protagonists' holidays and conference trips (Tigre, Mar del Plata, Río de Janeiro); Nicolás's father-in-law's luxury cars; and everyone's gorgeous homes and gardens. One has to learn not to overlook these signs, or to ignore the film's obviously negative attitude to them, though this is not easy with forms which, above all at particular times, may not encourage straightforward, allegorical readings. As Michael Taussig has written, '[a]bove all the Dirty War is a war of silencing . . . This is more than the production of silence. It is silencing, which is quite different. [. . .] the not said acquires a significance and a specific confusion befogs the spaces of the public sphere which is where the action is.'[59]

Does the film itself teach us to look differently? *Momentos* certainly requests a different kind of reading from us than earlier adultery films in order for its 'blameless' ending to make verisimilitudinous sense. Clearly, under all the given circumstances, Lucía *has* to return home at the film's conclusion; she must provide the military censors with their required 'positive ending';[60] her adultery finishes, and marriage is ultimately upheld – in any case, divorce is illegal and separation almost unthinkable, under Argentina's *patria potestad* laws, where women's legal status and right to hold wealth and property were diminished upon marriage until well after the *Proceso*. Mauricio noticeably doesn't greet his wife with the effusive forgiveness, blithe ignorance, or outright rage and fury normally confronting other returning film adulteresses. And this very lack of emotional expressivity at the end strips down what is at stake in the film's conclusion, laying bare Lucía's lack of freedom *as a woman*.

LA DONNA È MOBILE

During the early part of the *Proceso*, as Nissa Torrents reported, 'censorship and fear practically paralysed the [Argentine] film industry [. . .] by 1981, box office sales had decreased by 50 per cent in the provinces – 90 per cent in prosperous Mendoza – and by over 30 per cent in Buenos Aires', and yet *Momentos*, premiered in Buenos Aires on 7 May 1981, still broke even.[61] What changed in the period between the production of Bemberg's first two directed films was that there was a growing *apertura*, or liberalisation, as the military regime's control over cultural production began, very slowly at first, to crumble. This process had tentatively begun as early as 1979, when, for example, writer María Elena Walsh published an article in the cultural supplement of an Argentine daily newspaper entitled 'The nation, a garden of children', in which she indicated, subtly, that the collective fear of the time was giving way to an anxiety to reclaim freedom.[62] Two years or so later, Walsh wrote the feminist lyrics for the song *Señora mía* (*My Own Woman*) which accompanied the closing credit sequence of one of the two versions in circulation of Bemberg's *Señora de nadie* and which announced in unequivocal terms the film's association with the consolidation of cultural freedom which Walsh's article had courageously begun to announce.[63] The filming of *Señora de nadie* took place between December 1981 and January 1982 and it received its premiere in Buenos Aires on 1 April 1982.[64] The very next day every newspaper in the country, and many outside of it, was reporting that the Argentine armed forces had begun the reconquest of the Malvinas/Falkland Islands which, as well as ultimately hastening the military's decline and the country's return to democratic rule, rather eclipsed the media impact of the film.[65]

As I have shown earlier in my discussion, all three of María Luisa Bemberg's first feature films contain striking images of female stasis. The fourth film *Señora de nadie*, the second one she directed, is no exception to this rule. This film echoes in a number of ways some of the themes of *Crónica de una señora* and part of the storyline and ironic, though melodramatic, tone of *Triángulo de cuatro*. The protagonist Leonor (brilliantly played by Luisina Brando) discovers that her wealthy architect husband Fernando (Rodolfo

Ranni) is having one of a series of affairs with a 'liberated' girlfriend (Susú Pecoraro, who went on to play the title role in *Camila*). As Leonor's world falls apart, she seeks time for herself, initially leaving her two sons to be cared for by their father. She has sexual liaisons of her own, including briefly with her husband;[66] but most importantly she becomes much more self-reliant, making friends in her own right (most notably her gay friend Pablo, played by Julio Chávez, whom she meets at group therapy sessions) and gradually discovers that, though life as a single working mother is not easy, it is better than life as an ignorant, deceived and 'kept' woman.

Unlike the earlier films which tend to *close* with their most graphic displays of female entrapment, this film *begins* its pre-credit sequence with its own audio-visual figuring of the protagonist's 'symbolic death'. The camera focuses on a noisy electric ceiling fan and, as it pans down and to the left, past family photographs on the wall and a bedside table, and finally alights on a bed, we realise that over the sound of the fan we have also been hearing the breathy cries of a naked (male–female) couple who are making love there. As they separate, all his passion spent, the man rolls out of shot and the camera focuses on the woman. Her electronic alarm clock goes off. She reaches across to switch it off and is caught, with her back turned, in a freeze frame. The sound of the beeping alarm also 'freezes', becoming one continuous noise, and thus resembling the tone of a hospital heart monitor when the 'flat-line' signalling cardiac arrest is shown on the screen. The image then fades to black, the noise of her 'wake up call' goes silent and red 'chalk writing' appears, literally spelling out (with a suitably dissonant chalk-sound effect) the title of the film, along with its metaphoric didactic intentions.

While *Señora de nadie* appears much less interested in the art-cinema modality of *Momentos*, despite a few touches (the deliberate confusion of the film's central flashback sequence, in particular) it maintains nonetheless a similar phenomenological interest in scrutinising again and again, with different shot lengths and in extremely slow-paced sequences which seem to contribute little to the film's 'plot', its protagonist's facial and bodily reactions to the twists and turns of her new situation. Luisina

Luisina Brando as Leonor in *Señora de nadie*

Brando's astonishing performance needed to be much more subtle for the multiple physical registers of the second directed film, compared with the narrower expressive range (emotional 'frozenness' to slight 'thawing') required of Graciela Dufau in the first film. Brando went on to repeat her success with Bemberg, as an extremely 'physical' actress, in two further performances: in *Miss Mary* (1986) as the mistress of the family patriarch and more notably as Doña Leonor in the final directed film, *De eso no se habla* (*We Don't Want to Talk About It*) (1993).

Unlike Bemberg's earlier adultery movies, it quickly becomes apparent that *Señora de nadie* is interested in investigating the (post-marriage) 'after' phase of the woman character's life. It studies in particular detail the slow and difficult 'awakening' of its neophyte feminist heroine. The character of Leonor is frequently shown in bed, either sleeping or on the edge of sleep or, alternatively, complaining of tiredness. In one beautifully shot and acted early sequence, after Leonor has had the extremely painful experience of leaving the family home following the discovery of her husband's infidelity, she goes to stay in her parents' house. The next day, in a huge, bright and airy room, watched over by her concerned mother and step-father, Leonor wakes up before our eyes on the family couch, finds herself in her new life and slowly 'discovers' her body, which from then on in the film will frequently be less covered up as she adopts lighter clothing for everyday wear, as well as for socialising (this film is shot in spring and summer in contrast to *Momentos*). Leonor gradually acquires more energy and zest as the film progresses but her three 'independent' sexual experiences (once with a man she is showing round a house in her new capacity as an estate agent, once with her husband who falls for the 'rejuvenated' version of his wife, and once with a man at a party towards the very end of the film) seem to weary her once more.

Luisina Brando and
Julio Chávez in
Señora de nadie

Señora de nadie is not, then, an unequivocally Utopian feminist film. It will still scan and frame almost as many images of limits and thresholds as *Momentos* did before it, one of its two versions ending on a similar shot of a window as in the first film, though this time the window (of Pablo's house not of the marital home) is seen from the outside. As I have just begun to suggest, though, the threshold explored in greatest detail in Bemberg's film, is the one which separates women and men's bodies. Not only does the film repeatedly show Leonor engaged in sexual activity with men, from the opening sequence onwards, it also shows her on a number of occasions in very close, physical proximity to Pablo. In an early sequence, at one of their group therapy meetings, we see them standing separately, some distance away from one another, with their eyes closed, touching their own faces and gently being manoeuvred by the group leader into forming a pair. This is the moment where they 'meet' for the first time, unable to see one another, feeling one another's faces in a relationship of non-sexual reciprocity and trust. Interestingly, immediately after this scene, Leonor meets the man with whom she will initiate her first sexual affair since she left her husband. In a later sequence, very near the end, before Pablo is beaten up, Leonor and Pablo are shown lying on the bed together and Leonor gently caresses the gay man's back as she comforts him over the trials and tribulations of his relationship with his violent partner (with which, we may assume, Leonor is able to empathise to a certain extent: she has already revealed at the group therapy sessions that her father used to beat her mother, before he left them – *desapareció*). Again, this is a sequence which precedes another of Leonor's disappointing heterosexual encounters.

Approximately one hour into *Señora de nadie*, however, comes one of the most Utopian and uplifting scenes of any Bemberg film. Leonor and Pablo have been sitting in a café and Pablo has just invited her to move in with him, solving at a stroke the accommodation difficulties she has experienced since moving out of the marital home with no legal right to any of her husband's property or money. In their mutual joy they seize hold of one another's hand and rush out of the café into a summer rainstorm. A tracking camera follows their hasty progress down the street, as they shriek and laugh, begin to dance, their soaked clothes sticking to their bodies. This rain dance precedes by five years another film sequence with a very similar sensibility, shot by Spanish director Pedro Almodóvar, involving two of the protagonists of his 1987 film *La ley del deseo* (*The Law of Desire*). The gay lead, also named Pablo, was played by Eusebio Poncela and his transsexual 'sister' Tina was played by Carmen Maura. Bemberg's sequence, along with others in her film, provides a moving picture of a post-second wave feminist ideal of an intimate, solidary relationship based on pure emotion and trust, for women and men struggling to break free from preexisting gender roles.[67] Much of the rest of the film, however, appears less convinced, outside of these Utopian moments, that such relationships really are possible, particularly when they involve sexual contact. Almost immediately after the sequence in the rain, Leonor meets her husband at a party and he sets out to seduce her and succeeds until she discovers that he is continuing to deceive another woman to whom he has some kind of commitment.

In an essay which treats questions of film authorship, Victor Perkins writes that 'in order to recognise *particular* sets of choices, one has to have some sense of *available* choices'.[68] The *intimista* style proves a very useful 'choice' for María Luisa Bemberg's early scripts and directed films; once mixed with some art-cinema styling and concerns, it provides her with a reasonably low-budget, relatively high-prestige form of film-making which has international possibilities and aspirations.[69] It also enables her and her collaborators, against a difficult political backdrop, to experiment with feminist representation (in particular with filmic point of view in its broad sense) in order to examine *cinematically* questions of feminism and of male and female sexual relationships; time and time again, she 'chooses' to return to dissect her idea, adapted from de Beauvoir, that 'Women must stop feeling like children who pass straight from the tutelage of their fathers to the tutelage of marriage.'[70] After *Señora de nadie*, though, the film in which a female character finally does manage to put a full stop to this seemingly endless tutelage and begins the difficult process of transforming her feelings, Bemberg turns away from the form, declaring that:

A woman director ought to try to grow with each film. I felt that in *Momentos* and *Señora de nadie*, the 'intimist' world of the woman had turned out to be too comfortable for me. I could have carried on making that kind of film.[71]

Despite her successful change of tack, Bemberg's later film protagonists continued to populate stories of female transgression, although there was a 'flight' from the contemporary world in the change to period drama begun with *Camila*. It is indeed arguable, though, as to whether or not the relatively pessimistic, or at best uncertain, endings of the first feature films were ever positively 'redressed'. For Bemberg's film heroines, intimate transgressions provide no real way out of patriarchy in and of themselves, a consistent 'message' ably intimated not just by their 'stories' but also by the very form and style of those films with which their maker began and then continued her successful career.

NOTES

Many thanks to Sebastián Guerrini for his invaluable help in obtaining video copies of the scripted films, and thanks also to Pilar Sabugo and John King.

1 '8 preguntas a escritoras, actrices, mujeres de ciencia, de las artes, del trabajo social y del periodismo', *Sur*, 'La mujer', nos 326–8, September 1970–June 1971, pp. 193–253, pp. 198–9.
2 My translation, as are all translations into English in this chapter, except where otherwise stated. 'Mientras el matrimonio siga siendo la mejor "carrera" para una mujer, la mejor solución a sus problemas afectivos y económicos, mientras se sienta insegura, indefensa, dependiente de su marido, viviendo por procuración, pienso que el divorcio le sería perjudicial. Primero que sea autónoma, vertical. Recién entonces el divorcio debidamente legislado hará de ella, si lo desea, una mujer libre y no una víctima.' Ibid., p. 199. Interestingly, these views are almost exactly echoed by Bemberg in her interview with Nissa Torrents as divorce was being legalised once again in the late 1980s. Nissa Torrents, 'One woman's cinema: interview with María Luisa Bemberg', in Susan Bassnett (ed.), *Knives and Angels: Women Writers in Latin America*, Zed Press, London, 1990, pp. 170–5, p. 172.
3 According to Clara Fontana in her invaluable book on Bemberg which was

based on a number of interviews with her, *María Luisa Bemberg*, Centro Editor de América Latina, Buenos Aires, 1993, p. 12.

4   Ibid., p. 14.

5   'La mujer', op. cit., p. 198.

6   According to Clara Fontana, op. cit., p. 17.

7   Nissa Torrents, 'Contemporary Argentine cinema', in John King and Nissa Torrents, *The Garden of the Forking Paths: Argentine Cinema*, British Film Institute, London, 1987, pp. 93–113, p. 100.

8   Reported by Caleb Bach in 'María Luisa Bemberg tells the untold', *Americas* 46, March/April 1994, p. 21.

9   Clara Fontana has also noted these in passing, Fontana op. cit., p. 12.

10   Indeed, in the next sequence, we hear Fina's children being taught French conjugation by their French governess.

11   Interestingly, Friedan recounts in her introduction an anecdote about how, when asked by a census taker what her profession was, she replied 'housewife' despite the fact that she was working as a writer on this book at the time, Betty Friedan, *The Feminine Mystique*, W. W. Norton and Company, New York, 1963, 1974, p. 6.

12   Clara Fontana, op. cit., p. 11.

13   'La mujer debe tomar conciencia de la "condición femenina", o sea del estado de dependencia política, social y económica en que se encuentra. El primer paso para lograr un cambio es desear ese cambio.' *Sur*, 'La mujer', op. cit., p. 199.

14   Exhibition programme cited by Clara Fontana, op. cit., p. 19.

15   'Bemberg enfrenta al espectador y sobre todo a la espectadora, con un hecho encubierto por las prácticas sociales: el pretendido "mundo de la mujer", no es "de la mujer". Es un mundo de cosas, objetos, mercancías. La mujer es apenas un instrumento mediador.' Loc. cit. Bemberg wrote and directed a second documentary short, on a similar theme, in 1978: *Juguetes (Toys)*.

16   'Otra vez la protagonista, ahora en la piel de Thelma Biral, busca como Fina en *Crónica* . . . el refugio de la infidelidad. El trazado es poco convincente y difícilmente audaz. Le falta la dimensión conceptual que en algunos casos, el de *Crónica de una señora* es uno, hacen [*sic*] de una historia menor un arquetipo relevante de un conflicto humano y social. *Triángulo de cuatro* es un drama común entre gente frívola y algún toque crítico no la rescata de la trivialidad.' Clara Fontana, op. cit., p. 20.

17   Reported by Luis Trelles Plazaola, 'María Luisa Bemberg', *Cine y mujer: en*

América Latina directoras de largometrajes de ficción, Universidad de Puerto Rico, San Juan, 1991, pp. 105–25, p. 105.

18 There are further allusions to Fellini's *La dolce vita* in *Triángulo*. We discover that Martín likes to record sound effects from nature like Marcello's friend Steiner who commits suicide in the 1960 film. This is treated much more lightly in Fernando Ayala's movie.

19 There are other sequences where Teresa 'directs' humorous scenes with Felipe in the photographic studio space of her flat, including one in which she pretends to be his *geisha*.

20 I base this observation, and others in this chapter, on Murray Smith's extremely useful theories of 'alignment' and 'allegiance' in film narration in his book *Engaging Characters: Fiction, Emotion and the Cinema* (Oxford University Press, Oxford, 1995): '[*Alignment*] describes the process by which spectators are placed in relation to characters in terms of access to their actions, and to what they know and feel. The concept is akin to the literary notion of "focalisation", Gérard Genette's term for the way in which narratives may feed story information to the reader through the "lens" of a particular character', in film largely through *spatio-temporal attachment* and *subjective access* (Smith, p. 83). Meanwhile, *allegiance* 'pertains to the moral evaluation of characters by the spectator' and 'depends on the spectator having what she takes to be reliable access to the character's state of mind, on understanding the context of the character's actions, and having morally evaluated the character on the basis of this knowledge'. The word 'moral' is used by Smith rather than 'ideological' because, with respect to characters, 'ideological judgements are typically expressed as moral evaluations; and secondly, assessing the overall ideology of a text may involve factors other than those pertaining to its characterological structure' (Smith, p. 84).

21 '[M]e bastaron estas dos películas para darme cuenta, y lo que digo no implica un juicio de valor sobre esos films, de que nunca nadie iba a interpretar como yo lo que yo había escrito', Clara Fontana, op. cit., p. 20.

22 Here I allude to Timothy Corrigan's understanding of the modern 'commerce in auteurism', which takes place as much in press and academic interviews, and in other seemingly peripheral items of film culture, as it does in the physical distribution and consumption of actual film texts, especially since 1970. In the chapter 'The commerce of auteurism' in his book *A Cinema Without Walls: Movies and Culture after Vietnam* (Rutgers University Press, New Brunswick, 1991, pp. 105–27), Corrigan advocates the analysis of directorial

interviews in order to investigate the kinds of 'commercial dramatisations of self' (pp. 10–89) which are routinely articulated in this ubiquitous format. I have discussed Corrigan's work and its implications for the future study of film authorship in some detail in an article for *Screen* vol. 41, no. 1, 2000: 'www.auteur.com?', pp. 121–30.

23 Bemberg in 'Pride and prejudice: María Luisa Bemberg, interview with Sheila Whitaker', in John King and Nissa Torrents (eds), op. cit., pp. 115–21, p. 115.

24 Ibid., p. 116.

25 'Yo creo que la primera película se hace en la máquina de escribir. Cuando uno escribe, por ejemplo, "amanece, aparece en el fondo la silueta de una figura que avanza hacia la cámara" yo ya la estoy filmando, estoy encuadrando. Concluí entonces que si yo quería que la película reflejase fielmente lo que yo había visualizado no tenía más remedio que ponerme a dirigir.' Bemberg in Luis Trelles Plazaola, op. cit., p. 111.

26 Ibid., p. 113.

27 '[Películas que] sólo pudieron ser concebidas por mujeres y hasta me atrevo a decir por mujeres que sublimaron su descontento en fuerza creativa': Clara Fontana, op. cit., p. 8.

28 'Se filmaba la escena de *Crónica* . . . en que Fina se augustia al percibir la realidad de su existencia vacía. Según cuenta Bemberg, que siempre asistía a las filmaciones, como autora pensó que para dar convicción a la escena se imponía hacer un primer plano muy especial. No pudo convencer a de la Torre, que sentía una antipatía por Fina, ese personaje al que Bemberg consideraba víctima de las circunstancias. Como para consolarse comentó el hecho al iluminador, que era Juan Carlos Desanzo. Desanzo le contestó: "¿Por qué no dirigís vos?" "Mi reacción" comenta Bemberg "fue . . .". "¿Yo, mujer, . . . dirigir? No sé nada de técnica".' Clara Fontana, op. cit., pp. 18–19. Caleb Bach is less circumspect: 'Believing that "no man could understand what was happening with the new awareness of women", she decided to go behind the camera herself.' Bach, op. cit., p. 2.

29 'Adultery "decriminalised"', Clara Fontana, op. cit., p. 22.

30 Tony Tanner, *Adultery in the Novel: Contract and Transgression*, The Johns Hopkins University Press, Baltimore, 1979, p. 15.

31 Bryan S. Turner, *The Body and Society*, Sage, London, 1996, p. 23.

32 Ibid., p. 3.

33 Loc. cit.

34 'These socio-economic changes are furthermore closely associated with what Anthony Giddens has called *The Transformation of Intimacy* [Polity/Blackwell, Oxford, 1992], in which self-understanding, individualism and self-realisation are expressed through interpersonal relations based on pure emotion, non-utilitarian trust and interpersonal intimacy' (Turner, p. 3) and no longer on a property contract. In his 1992 book, Giddens connects these changes to the emergence of second wave feminism, and writes: 'Fundamental features of a society of high reflexivity are the "open" character of self-identity and the reflexive nature of the body. For women struggling to break free from pre-existing gender roles, the question "Who am I?" which Betty Frieden [sic] labelled "the problem that has no name" comes to the surface with particular intensity' Anthony Giddens, op. cit., p. 30.

35 See Clara Fontana for her anecdote about how Bemberg's film *Momentos* could be a 'reinvention' of Torre Ríos's adultery film *La vuelta al nido*, freed from its negative moral connotations, op. cit., p. 24. Meanwhile, see Ana López's discussion of the Argentine *cinéma d'auteur* in which she traces the connections between the different generations and, in particular, points out that Torre Nilsson's creation of his own production company created a commercially viable 'art-cinema' production model to be copied by Ayala and Olivera with their Aries Cinematográfica company (which produced Bemberg's *Triángulo*) and I would argue, in due course, by Lita Stantic and Bemberg with their GEA Cinematográfica, 'Argentina, 1955–1976: the film industry and its margins' in King and Torrents, op. cit., pp. 49–80, pp. 54–9 (and on de la Torre, p. 77).

36 Annette Kuhn, *Women's Pictures: Feminism and Cinema*, Verso, London, 1994, p. 135.

37 In the interview with Caleb Bach, Bemberg is quoted as follows: 'my first film has the influence of Michelangelo Antonioni in which very little things suddenly become relevant, objects for instance. The one who influenced me most, his words – *Notes on Cinematography* – that's Robert Bresson. He's my master.' Caleb Bach, op. cit., p. 4.

38 'Bemberg lo reinventa al quitarle toda connotación moral. El adulterio se esfuma. Nadie transgrede nada. El conflicto pasa por los sentimientos, no por la moralidad.' Clara Fontana, op. cit., p. 24.

39 '[T]iene clara conciencia de [. . .] "género femenino".' Ibid., p. 22.

40 'El adulterio de una mujer visto por otra mujer.' There are no 'intradiegetic' female characters who witness the affair, so the marketing tag clearly refers to Bemberg's role as director.

41 One might convincingly argue that this is a Bergmanesque style heavily inflected, not only by the 'women's film', but also by the style of Woody Allen whose films Bemberg claimed to like in numerous interviews (see Luis Trelles Plazaola, op. cit., p. 115), although *Momentos* itself owes little to that film-maker's humorous treatment of adulterous relationships (unlike Bemberg's second directed film, the heavily ironic *Señora de nadie*). A Bergman movie receives a mention in one of *Momentos*'s sequences. Roughly an hour into the film, the two lovers are deciding which film to go to see to fill one of their increasingly empty evenings in Mar del Plata. Lucía first suggests *Kramer versus Kramer* (US, 1979, Robert Benson) which Nicolás has already seen and liked. She then enthusiastically suggests Bergman's *Cries and Whispers* (*Viskningar och rop*) (Sweden, 1972), but he expresses his derision at her taste until he sees he is wounding her.

42 This connects Lucía, in particular, to another of Bemberg's characters, Miss Mary, whose younger lover was killed, leading her to seek out that kind of passion once more. Sigmund Freud, 'Remembering, repeating, and working-through (further recommendations on the technique of psycho-analysis)' in *The Standard Edition of the Complete Psychological Works of Sigmund Freud*, Vol. XII, The Hogarth Press, London, 1958, pp. 145–56.

43 Anthony Giddens, op. cit., p. 8.

44 *Nosotros* (composed by Pedro Junco; most well known in the version sung by Los Panchos): 'We love each other so much, but we ought to separate. Don't ask me why, it's not for the lack of love – I love you with all my soul [. . .], and in the name of this love, and for your own good, I say goodbye.' Nicolás reacts violently to her attempt to let him down gently, though he is full of remorse for hitting her and she seems to forgive him.

45 Almirante Emilio Massera decreed in May 1976, at the beginning of the military dictatorship, that in Argentine cultural texts 'in all cases, the resolution of the issues must lead to a positive ending', documented in Andrés Avellaneda, *Censura, autoritarismo y cultura: Argentina 1960–1983*, Vol. 2, Biblioteca Política Argentina, Buenos Aires, 1986, p. 155.

46 Tony Tanner, op. cit., p. 376. Here Tanner alludes to Michel Foucault's well known essay 'Préface à la transgression'.

47 Bemberg herself once said that '*Momentos* begins with a euphoria which gradually becomes a *noia*, a kind of asphyxia and anguish.' ('Es una película que comienza con una euforia y poco a poco se va transformando en una *noia*, una asfixia y angustia.') in Luis Trelles Plazaola, op. cit., p. 114.

48 Part of a quotation from Bemberg's film *Camila*, where the character of the mother states: 'marriage is like the nation [. . .] The best jail is the one you cannot see' ('el matrimonio es como el país [. . .] La mejor cárcel es la que no se ve').

49 Bemberg wrote the script for *Momentos* with the credited collaboration of therapist Marcelo Pichon Rivière, the son of a famous Argentine psychoanalyst, probably to lend the psychoanalytic references greater credibility.

50 '[H]abía realizado antes films como *Momentos* y *Señora de nadie*, donde introduce con cierta superficialidad ambientes de la alta burguesía argentina (que conoce bien porque son los suyos), y un feminismo tenue, apto para la hora del té.' José Agustín Mahieu, *Panorama del cine iberoamericano*, Ediciones de Cultura Hispánica, Madrid, p. 50. This does echo Bemberg's own remarks about the film in Sheila Whitaker's interview. See note 23 above.

51 In the interview with Luis Trelles Plazaola, Bemberg gives her own interpretation of *Momentos*'s ending: 'I believe that for [Lucía] that window is closed and she returns to her marriage because she has no way out.' ('Yo creo que para esa mujer esa ventana está cerrada y vuelve a su matrimonio porque no tiene salida.') in Luis Trelles Plazaola, op. cit., p. 117.

52 'Fue un gran bajón porque me había dado cuerda para largarme a hacer esta película y me dijeron que no se podía hacer. Me dieron tres razones: la primera, porque era un pésimo ejemplo para las madres argentinas; la segunda, es que hay un maricón – "Yo, señora, prefiero tener un hijo con cáncer a que sea maricón"; y la tercera, es que la dirige una mujer.' Ibid., p. 113.

53 Foucauldian 'regimes of truth' are 'encased in institutional structures that exclude specific voices' (Ella Shohat and Robert Stam, *Unthinking Eurocentrism: Multiculturalism and the Media*, Routledge, London, 1994, p. 18), yet do not simply function to repress, but also to produce the forms that specific cultural products take.

54 Sarah A. Radcliffe, 'Women's place/El lugar de mujeres: Latin America and the politics of gender identity' in Michael Keith and Steve Pile (eds), *Place and the Politics of Identity*, Routledge, London, pp. 102–16, p. 106.

55 Mary-Beth Tierney-Tello, *Allegories of Transgression and Transformation: Experimental Fiction by Women Writing under Dictatorship*, State University of New York Press, Albany, 1996, p. 142.

56 Luis Trelles Plazaola, op. cit., pp. 117–18.

57 There was some press interest, though, in the 'nude scenes', and at least one newspaper chose to stage a discussion about Miguel Angel Solá's brief total

nudity in the 'breakfast in bed' sequence in *Momentos*, 'Actores critican el desnudo de Solá', *ASI en CRONICA*, Buenos Aires, 17 May 1981, p. 8. (This newspaper is mentioned by the character of Julio in *Señora de nadie*.) The only negative comments that the journalists managed to gather, however, were ones from a few actors, including Graciela Borges, who on balance criticised the film, generally in a rather mean-spirited fashion, for playing somewhat too safe in these sequences. (My thanks to John King for providing me with a copy of this article.)

58   'La tendencia a gastar, a viajar, a evadirse, era tal vez una necesidad colectiva luego de los grandes miedos del período '70/78. Esta soledad vuelta sobre sí misma, sin vida pública, privatizada, encontraba un escape a su angustia, una suerte de compensación que le ofrecía la política económica [con el fenómeno denominado 'plata dulce'].' María Sáenz Quesada, *El camino de la democracia*, Tiempo de Ideas, Buenos Aires, 1993, p. 126.

59   Michael Taussig, *The Nervous System*, Routledge, New York, 1992, p. 26, cited by Diana Taylor, *Disappearing Acts: Spectacles of Gender and Nationalism in Argentina's 'Dirty War'*, Duke University Press, Durham and London, 1977, p. 287, see note 16.

60   See note 45.

61   John King and Nissa Torrents, op. cit., pp. 93–113, p. 103. Bemberg herself states that *Momentos* and *Señora de nadie* both broke even, Luis Trelles Plazaola, op. cit., pp. 119–20.

62   María Elena Walsh, 'El país, jardín de infantes', *Clarín*, circa mid-1979, as reported by Sáenz Quesada, op. cit., p. 126.

63   The music for the song was composed by Luis María Serra, one of Bemberg's regular collaborators. Alberto Ciria has briefly discussed the matter of the film's two endings as follows: '*Señora de nadie* ends with two codas. In the first, Laura [*sic*: Leonor, the protagonist] consoles Pablo [her gay friend] (who has been brutally beaten up by his violent lover), and the two sleep in the same bed, like good friends. In the second, Laura and her sons have moved into a new apartment and the film plays out with the soundtrack of the song *Señora mía* [. . .] which underlines the theme of women's independence outside of the confines of marriage.' '*Señora de nadie* termina con dos codas. En la primera, Laura [sic] consuela a Pablo (quien ha sido golpeado duramente por un amante violento), y los dos duermen en la misma cama, como buenos amigos. En la segunda, Laura y sus hijos ocupan un nuevo departamento con el fondo sonoro de la canción *Señora mía* [. . .] que subraya el tema de la independencia de la mujer

fuera de los límites asfixiantes de la institución matrimonia.' Alberto Ciria con Jorge M. López, 'Historia, sexo, clase y poder en los filmes de María Luisa Bemberg' in Ciria, *Más allá de la pantalla: Cine argentino, historia y política*, Ediciones de la Flor, Buenos Aires, 1995, pp. 153–77, p. 156. The commercially distributed VHS version (AVH, Buenos Aires) does not incorporate the song and, like *Momentos*, ends with a shot of a window (this time shown from the outside), following on from the sequence of Leonor and Pablo in bed. In a letter from María Luisa Bemberg to John King, dated 11 August 1992, the director expresses her clear dislike of the second ending, with Walsh's song an 'ideological concession' to the idea of the 'woman triumphant'. (I am very grateful to John King for giving me a copy of this and other Bemberg correspondence.) Unfortunately, I have not managed to discover yet which of the two endings was used for the film's cinema release, or why the film has two versions in circulation. I do, however, concur with Bemberg's own assessment of her endings: the platonic bed sequence more neatly rhymes, inversely, with the film's precredit sequence.

64 Clara Fontana, op. cit., p. 59.

65 Sáenz Quesada, op. cit., p. 159.

66 This and other details and, in general, the film's tone, are strikingly reminiscent of Ingmar Bergman's *Scener ur ett äktenskap* (*Scenes from a Marriage*) (Sweden, 1972).

67 This kind of ideal relationship chimes with Gidden's idealised depiction of certain kinds of modern 'interpersonal relationships'. See note 34.

68 My emphasis: V. F. Perkins et al., 'The return of *Movie*', *Movie*, no. 20, Spring 1975, p. 12.

69 Both of the first directed films were shown at international festivals, including Huelva, Spain, Chicago, Cartagena, Colombia, Taormina, Italy and Panamá, winning prizes for acting and direction, Clara Fontana, op. cit., p. 62.

70 Bemberg, 'La mujer tiene que dejar de sentirse una "menor de edad que pasa de la tutela paterna a la tutela marital"', La mujer, op. cit., p. 198.

71 'Una directora tiene que intentar crecer con cada película. Sentí que en *Momentos* y *Señora de nadie* el mundo intimista de la mujer me quedaba super cómodo. Podía seguir haciendo este tipo de película.' Luis Trelles Plazaola, op. cit., p. 115.

FOUR

ON *CAMILA*: THE RED, THE BLACK, AND THE WHITE

Alan Pauls

Every true passion thinks just of itself.

Stendhal

We should perhaps treat the release of *Camila* as an event. There is more than one reason for this statement that some might consider somewhat hyperbolic. (We consider that Argentine cinema lacks events and instead is made up of workmanlike films that purport to offer an image of a film 'industry'.) For one thing, there is the scope of its production (shared with the Spanish company Impala that supplied the lighting cameraman and the actor Imanol Arias), which reconstructs in minute pictorial detail scenes of Buenos Aires in the mid-nineteenth century. Furthermore, there is the commitment to a genre, melodrama, which is radically different to the tone of the two previous pictures of María Luisa Bemberg. This is a genre that Argentine cinema purports to avoid out of a sense of decorum yet still cultivates in a worthless way. From the first to the last frame, *Camila* is a melodrama but its virtuosity lies in the fact that the melodramatic mode is an aesthetic choice rather than an accidental outcome. *Camila* explores the terrain of melodrama, *works* its conventions and its rhetoric; for that reason, it is far removed from that degraded version, the soap opera. The first question that *Camila* raises is: why this leap from domestic bourgeois fictions to such a broad sweeping tale, full of novelistic incident and romanticism? What happened to the director between *Señora de nadie* (1982) and this *Camila*?

'I felt that I had fulfilled an obligation', says María Luisa Bemberg, 'an obligation that I had with regard to the situation of women in society. This made me denounce the systematic denegration of women, their social, economic and emotional dependency, in fact everything that stood in the way of women's freedom. For that reason, my previous films are portraits of alienated women who, particularly in *Señora de nadie*, try to affirm themselves gradually as autonomous individuals. Then I began to feel rather bored, I felt that I was in danger of repeating myself or of becoming too comfortable, which are two great dangers for a professional who wants to grow. I don't use the term artist since I'm somewhat afraid of it; let's call me instead a 'teller of tales'. Then Lita Stantic [the executive producer of *Camila*] suggested the story of Camila O'Gorman. She made it something of an issue of pride by saying: 'Even the critics that most respect your work say that you don't know how to tell a love story, that you're too sceptical.' And I accepted the challenge, picked up the gauntlet and thought, 'let's see if I can tell the story of a passion'. Two things really attracted me to the project: the worlds that I was gradually discovering as I got to understand Camila O'Gorman better, and the fact of engaging with our past, with that ambivalent, fractured identity that all of us Argentines should recognise if we wish to study our roots.'

Historical accounts confirm the scandalous passion of the adolescent girl from Buenos Aires and the Jesuit priest. Their pages tell of the fatal challenge that the lovers posed to the institutions and power of their time and allude, with the necessary austerity of chronicles of the past, to the final tragedy. But they modestly omit the details. Here history and fiction begin to fork: 'Lita first brought me the beautiful book of Enrique Molina, *Una sombra donde sueña Camila O'Gorman* (*A Shadow Where Camila O'Gorman Dreams*), which is a prose poem. For that reason it was impossible to adapt, since it was pure language. So we had to invent everything, except certain historical references that are contained in the memoirs of Captain Reyes, which is the source that all the historians use. It is known that he was a Jesuit attached to the Iglesia del Socorro, and that she sang in the church choir. It is known that they ran away on 12 December 1847 and that they set up a school in Goya. Other authentic details are the false names that they used, the denunciation of Father Gannon and their execution by firing squad in Santos Lugares. All the rest, as I say in the film, is a free version.'

For the historical reconstruction, Bemberg asked the help of the feminist historian Leonor Calvera. Calvera consulted archives and read the history books and memoir accounts. By elucidating the past, she prepared the-ground for the fiction. 'The fact of working with an historical era restricts you a great deal. We took a trip to Córdoba to look for locations, but it was all too Spanish, it was earlier than what we needed. We went to Colonia, travelled around a great deal and finally found that very beautiful house Chascomús, which we turned into the O'Gorman family house in Buenos Aires. We had thought of using the Pueyrredón Museum, but they did not let us have it: perhaps they did not like the script. Anyway, I'm pleased, because the Pueyrredón Museum is too well known and that would have detracted from the story's veracity. I think that the place we chose has a like-ness to the exteriors of houses painted by Figari. That was my challenge with respect to historical reconstruction: that people should stop looking at the characters from the outside, should not see them as dressed up, but rather engage with the story.'

History, we know, is a 'virile' genre. Argentine cinema has managed to stress this adjective to ridiculous lengths, with bronzes, statues, hieratic and paternalist great men and energetic postures. The foundational myth of historical heroism coincides suspiciously with a masculine myth: Cabral sacrificing himself for San Martín. What is there left for women in this uni-verse of boots and sabres, these almost parodic emblems of virility that the films of Torre Nilsson exalted? 'To some extent', Bemberg states, '*Camila* projects a feminine gaze onto history. There is no doubt that she is the pro-tagonist of the film. I was interested in dissolving the 'feminine' myths of a languid girl, with a blank expression, who dies for love. I wanted a person who was bold, brave, daring, a liberated woman *avant la lettre*. As a femi-nist, I was interested in offering images of women that were different to the traditional stereotypes, that the historians themselves had helped to reinforce. Busaniche, Gálvez, Ibarguren talk of the 'sweet, innocent and pure Camila, who was seduced . . .'. What if it was the other way round? It's the old story of feminine passivity faced with virile aggression. I thought: a traditional, Catholic, virgin, controlled, repressed girl who managed on her own to go and live with a priest. . . . What balls she must have had! Then I knew that she was not a traditional woman who stayed in her allotted place, but that she had broken all the barriers. A woman with a lot of courage, a lot of vitality and with strong views: quite simply, a free person. And there are few free women in cinema.'

Which of the O'Gormans, that family ruled by the will of a despotic father (Héctor Alterio)   whose image is often juxtaposed with a portrait of

Forbidden love in *Camila*

Rosas – embodies that freedom and opens the way for Camila's destiny? It is the grandmother, La Perichona (Mona Maris), in whom the feminine and desire are dangerously confused with dissidence and scandal. It is she who *marks* Camila when she asks her, at the beginning of the film, if she likes love stories? The very young Camila, who is surprised at the arrival of this ghostly character, hesitates: 'I don't know', she says. However, this scene condenses and anticipates all the subsequent development of the tale: La Perichona appoints Camila as her successor. If the child Camila 'does not know', the spectator, by contrast, already knows and it is in this play of distance between the knowledge of the characters and that of the viewer that the dynamic of melodrama is established. In more than one sense, La Perichona is the 'author' of Camila, her mentor in passion: by entrusting to her her own legacy of transgressions, she sketches out a genealogy which mocks paternal authority and family honour. The last meeting between Camila and her grandmother is exemplary in this respect. Confined by her son to a remote corner of the house – her 'illness', of course is contagious: Camila is the first to be affected – La Perichona anxiously awaits the visit of Liniers, her ex-lover, who has been dead for years and she shares with her granddaughter the art of impatience. Instead of 'bringing her back' to reality, Camila fuels her imaginary world and takes part as a character in the 'representation'.

'Love stories', furthermore, are no longer a matter of indifference to her. She receives them periodically from the bookseller Mariano, who slips romantic novels into her hand with extreme caution, as if they were antigovernment pamphlets. The comparison is not fanciful: the bookseller will become the first victim of the repression and, faced with his severed head, Camila will glimpse the severity of her own 'deviance'. Liniers is already a figure in a daguerreotype, la Perichona is consumed by delirium, but Camila does not seem to pay much attention to these dangers. As both an accomplice and a disciple of her grandmother, how can Camila challenge what La Perichona proclaims in her dementia, which is nothing more than the right to desire, outside confinement, and also the right to madness when later it will be she, Camila, who, alongside Ladislao, will become the protagonist of a fiction of love woven with false names? 'Passions cannot be

Susú Pecoraro in *Camila* (BFI stills library)

explained: destiny marks them out', says Bemberg. 'I think that the scene where she has her eyes blindfolded and she touches Ladislao is like a representation of fate, which is blind. But of course La Perichona has influenced Camila, she has made her a captive audience and filled her head with impossible love stories. And what is more impossible than a priest? But that would be another film, a Rohmer-style film, which would explore and dissect the behaviour of the lovers to see to what extent the forbidden attracted Camila and became one more stimulus for her to approach and walk the edge of the abyss. Perhaps Camila might have spent her life dreaming of an impossible love, going to confession, casting little glances in church, perhaps stealing a furtive kiss, but what happens is that she meets a man who tells her, "I am not one for secret loves". And that is a moral attitude that seems very important to me, because this man is prepared to pay for the price of his love: there is no hypocrisy. When he understands that the church does not allow him to serve God and his love at the same time, he leaves the chalice, takes off his cassock and abandons everything. This is an act of moral honesty that seems very necessary.'

To narrate the story of a passion is, to some extent, an exercise in domestication. The law of melodrama is severe: the more excessive the passion, the more 'controlled' the story must be, the more the rapture must be contained and the outbursts rationalised. *Camila* draws with rare wisdom on melodrama's sense of narrative construction, its ability to measure out the effect and the affect, employing that intensity of structure that characterised novels of the nineteenth century. (María Luisa Bemberg defines it as 'a kind of control of excess.') 'I knew', she says, 'that the story divided into three parts: Buenos Aires, Goya and Santos Lugares. I wrote the script four times with Docampo Feijóo and Stagnaro. Then it occurred to me to use a fragmented structure: start in Goya and then do a flash back. They really liked the idea and we began a fifth version as a *racconto*. I let it rest for a week, I read it and didn't like it. It seemed too capricious and artificial, it didn't have any foundation. Then I took over the script alone and rewrote it a further two times. I began work in cinema as a scriptwriter and I know that if a script is not rigorous and tightly written, then it is very difficult to make a good film, however talented the director. It's like the architectural foundations for a house. What's the point of putting in Carrara marble if the foundations are bad? What's important, and this only a director can do, is to have the whole film in your head, like a map. Then, with that security, you can follow intuitions and diversions, but always having in mind what it is you want to tell: not getting lost, not trying to tell seventeen things at the same time. In *Camila*, I wanted to explore one or, at most, two things: the abuse of power as a subtext and the story of a passion. With these goals clear, a film is like a yacht, you have to steer with the sails tight, on one course.'

How to represent love, when love is always *already* a representation? Don't lovers 'make scenes'? Love is a love scene; it is impossible to think of it outside this dramatic frame. But alongside scenes, there are episodes, sequences of love. Melodrama provides the most complete model of this narrative expansion of love and has laws to regulate its economy. Some time back, in a press conference, María Luisa Bemberg had categorically affirmed her allegiance to this dramatic economy: 'I hope that I have the courage to develop a melodrama right to the end.' *Camila* is the dramatisation of this courage: 'When I said that, I was thinking of melodrama in terms of exaggeration, as a total exaltation, without any of the reticence that a colder, more detached, mind might use to interpret this sort of behaviour. I did not want to keep my distance, because, sceptic as I am, I would have started to probe, as I did in *Momentos*, which is a film made through a magnifying glass, a film of observation. In this instance, I did not want to lose those gusts of exaltation. I decided to get inside that situation of love's madness, to give truth to the phrase, "to lose one's head through love" and try not to worry if I became excessive: *I did not want to be afraid of excess*. If we need sobbing violins, I thought, well then, let them sob. And I think this lack of fear is what allowed me to film everything to the limit and to make the result credible and moving'. Like *The Woman Next Door* and *Adèle H* by Truffaut, and like Polanski's *Tess*, *Camila* is a film that has no shame. Not because it contains daringly erotic scenes, but because it is brave enough to sustain a discourse which – Barthes has already said it – is not contemporary, is currently discredited and is marginal to all forms of science, knowledge and the arts. For María Luisa Bemberg, 'not to be afraid of excess' is to have had the courage to immerse herself in this profoundly devalued genre and to have wrested from its codes a truth which is often trivialised. Fanny Ardent made the point in *The Woman Next Door*: 'I can only repeat phrases from the most banal songs: "don't leave me", "I miss you", "I love you". That's where the truth is.' '*Camila*', says Bemberg, 'is a film with much less distance than *The Woman Next Door*, where everything is seen as if from the outside, with those aerial shots of the ambulance and with that narrator who seems somewhat like Truffaut himself. It's a reflection on passion, on the inevitability of passion. I think that *Camila* might be seen as closer to *Adèle H* in the sense that it is not so much a reflection on passion as a submission to passion. If the film has a reflective part, this concerns the nature of violence. In any event, these analogies are *a posteriori*. When I begin to incubate a film, even though I'm a regular film-goer, I stop going to the cinema altogether. I only feel the need to be alone, shut up inside my house, in silence or listening to music. Certain musicians such as Mozart, Wagner and Bartok help me to visualise images. At that moment, other people's films bother me, they interfere: *I don't want anything outside me to influence me.* I don't look at other people's images, for once they have been given form by someone else, then they are no longer any use to me. I get inhibited if I think of other films and one has to be as free as possible in order to create.'

Susú Pecoraro and Imanol Arias in *Camila* (BFI stills library)

'In Paris, love is the child of the novel', Stendhal writes. Geography matters little: it is accidental. In *Camila*, love is also a branch of an extensive tradition, which includes, of course, *Scarlet and Black*. Like the O'Gorman house, which evokes or copies Figari, like the tone and light of the film which deliberately appropriates the tone and lithography of Peregrino, Camila's passion is *read* in the books that she secretly devours. And just as Camila herself receives her lover's education from her grandmother and fulfils her mandate of passion, María Luisa Bemberg (although her words about creative isolation might seek to deny this) also inherits the knowledge about sentiment that a whole century disseminated in novels, *feuilletons* and melodramas.

To say that *Camila* only deals with two themes is a modest declaration of principles that the logic of melodrama undermines. *Camila* also talks, in its own terms, about sex, the family, Oedipus, society, masters and servants, priests and the problems of a vocation and homosexuality (although the brother, Claudio Gallardón, is a sort of sexless double of Ladislao). *Camila* weaves all these elements into a web that both displays and hides them, using the false naiveté with which melodrama presents its knowledge about the world: a circular knowledge interspersed with gusts of emotion. But María Luisa Bemberg is stubborn in this respect: 'I am not an intellectual, I'm someone who works on dramatic intuition. My first question is "what" and the second "how"; and that is always determined by the theme. Here what I wanted to tell was the amorous disorder of two young lovers in nineteenth century Río de La Plata with all its undercurrents of violence: the purity of these two beings, their lack of awareness. I knew that with this story, *I had to bring the characters close to the spectator*, put them in close-up, so that it would almost be possible to see the beating of their hearts. And that determined the camera placement, the colours, the frames, the rhythm, the music.' Susú Pecoraro's acting is decisive in establishing this closeness between characters and spectators. Her Camila (and perhaps the highest compliment that can be paid to her is to say that she has made the part of Camila her own; after her performance it is impossible to imagine another actress in the role) very effectively combines stubbornness and despair, tension and an inflexible dignity. She is both subject and object of the

Susú Pecoraro and
Imanol Arias in
Camila (BFI stills
library)

passion that drives her and perhaps the key to her performance lies in maintaining this delicate balance.

Susú Pecoraro is a force that blows through the film like a tornado, dragging it in her wake; most of the emotion the film generates comes from her face (the intensity of her fury) and the energy of her body. Think of the declaration of love scene in the confessional where Camila takes on the function that the code of love usually reserves for men. She admits to Ladislao that she loves him, but refers to him in the third person: 'I love him father', she says to him, 'but he cannot marry'. We just have to think of Camila's face that can only be glimpsed through the confessional grille ('just her pleading eyes and her fresh and sensual mouth, quite irresistible', adds Bemberg) and, in counter shot, the terrified, fascinated expression of the priest, to realise how one actress can give *body* to a text, while another might fail completely. Susú Pecoraro, without any further gesture, but also without wavering, declares her love and makes this declaration an amorous imperative, with no possibility for resistance or escape.

And the colours? *Camila* also tells a chromatic story, the red of the emblem on the black clothes of the priest and Camila's father, the black on the white of Camila, the white blindfolds over Camila's eyes and the black blindfolds of the firing squad execution. 'Colours also play a part in the way I map the film in my mind during that voluntary preparation period in hibernation. Things emerge slowly. Obviously the red blood of Rosas is both violence and passion, which are the two axes of the film. Black is an ecclesiastical colour, the colour of authority and patriarchy (Alterio is always dressed in red or black). As for purity, well, it might seem a bit obvious, but there is no better colour than white to express this. There are also the chromatic tones of the film: at first, warm and golden (I showed the lighting cameraman many lithographs and prints of the period). Then gradually everything darkens and, at the end, in prison, there are greys, ochre, sepias. The only thing to stand out are the pink flowers on Camila's dress, a dress made for a party (we see her sewing it in the country), never suspecting that this will be the dress that she dies in. I was looking for the counterpoint between the dramatic force of a rifle and this simple dress with its little flowers, very fragile, very feminine.'

The subject of love, writes Barthes, is suspended far from human concerns, by a tacit decree of insignificance: it is not part of any repertoire or any refuge. Like this subject, *Camila* is a *solitary* film. It is not weighed down by immediate concerns or by opportunism. At a time when Argentine cinema seems to feel an imperative to be 'committed', often mistakenly, *Camila* is a film that, like the passions in Stendahl, only thinks of itself. It is made with great freedom, with great pleasure and with the emotion that only freedom and pleasure can provide. For these reasons, *Camila* is more than a film, it is an event.

This chapter was translated by John King. The original version appeared in Cine Libre, *July 1984, pp. 4–7.*

FIVE

RE-ENGENDERING HISTORY: MARÍA LUISA BEMBERG'S *MISS MARY*

Elia Geoffrey Kantaris

The late Argentine film director, María Luisa Bemberg, is probably best known for her massively popular post-dictatorship film of 1984, *Camila*. This film, which carefully deploys a popular melodramatic idiom, was seen by over two million Argentines on first release and received wide international distribution.[1] Bemberg's following feature of 1986, the much starker yet thematically more complex *Miss Mary*, was less immediately popular, although it certainly confirmed Bemberg's position as one of Argentina's top directors. This chapter will concentrate on the latter film in an attempt to show how Bemberg's thinking about the intersection of diverse fields of power – political authoritarianism, neo-colonialism, and the gender system – is linked to a subtle reworking of the twin representational systems of history and cinema.

Miss Mary as a film speaks a somewhat different language to *Camila*, and I do not merely refer to the film's bilingualism with its extensive use of English as signalled by the title, a fact which itself acts as a forceful allegory for the power relationships surrounding Argentina's historical insertion within world economic and political systems. Even in more general terms, *Miss Mary* moves away from the carefully applied melodramatic idiom of *Camila* into an equally subtle but perhaps more complex engagement with the historical dimensions underlying a network of patriarchal power extending from family, to social class, to a whole socio-economic system together with its geopolitical determinants. Both films operate a temporal displacement of the gendered politics of authoritarianism: *Camila* deals with family and national romance during the mid-nineteenth-century dictatorship of Juan Manuel de Rosas, while *Miss Mary* is set in the 1930s and 1940s during the Infamous Decade of unconstitutional rule by the conservative land-owning oligarchy in Argentina. Through such displacements, the films impose a double reading: the bloody dictatorship of the late 1970s and early 1980s is compared with a previous period of dictatorship and is impeccably reconstructed. It is as if the films were summoning the past, its exclusions, gaps and repressions, to make it account for what has been silenced within the present. That the films should open up, from the outset, the gendered dimension of those repressed spaces is characteristic of Bemberg's work which carefully re-deploys the *genre* of historical reconstruction, re-engendering it as refracted history of the present.

Camila is based on a 'true story', set in 1847, of a young woman from Buenos Aires, Camila O'Gorman (Susú Pecoraro), who became the lover of a priest, Ladislao Gutiérrez (Imanol Arias). After eloping together, they are eventually caught and executed, despite the fact that Camila is pregnant. Although they are executed for sexual immorality and blasphemy, the film suggests that the making of the issue into one of national authority (it is the dictator Rosas who orders their capture and signs the death warrants, while even Sarmiento makes political capital out of the affair from his exile in Chile) points to the symbolic threat the affair represents to the patriarchal fundamentals of family, church and state. The allegorical simplicity of the film gives an impression of power functioning vertically within a simple metaphorical structure of substitutions: one kind of father substitutes seamlessly for another, so that Camila's father Adolfo (Héctor Alterio) comes to stand for, and wields all the functions of, the political and ecclesiastical fathers, whether the dictator Rosas, or ultimately God the father himself.

The family is thus seen as a structure of social and political control, regulating female sexuality in the form of ordered procreation and is the basis for the institutions of church and state: this is why Camila's sexual transgression with the priest is seen as such a precise moment of ideological threat to those institutions, repeating her grandmother's earlier sexual transgression with Viceroy Liniers, for which she is locked up for life in the *mirador* of the family's country house, forming something of an Argentine version of 'the mad woman in the attic'. The metaphorical structure of substitutions is expressed very tersely by Camila's mother when she ironically summarises her husband's arguments about the necessity of marriage for a young woman by saying: 'El matrimonio es como el país, y la mejor cárcel es la que no se ve.' ('Marriage is like the nation, and the best prison is the one that is invisible.') Such prisons abound in the film and it is women who are locked up in them. Moreover, the state's need to punish unregulated sexuality is explicitly paralleled with the misogyny encoded within the psychic drama of the mother–son relationship, so that Adolfo continually draws parallels between the wayward sexuality of his daughter and that of his mother. Father/son and state are bound up within the same repressive structure in this film; it is for this reason that Adolfo's punishment is so severe and that he himself urges the state to punish Camila's sacrilegious liaison, refusing to intercede on Camila's behalf.

In *Miss Mary*, the more or less simple vertical structure of *Camila*, with its binary model of the functioning of power-as-repression, is replaced by a more subtly evoked metonymic web of interlocking power structures, as befits the different historical periods Bemberg is examining: the brutal authoritarian regime of Rosas in *Camila* and, in *Miss Mary*, the Infamous Decade, when the land-owning oligarchy, essentially driven by economic and class interests, breached the constitution in order to hold on to political power in the face of the rising tide of populism. In *Miss Mary*, then, the father is no longer depicted as the angry repressor, thundering from the pulpit or issuing decrees. Johnny, who is the son in the family for which Miss Mary Mulligan works as an English governess, puts this very succinctly when he says: 'My father is never very angry. He doesn't have to be.'

The networks of power in *Miss Mary* may be ruthless in their effect on all of the women characters, but they are quietly efficient in their decentred modes of operation. They extend from family and honour, through gender, race, language to social class and, crucially, colonialism and neo-colonialism in the subtle examination of the relationship between Argentina and Britain during the 1930s and the Second World War. All of this is made even more

A portrait of an oligarchic family in *Miss Mary*

complex because of the film's ingenious narrative technique involving the use of extended flashback representing Miss Mary's, and later, Johnny's, reminiscences about the period from Miss Mary's arrival in Argentina in the summer of 1938 until her imminent departure at the end of the Second World War on the eve of the new Peronist era in Argentina. These flashbacks function to reconstruct social history from a female perspective whilst also revealing the entangled complicity of Miss Mary's own ideology and her perilous sense of self-identity as an old maid clinging on to her colonial notions of Britishness as her only real form of social power; indeed, one of Miss Mary's first thoughts in the film as she thinks back over her time in Argentina is 'Perhaps you should have gone to India, Miss Mary. There at least it's clear who the natives are.'

Miss Mary, then, is the story of a prim English governess, played by Julie Christie, who is employed by a rich Argentine family to look after and teach

English to their three children, two daughters, Carolina (Sofía Viruboff) and Terry (Barbara Bunge) and a son, Johnny (Donald McIntyre). It is also a devastating portrait of upper-class Argentine society and morals and of the position of women within the closely circumscribed confines of the Argentine elite. Its setting during the Infamous Decade, 15 years, in fact, is framed by the overthrow in 1930 of the populist Radical President Hipólito Irigoyen by the conservative forces under General Uriburu and the Peronist revolution of 1945 which so cunningly established its power base among the emergent industrial working class. The film is actually preceded by the following text projected on screen:

> On September 6 1930, in Argentina, an ultra right military coup led by General Uriburu overthrew the democratic government of President Irigoyen.
>
> The Argentine upper class, economically and culturally influenced by the British Empire, wholeheartedly supported this breach of constitutional rule.
>
> Through fraud and repression, the Conservative Party remained in power for 15 years.

The film is evidently an examination of the social codes and mores which made possible such a long period of right-wing unconstitutional rule and its relevance to the ultra-right regime of the 1970s and 1980s, as well as to the colonial complexities of the Malvinas/Falklands conflict between Argentina and Britain, in the aftermath of which the film was produced, is self-evident. What is really important about *Miss Mary*, however, is its exposure of the way in which the military and paternal authoritarianism of the period is inevitably bound up with the control and circumscription of women. The film not only examines Miss Mary's suppressed sexuality and her internalisation of the authoritarian values of the British Empire but also, and perhaps more centrally (and this is in fact autobiographical for Bemberg), it examines the progression from female childhood to womanhood in that we see various stages in the development of the young girls and the boy who are in Miss Mary's care.

We see the girls' natural rebelliousness and exuberance slowly being quashed by the increasing restrictions placed on their sexuality as they grow older. We see the devastating, terrible neuroses that they develop, in

their failure to accommodate their interior emotional lives to the strict for-
malisms and manners of the society around them. That the women are
caught in a vicious circle is clear from the fate of the mother, Mecha (Nacha
Guevara), locked into a stifling, repetitive routine, her only relationship
to her husband Alfredo (Eduardo Pavlovsky) being that of decorative
adjunct in social functions now that she has fulfilled her reproductive role.
It is interesting here to look at what Bemberg herself has to say about the
women in this film, from an interview she gave to Nissa Torrents:

> In my films, women always rebel. Against their husbands and families in
> *Momentos* and *Señora de nadie*, and in a larger field in *Camila*, against the family,
> the state and the church. In *Miss Mary*, the governess, not such a young girl,
> intends to rebel but, like the other women in the film she is defeated. Nobody
> makes it. The atmosphere is too oppressive, too rigid. The class pressures are
> too strong. The mother might have become a good pianist had she been born
> elsewhere. That is why I have her always playing the same piece by Eric Satie.
> To indicate the crippling circularity of her existence [. . .].
>
> [T]he class [*Miss Mary*] represented at that point in history was a class which
> refused all public shows of affection, of sentiment. It is a film about a great
> emptiness. The lack of spiritual values and tenderness is overpowering. Appar-
> ent and actual luxury, but a great void. Form, appearances are all.[2]

What Bemberg does not say explicitly here, but what is shown as implicit
within both *Camila* and *Miss Mary*, is that patriarchy actually *depends* on
this kind of circumscription of women, particularly of their sexuality, for
its very continuation and existence, through the control of reproduction.

Miss Mary begins with a pre-credit sequence set in 1930 on the night
after Uriburu's overthrow of Irigoyen, eight years before Miss Mary's arrival
in Argentina and hence outside the film's subjective flashback framework.
The two little girls are with a previous English nanny, preparing to go to
bed. It is worth dwelling a little on this sequence since it orchestrates a
whole constellation of social and psychic forces which demonstrate how
the manifestations of patriarchy, from family to religion to state, are pred-
icated on and depend upon the psychic enclosure of women and women's
sexuality.

First of all we have the bedrock of religion with the little girls saying their bedtime prayers kneeling before an imaginary and appropriately infantilised male Christ figure ('gentle Jesus meek and mild'), the ideological effects of which are clearly understood by the father who, at a later stage in the film, tells Miss Mary that 'religion keeps women out of trouble'. Then the mother comes in, dressed up, made-up, painted, with her hair styled, and the girls rush to her and immediately emphasise her status as mere spectacle, as receiver and object of the gaze: '¡Qué linda que estás mamita!' ('How pretty you are, mummy!'), followed by her reply 'Cuidado, no me despeines' ('Careful, don't mess up my hair'). The spectacle of woman is however immediately shown to be in the service of the most crudely political manifestation of patriarchy – the military dictatorship whose overthrow of the civilian government the parents are going out to celebrate.

Nacha Guevara as the lonely wife in *Miss Mary*

To complicate matters further, this triumph of authoritarian patriarchy is immediately linked to the psycho-sexual repression of the girls. As the mother leaves she tells the girls to remember to look under the bed, a phrase that is repeated at several points in the film, giving it an ominous psychic force. What are they to look for? Might there be reds under the bed, terrifying men waiting to punish the girls sexually? Sure enough, as the eldest girl asks who Uriburu is, the nanny is tying the sleeves of the younger girl's nightdress, a clear symbol of sexual shackling as John King points out,[3] to prevent her hands from wandering in the night, perhaps discovering her own body. The nanny further links Uriburu's military triumph to the sexual repression of the girls by telling them that the populist Irigoyen was a 'rabble-rouser' and, crucially, 'a chaser after little girls'. The effect of this psychic coupling of populism with frightening sexuality is very clear. The eldest girl says to the nanny, 'Please leave the door open, I am a little girl': she is now frightened of the bogey-man Irigoyen who has been psychically transformed into a sexual monster.

When the nanny leaves, however, the girls, despite the sexual shackling, get into the same bed together, partly because of the subtle sexual terrorism of the mother and the nanny. They then begin to sing the words of a popular song from the United States and it becomes clear to what extent they are already unconsciously internalising their future role as sexually mature young women. The words of the song are:

> Ain't she sweet, she's coming down the street
> Now I ask you confidentially, ain't she sweet.
> Ain't she nice, look her over once or twice
> Now I ask you very confidentially, ain't she nice.
> Just cast an eye in her direction
> Oh me oh my, ain't that perfection.

The North American popular song sums up very clearly that their rôle, like that of the mother, will be as aestheticised sexual objects, 'sweet', to be looked at. And indeed, in a later scene, Miss Mary says to the two girls, now older, 'Little girls should be seen and not heard.' The importance of the lyrics, and they are repeated twice as the background music to the credits, is that they highlight very precisely the role of woman as spectacle, a theme repeated throughout Bemberg's films and indeed one which has well known consequences for the portrayal of women in cinema generally as has been famously addressed by commentators such as Laura Mulvey:

> In a world ordered by sexual imbalance, pleasure in looking has been split between active/male and passive/female. The determining male gaze projects its fantasy onto the female figure which is styled accordingly. In their traditional exhibitionist role women are simultaneously looked at and displayed, with their appearance coded for strong visual and erotic impact so that they can be said to connote *to-be-looked-at-ness*.[4]

Bemberg's films are acutely aware of the gendered gaze, that women are to be seen, but that their own active gaze must be rendered invisible within the masculine order of signs, and she carefully underlines this theme with devices that impede the woman's own gaze. The clearest example of this is the use of the blindfold in *Camila*, during the scene portraying a game of blind-man's-buff, with more than a hint towards a visual parody of Sternberg's film of 1934, *The Scarlet Empress*. When Camila, there, does remove the blindfold, her look is challenging because it signals not only her sexuality, but a precise moment of ideological threat within a system that depends on the shackling of female desire along with her gaze.

I shall discuss the symbolisation of shackled vision in *Miss Mary* in a moment, but before I do so I want to take one more instance of the strict codification, and ultimately silencing, of the female body, or, to be more precise, that barring of the woman's access to her own sexuality, her *jouissance*, which is characteristic of a social regime that attempts to tie that sexuality to reproduction. This is the occasion of Carolina's first period. Terry, the younger daughter, bursts into Miss Mary's room exclaiming that Carolina is dying because she has blood on the sheets on her bed. Miss Mary hurriedly cleans up, explaining with embarrassment that Carolina is now a woman which means that she is capable of having a baby. Carolina's reaction is to start dancing for joy: 'Let's celebrate, let's have a party!', she exclaims. 'Never', answers Miss Mary, 'you're not to talk about this.' 'Why?'

'Because it's a secret among women.' 'Why?' 'You have to stay in bed for three days.' 'For three days? Why?' 'Because you are unwell!' 'I'm not unwell!' 'Yes you are. Don't argue.'

Menstruation, of course, has always been symbolised, at least within the masculine imaginary, as that frightening excess over reproduction, that dissemination or loss of the unitary self in bodily flux which threatens the reproduction of the self-same. The menstruating woman is 'unclean' or 'unwell', the blood disturbs the field of vision and must be hurriedly removed from sight, unlike the heroic blood of those men wounded in battle, blood which comes to symbolise and in a sense construct the nation. It is in this sense that the woman's body is barred to herself, just as surely as Carolina's hands carefully placed by Miss Mary on top of the sheets as she tucks her back into bed during this sequence symbolically prevent the sleeping girl from knowing and inhabiting her own body. The body is rendered insanitary, an object of self-loathing, or as Miss Mary tells the two girls when she accidentally stumbles across them kissing each other in a make-believe Hollywood-inspired doctors and nurses game (with some dead flies as patients): 'You are not to kiss on the mouth.' 'Why?' 'Because it is unhealthy.' 'Why?' 'And you are not to play with flies.' This translates into the mother's obsessive swatting of flies so that a network of symbols is set up associating feminine sexuality with dirt, with the abject, with something that needs to be cleaned up and regulated. It also translates into a devastating series of neuroses, from the mother's incessant repetition of the Satie piece to, later, Carolina's kleptomania and the recommendation of her psychiatrist to copy out word for word the telephone directory on a typewriter. As Jacques Lacan once said, 'the Law of the Father is a letter that never ceases to write itself in the unconscious'.

Interestingly, among the objects that Carolina compulsively steals is a pair of theatre binoculars, clearly suggesting a symbolic attempt to appropriate the gaze. Indeed, within the genre of historical reconstruction which Bemberg chooses, it is the theme of vision which calls into question the modes of feminine (self-)representation and which implicates the cinematic medium itself. In *Miss Mary*, the shackled gaze is cleverly symbolised by the use of veils and dark glasses, particularly in a complex sequence of

Eduardo Pavlovsky and
Julie Christie in
Miss Mary

reminiscence and flashback showing the enforced marriage of Terry after an unfortunate adolescent sexual adventure.

The sequence starts in the church where we see the veiled woman being handed from father to future son-in-law entirely against her will. Miss Mary, herself veiled in the congregation, gazing at the mummified faces of Terry and her mother (the latter wearing dark glasses), thinks to herself: 'They look all alike, these *señoras* with their sad, painted faces. So . . . arrogant. And so helpless. What a waste.' In flashback, we see the mother compulsively repeating the same tune on the piano, several years earlier, wearing absurdly large dark glasses, then the mother at dinner, still wearing the glasses, going off to cry in a small enclosed room she calls the 'crying room', followed by her once more playing the piano and obsessively swatting flies. As in *Camila*, we have an emphasis on women enclosed within confined spaces, linked to the problematic position of the mother, who has now served her purpose, to provide children for the male. Within the disciplinary regime of *Miss Mary*, however, that enclosure is self-imposed, an ambiguous form of refuge, like veils and dark glasses themselves which are both a form of protection *from* the male gaze *and* the rendering passive or neutralisation of the (castration) threat encoded within the active female gaze. The problematic role of the mother and motherhood in general, within the feminine masquerade is cleverly framed by the flashback technique so that the sequence begins and ends with the church scene in which we see patriarchy reproducing itself in an enforced public act of handing over the veiled woman.

At the end of this long sequence, the organ music played as Terry and her new husband leave the church is the nationalistic British tune *Land of Hope and Glory*. This is a good example of the way in which, at every juncture, Bemberg links her feminist concerns into a broader critique of power relationships both at a national and geopolitical level, of which there are countless examples, from Miss Mary's refusal to speak Spanish ('That's the strength of the British Empire'), through her indulging in fictive stereotypes of Argentine identity in her desperate letters home ('The whole family danced the tango to the sound of throbbing guitars'), to the father's declaration to his future son-in-law that Argentina would have been much better off had the British succeeded in colonising the country during the two failed attempts at the beginning of the nineteenth century.

Mary Anne Doane has shown that the trope of the woman wearing glasses in cinema always has something to do with signifying the woman's look or lack of look. The dark glasses in the sequence analysed above function as veils to render invisible the female gaze as well as to provide an ambiguous form of protection from behind which the woman can look out at the world without her gaze functioning as a threat to the male symbolic order. *Transparent* glasses, however, particularly reading glasses, serve to heighten the gaze and are often linked to a woman's active appropriation of it within an intellectual framework – her attempt to negotiate a space for herself within the masculine symbolic order of writing. Miss Mary herself wears glasses, and Bemberg cleverly plays on the threat that the woman's appropriation of the gaze presents to the very ideology of representation within masculine cinema, because it is precisely her gaze, signified by the putting on or removal of glasses or of the veil in the church, that frames many of the flashbacks within the film. It is thus clearly the woman's gaze, and of course implicitly the gaze of the woman director, that re-engenders history.

The 'problem' of feminine sexuality and feminine desire within patriarchal structures that bind it entirely to paternal filiation is emphasised in the film by a repetition of the infamous Freudian question '*Was will das*

María Luisa Bemberg and Julie Christie on location for *Miss Mary*

Weib?' (What does woman want?). Johnny, talking to Miss Mary after the wedding about Carolina's psychiatric problems, asks with concerned incomprehension, 'What does she want?'. The scene immediately cuts to a flashback of the father, Alfredo, shouting '*¿Pero qué mierda querés?*' ('What the hell do you want?') as he beats on the door of the room where Carolina has locked herself away in her defiant refusal to attend her younger sister's wedding. It is significant that Carolina's refusal should take the form of her deliberately smudging the carefully applied make-up on her lips and face, rendering her mouth bloodied and monstrous, and so revealing the symbolic (and actual) violence underlying the enforced feminine masquerade. As the camera pans out from a close-up of her smudged face, the frame reveals that she is once more typing out the names from the telephone directory while her brother, standing outside the locked door, tries in vain to coax her out of the room.

The culmination of the theme of gendered vision in Bemberg's work – which is fundamentally that of the status of woman as passive object of desire/knowledge versus active desiring subject – must surely come in the later film *Yo, la peor de todas* (*I, the Worst of All*) (1990) about the seventeenth-century poet Sor Juana Inés de la Cruz. Her life was spent attempting to find an intellectual space within a society where knowledge bore an exclusively masculine sign, and Bemberg's interpretation of her forced abjuration of knowledge and learning uses one of the most devastating symbolisations of the destruction of the woman's gaze in the whole of cinema. After reading a forced confession of her sins, Sor Juana removes her reading glasses, fixes the presiding bishop for a moment and then brings her hand smashing down on the glass lenses, crushing them and releasing the blood with which she signs her abjuration of all knowledge: *Yo, la peor de todas* (*I, the Worst of All*).

Bemberg's challenge to the representational systems both of cinema and of history, let alone of the film of historical reconstruction, does not come in grand sweeping gestures like those of Fernando Solanas's 'Third cinema', or Eliseo Subiela's nightmares of urban dissolution or neo-surrealist experi-

Julie Christie and
Donald McIntyre in
Miss Mary

mentation with the very language of cinematic representation. It comes, rather, in her detailed reconstruction of women's history which, through the careful interweaving of themes and symbols, attempts to lay bare the mechanisms of patriarchal power as well as the mechanisms governing the visual ideology of cinema. This gives her cinematography a particular analytic power in terms of its political reach. Although *Miss Mary* isolates the historical moment in which it is set by emphasising its framing by populist periods of government (Irigoyen and Perón), it nevertheless invites a reading that extends, like *Camila*, to the period of dictatorship that had ended only a few years prior to its first screening. Indeed, the internal references in the film to the nineteenth-century British attempts at colonising Argentina could only be read by an Argentine audience watching the film in 1986 as allusions to the colonial Malvinas/Falklands conflict that had marked the end of the dictatorship. In attempting to isolate and analyse a period of right wing, nationalist and oligarchic rule in terms of the psychic, gendered and even geopolitical mechanisms underlying networks of social control, *Miss Mary* moves the debate and national self-examination in post-dictatorship Argentina on from mere denunciationof repression to an attempt to understand some of its wider social and historical co-ordinates.

First published in Women's Studies *(vol. 29, pp. 5–18, 2000).*

NOTES

1 John King, 'Assailing the heights of macho pictures: women film-makers in contemporary Argentina' in Susan Bassnett (ed.), *Knives and Angels: Women Writers in Latin America*, Zed Books, London, 1990, pp. 158–70.

2 Nissa Torrents, 'One woman's cinema: interview with María Luisa Bemberg' in Susan Bassnet, op. cit., pp. 171–5.

3 John King, op. cit., p. 166.

4 Laura Mulvey, 'Visual pleasure and narrative cinema' in Gerald Mast, Marshall Cohen and Leo Braudy (eds), *Film Theory and Criticism: Introductory Readings*, 4th edition, Oxford University Press, Oxford, 1992, pp. 746–57.

SIX

MARÍA LUISA BEMBERG'S INTERPRETATION OF OCTAVIO PAZ'S *SOR JUANA*

Denise Miller

In 1990, María Luisa Bemberg made a film about the life of the Golden Age poet and Mexican nun, Sor Juana Inés de la Cruz (1648–95), who is considered to be the most significant woman writer in the entire Latin American colonial period. It is based upon Octavio Paz's 1982 biography which seeks to explain why she renounced her poetry and ideas, by signing at the end of her life, a confession that she, 'the worst of all', was un-worthy. Originally, Sor Juana had been a lady-in-waiting at the court and had then entered the convent to gain the space to read and to write. Her legendary erudition and wit secured her the patronage of a succession of viceroys who delighted to attend her salons or *audiencias* behind the bars of the convent's visiting room or *locutorio*. Paz's contention is that her final renunciation of all this learning was the result of having been caught up in an argument between powerful men but that nevertheless it was an argument in which she chose to intervene: in producing a critique of a Portuguese priest's sermon. This was Vieyra who was closely associated with the interests of the Mexican church, whose tolerance she thereby forfeited. Bemberg, however, sees Sor Juana here as a pawn in their game of intrigue and specifically as a woman pitted against men. Her agenda is specifically valid in this case; according to Stephanie Merrim, Paz himself has paved 'the way for a more enlightened feminist understanding of its subject'.[1]

In unravelling the historical and social context in which Sor Juana lived,

Paz is dealing meticulously with a local analysis of the nun in order to get to the truth of her, whilst Bemberg, the popular film-maker has something wider to say and to a wider audience.[2] The film as a text has its own validity and must condense the scholarship of those such as Paz which ranges in erudite and close scrutiny over the entire history of western (and sometimes eastern) literature as we know it, up to the seventeenth century. A comparison of both texts deals therefore with mediated images of Sor Juana, and not with Sor Juana herself, and so whether or not she did indeed 'revise patriarchal concepts' is not its primary point.[3] It is clear however that Paz very much approved of Bemberg's venture and its product.

Octavio Paz's book has the stated aim of resurrecting the truth of Sor Juana's final days and accordingly the impetus of the film is towards a final image of renunciation, as evidenced by its emblematic title: the last words of her confession.[4] His contention is that as a victim of a subtle intrigue on the part of the church she was condemned to sign her confession out of sincerely felt guilt, but a guilt that was not true to her maintained beliefs, and that on that day she was neither 'enchantingly good' nor 'arrestingly saintly' as her erstwhile biographers would have us believe.[5] One question we must ask is, how 'enchantingly' does Bemberg present her?

The purpose of this chapter is not to investigate or even to précis his thesis but to present the argument that Bemberg's 1990 film version of his book is true in spirit to the picture of Sor Juana that Paz presents, whilst it is much more 'feminist' (and sometimes problematically so) in its approach to her final days. For he argues that Sor Juana transgressed and thereby offended the church solely in her wish to extend the bounds of permitted knowledge, whereas Bemberg suggests that the nun threatened the church as a woman and not least as one who was in love with another. (Her choice of actors here would appear to be deliberate. Assumpta Serna starred in earlier lesbian roles and Dominique Sanda in roles that can at least be described as sexually ambiguous.)[6]

María Luisa Bemberg has come to the book with her own agenda.[7] Prior to making this film she has moved the marginalised (usually women) into centre-frame. Her motive is political. This is clear in her discussion of the initial problems she had in placing a homosexual in *Señora de nadie* (1982):

María Luisa Bemberg confers with her art director, Voytek, on the set of *Yo, la peor de todas*

> The colonel said that he would rather have a son who had cancer than one who was homosexual so I couldn't do it. I had thought that both a homosexual and a separated woman were marginals and so in the film they get together.[8]

Bemberg's motive is also to universalise for she is used to taking a historical figure and pointing out a parallel, as she does in *Camila*, between Rosas's Mazorca gangs and the anonymous killers in the Dirty War: 'Over two million people wept at the story of Camila O'Gorman, which was their own story.'[9] Thus in an interview with her, in the context of her then proposed project of *Yo, la peor de todas*, Luis Trelles Plazaola can introduce her as having in common with other Latin American women directors, feminist themes, the fact that she focuses upon women who break convention and transgress the role expected of them in Latin American societies. She says in this interview: 'I also wish to create universal stories.' Tolstoy says, 'speak of your town and you will speak of the world if you speak in a universal way.'[10]

An evaluation of Bemberg's filmic interpretation begs a close analysis of one or two scenes each dealing with the three major areas of Paz's book that I understand her to treat: the intellectual debate over knowledge as transgression with the interrelated ideas that Sor Juana involves herself in this specifically as a *woman* and as a woman in love. Finally, these discussions have a bearing on their respective interpretations of her closing days. But as we are dealing largely with image, it is useful to start by observing the general impression the film gives and by analysing an early sequence in her cell and then an *audiencia* she later holds with the men of the church in which she touches upon her great poem *First Dream*.

What the film does do is to reinforce Paz's eloquent summing-up of Sor Juana, 'I see a woman lucid and whole.'[11] This is reflected not least in the formal composition of the entire film. Here for the first time Bemberg eschews the lavish *mise-en-scènes* of her former films. In answer to the contention that a convent film would necessarily be austere, hers is only one of two I know which avoids the temptation of a real convent and prefers the even clearer and bolder delineations of an abstract film set.[12] Nevertheless, what is rendered austere in outline is given vibrancy in Sor Juana herself who carries colour (though deep, not bright), in her blue and white habit against a usually much darker background. Moreover, Assumpta Serna the actress reinforces her beauty and poise, whilst Assumpta Serna the star brings 'always already' her vitality (as well as ambiguous sexuality as we have seen) to the role.

More specifically, both tones and sets seem to me to be remarkably faithful to the terms of Paz's discussion of her melancholy. He draws connections between *First Dream* of Sor Juana and Albrecht Dürer's *Melancholy 1* (1514) to reinforce his argument that Sor Juana is, unwittingly, one of the first moderns. They are both works that, spiritually, verge on infinity. *Melancholy 1* is prophetic of Sor Juana's poem 'in which the soul, lost in the geometric night and its prospects of obelisks and pyramids, looks on everything and sees nothing'.[13] Heinrich Wölfflin in his own examination of the painting points out that the term 'melancholic' had taken on ambiguous meaning by Dürer's time, meaning either 'sick' or earnest for the gift of intellectual work.[14]

Dürer's painting shows this ambiguity wonderfully. The figure of melancholy is hunched up in the left foreground of the frame but her eyes, gazing on nothing as they do, nevertheless have a wonderful energy. 'It is obvious that something is alive in this immobile figure; the tense glance, the tightly clenched fist are signs of willpower',[15] which energy is further reflected in the chaos of the intellectual instruments of compasses and geometric blocks, etc. around her.

Paz is alive to this ambiguity. Sor Juana's melancholy is not just that of the intellectual, and it seems to me a happy effect that Wölfflin's description of the tonal qualities of the etching, 'The light is not concentrated but broken-up; the main highlights are set very low',[16] have found their reflection in Bemberg's film whose increasingly sombre palette is true to the darkening tones of Paz's book, as melancholy is inscribed visually by Bemberg at the formal level of the text.

Furthermore, there is apt coincidence between the objects in Sor Juana's cell and those in Dürer's painting. Of them Paz says:

> This kind of collection is more closely related to the magician's cave than to the museum gallery . . . The collection and the library were her family . . . They were also her realm. A realm at once spatial and temporal, concrete and imaginary . . . reduced to a series of random and miscellaneous objects.[17]

Bemberg films 13 sequences in Sor Juana's cell and is aware of the particular passage quoted above, 'Octavio Paz speaks of Sor Juana's cell as an enormous matrix and designed in the round – like the mind of Sor Juana, like the world.'[18]

There is an early sequence in her cell which deals precisely with the objects within this 'world'. It is prefaced by the sombre lights of her confessional, in which figures of priest and nun are merely lighted silhouettes in surrounding darkness. She says significantly that she is only here (in the convent) according to his wishes, so that when we cut to the relief of the golden lights of her library, we understand that only in this 'secular world' where she is reading, is she free. The camera moves right with Sor Juana, brushing past a blue curtain and moving into the living space of the cell from where have emanated the extra diegetic sounds of (the vicereine playing) the strings of a harp. For a moment frozen within the frame is an ensemble remarkably similar to the cell of Dürer's melancholy: mandolin top left, books centre left and an obelisk in the top right-hand corner. The freedom of this is underlined by the vicereine's first words, 'I can't stand the bars of your audience room.'[19] There are few cuts at this point, with instead a mobile frame produced by circular camera movements, thus expressing a world much larger and more fluid than – an opening out beyond – the confines of a mere cell. The 'bitter path' Sor Juana has chosen to follow is mitigated by the delight she finds in her toys.

Nevertheless, ambiguity is present: whilst the film audience is introduced to vital information, 'They say that you have the largest library in the Americas – but that they are dangerous books',[20] we are led to talk of the Inquisition and the cross-cutting between vicereine and Sor Juana

Assumpta Serna as
Sor Juana in
Yo, la peor de todas

mediates a stark conflict between the vicereine's worldly sense of danger and the nun's innocence of it. This is rendered in a contrast of colours – that of the darker blue and grey tones both of Juana's habit and the background that frames her (the empty wall of her cell) – with that of the lighter golden tones of the close-ups of the vicereine, whose background of grey is alleviated by a bright orange mantilla carelessly thrown over the back of the chair in which she sits and dominates at least one-quarter of the frame. Similarly, the cross-cutting highlights the contrast of the feather in her cap versus the enclosing habit of Sor Juana.

Thus Sor Juana is trapped, and yet not trapped. Her demonstration of her toys, 'my glass, in which I read past and future . . . my metronome . . . my telescope . . . my lyre',[21] is true to Paz's own claim for her: They are her children, 'my pens, my writings . . . these are my children.'[22] This is a cell in which Sor Juana is most free in her unfree world and, if there is suggestion of melancholy in our common understanding of the word, there is also Dürer's other sense of the melancholic who is earnest for learning.

THE LITERARY DEBATE

Now we should look at Bemberg's treatment of Sor Juana as an intellectual. Paz is mostly interested in the literary argument surrounding Sor Juana: he therefore often deals in the abstract and this is an area that this film visually enters into, as we have seen, via an austere *mise-en-scène*. Narratively, it extracts from the actual literary debate those chapters dealing with Sor Juana's *First Dream*, for Paz her most important poem. One importance of it is in the nun's discussion of her wish to be free, where she cannot be. This reading was elaborated on many years ago by Paz in *The Labyrinth of Solitude* in 1950:

> They [Baroque artists in Mexico] were awakened intellects in a society that had been immobilized by the letter of the law . . . Sor Juana undertook the composition of her poem *First Dream* in an attempt to reconcile silence and poetry, illuminism and the Baroque.[23]

In the 1980s it is still vitally true to him. So in *Sor Juana*, he declares it is *not* an account of ecstasy nor mystical but wholly secular (hence dangerous) and in its gaze at vacancy is the first great modern poem, 'In one way or another, all modern poets have lived, relived, and recreated the double negation of *First Dream*: the silence of space, and the vision of non-vision.'[24] It is these limitations to reason that, he argues, are at the centre of Sor Juana's inner life. But, just as Dürer's melancholy is not necessarily, or wholly, sick, Sor Juana's non-vision is a statement of faith and hope, whose impulse is entirely 'upward'. It is a confession, but one that 'ends in an act of faith: not in learning but in the desire to learn'.[25] So that Paz refutes those critics who aim to link the ideas inherent in *First Dream* with her crisis of confidence of 1693.

Bemberg sets the discussion of this poem in the *locutorio*. What she does capture most forcibly is the 'silence of space' which the poem confronts. This is achieved very simply through ambient sounds which echo against a silence initially produced by, and working to confirm, Miranda's insinuation that she is attracted to the 'abyss'. The reverberating sounds of the rustling of her veil as, absorbing the implications of this remark, she leans against the chair, of the rustling paper, and finally of her own voice, also suggest the hollowness of the space. We see at the same time, as she is engaged in discussion (and therefore not alone), that Sor Juana is not free. Firstly, she is called from her studies to the visiting room by her amanuensis (a young novice). There is then a cutaway, shocking by juxtaposition, to the salon sequence itself in whose first scene the entire frame has the bars of the grille stretched across it, separating nun from clergy, men from woman. We see Sor Juana in long shot over the close-up shoulders of the man facing her. It is a motif of which Bemberg is fond and it is eloquent: such an image reinforces the later nub of the scene, that 'knowledge is always transgression. Especially for a woman', for men and woman are together in the same cinematic frame, yet separated within it. Furthermore, the audience is viewing the nun through the dominant (and domineering) perspective of the male whose shoulders literally entrap her.

The discussion concerns Phaethon, Paz's emblem for Sor Juana, who is a fit summary of the argument of *First Dream* for he represents the longing for knowledge and boundless daring that she and her poem do. The script has the nun clearly state that knowledge is always transgression, and more so in a woman.

Though Phaethon's transgression is central to Paz (for the nun's transgression is the will to knowledge and her defeat is the surrender of this quest to learn), it is not part of his argument at the stage of discussing *First Dream* that Sor Juana sees herself rebelling as a woman.[26] She didn't yet, according to him, believe that being a woman was a barrier to knowledge; the barrier was one universal to humanity: the body trapping the soul, and thus 'the daring of the soul, and the praise of the tragic figure of Phaethon are a true intellectual confession'.[27] For Paz, the realisation that she transgressed as a woman comes later, in the years immediately preceding her crisis.

So Bemberg has taken feminist liberties with Paz and merged two of his arguments in the dialogue she has accorded Sor Juana; one, that knowledge is transgression, with his second, later analysis of her crisis: her fatal understanding that this transgression was especially so as she was a woman.

FROM WHICH WORLD IS SOR JUANA TRANSGRESSING?

It is clear then that Bemberg's Sor Juana moves within a more intensely constricting world than in the one that Paz establishes. How is the more overtly feminist agenda set? The establishing shots are vital. They introduce us, not to a convent, nor more generally to the world of women, but to the world of men and their power: representatives of church, in the person of the archbishop, and of government, in that of the viceroy. After the credits (which are sober, white on black and against a background of music in a minor key), the first image is that of two wine-glasses in close up, on a table. The textual overlay informs us that we are in Mexico in the seventeenth century. The camera pulls back to reveal the owners of the glasses: the viceroy and the archbishop, their ensuing dialogue establishing and explaining a context of tension. They are discussing the prevalence of disbelief in Europe. The viceroy suggests that Spain sees itself as the champion of Catholicism, to which the archbishop roundly counters, 'It is.'[28] This man clearly will brook no dissension, although the viceroy pits Caesar against the archbishop's God, 'So God has ordained', by replying, 'and Caesar'.[29]

This context both of tension and rivalry, but between male institutions, is thus established. Only at this point is there a cut to a courtyard, accompanied by the extra-diegetic sound of female laughter. It is not one we typically associate with nuns and with convents. Furthermore, the colour tones are lighter. We are in a happier, carefree, feminine world, but it is threatened. Even when we cut to the isolation of Sor Juana in her cell where she is open to the feminine around her, indicated by the laughter coming through the open curtains, we learn with the next cut – to the nuns' assembly – that the convent is not thus open.[30] This scene twice returns us to a wide-angled shot of all of them in convocation – and contained by the frame – with the image, in deeper long shot, centre frame, of the two nuns heading the meeting. The demeanour of one – upright – indicates sternness, whilst that of the other – relaxed – suggests humanity. This is an interesting visual rhyme to the first image of the two men of power.

The next sequence introduces the idea that Sor Juana is a secular poet for her comedy is being performed in the courtyard. The church, in the person of Bishop Puebla, is framed behind and between the government, in the figures of viceroy and vicereine. This frontal shot directs how we see the next shot: framed now by the backs of the viceroy and vicereine, the view of the spectacle is through the censoring eyes of the church and is captioned by the archbishop's statement, 'This isn't a convent, it's a brothel.'[31] Now comes an immediate cut to the sequence of two nuns presenting the archbishop with a list of dissident nuns, who then wipes out the smell of these fellow, but female, conspirators with incense. From the first scene to this is thus established the male intrigue that frames the feminine world. (The femininity of this world is reinforced by the first meeting here of Juana and the vicereine. I return, below, to a closer discussion of this scene in the section dealing with their love.)

So the world of women is under threat from the world of men; in particular, a convent is threatened by the church. However, Bemberg's need to 'de-nun' her film from its start indicates a major difference in

On the set of *Yo, la peor de todas*

perspective between Paz and Bemberg. In her interview with Luis Telles Plazaola, she makes a telling comment: 'Nothing more boring than a convent and a nun of whom you see hardly anything, not skin, nor body, hardly her hands. I decided that I had to "de-nun" this film.'[32]

Paz disdains to say this, but it is true to Bemberg's own agenda to be a popular film-maker. Her universalising involves reaching a wider audience than his and also essentialises Sor Juana's condition as a *woman*. Her choice of actor, significant as we have seen, is specifically so in this respect, 'Assumpta Serna, the Catalan actress of *Matador* seemed perfect to me.'[33] The heroine in *Matador* is strong and man-killing. It is surely no coincidence, that it is in connection with this film itself that Bemberg herself talks of the universal, quoting Tolstoy in her support, as we have seen.[34] But for her, it is the feminist that is universal.

The 'universal' of which Paz talks is different. He discusses Sor Juana's longing for universality as an intellectual and her failure to get it: 'Spanish American culture . . . is always open to the outside world and has a longing for universality' and in the same breath that he mentions Sor Juana: 'Our culture, like a certain portion of Spanish culture, is a free election by a few free spirits.'[35] Bemberg chooses to mediate this visually as a woman who is trapped; so she 'de-nuns' her film by suggesting that women shared the same lot (in seventeenth century Mexico). She does this by focusing on the relationship between Sor Juana and the vicereine.

TRANSGRESSION THROUGH LOVE AND THROUGH KNOWLEDGE

LOVE

The first scene between these two, in the *locutorio* but alone, is about 15 minutes into the film and the longest so far (five full minutes long). In it the beginning of their 'relationship' is established: the cross-cutting between their mid-close-up images suggests reflections of each other and the camera looks always from one to the other through the separation of the bars in the foreground. The implication is that they are together but isolated and trapped in their own respective worlds. But this 'separation' is, paradoxically, what they share. The vicereine underlines this point, 'We live parallel lives.'[36] The audience is surely meant to feel Sor Juana's surprise that a woman of the world can be as trapped as a nun. The 'de-nunning' works both ways: all women are trapped, like nuns, or nuns are freer than most women. Whichever way you read the paradox, for Bemberg the convent can now be used as metaphor: as a woman's space, but one hemmed in by men. She has essentialised the particular, local condition of Sor Juana in the vicereine who in all her glory is likewise trapped. In fact every time the camera cuts to her, we not only look at her (from Sor Juana's perspective) through the bars of a grille but also as framed by the bars of another grille behind her and where the only visible sign of artificial or extraneous lighting is thrown on to the bars themselves. This is gilded paralysis. Certainly, Paz himself sees a connection between the vicereine's courtly activities and Sor Juana's continuous literary correspondence, 'In both instances busyness concealed an internal emptiness.'[37]

But how exactly do these two women, who are so trapped, *transgress?* Through their intimacy, suggests Bemberg, which is verging on love. What Paz suggests about their love is, of course, complicated. He does not dispute that Sor Juana may have been in love with the vicereine but he argues that firstly, the evidence is inconclusive and that secondly, expressed as it seems to be in the poems Sor Juana addressed to the vicereine, such a love would not have been understood as threatening or rebellious at the time; she was writing within the accepted boundaries and according to the mores of the courtly love tradition where the beloved was always female and always unavailable.[38] In short, for him, Sor Juana denied her sexuality and 'her erotic life was almost entirely imaginary' but he underlines 'not for that reason any less real or intense' and 'perhaps without love affairs but not without love'.[39] This is the cue that Bemberg takes from Paz but links it to his separate idea (outlined above but discussed more fully below) of her *knowledge* as transgression.

The 'love' scene in which the vicereine orders Sor Juana to take off her veil takes place about an hour into the film and is arguably long: five minutes. Little is spoken with much thereby suggested and working on an erotic level. Bemberg takes the suggestiveness of Paz's 'she lived among erotic shadows' and makes the shadows more corporeal.[40]

Again in the nun's cell the vicereine explains that she has often wondered what Juana is really like when nobody is looking at her. Accordingly the camera now requires that we look at Sor Juana in a new way. The question we need to ask of this scene is whether Bemberg is coming up with anything new (in attempting a rereading of their relationship and a feminist rereading of Sor Juana generally) or merely *formally* reinforcing the dominant ideology? In *Female Desire* Rosalind Coward maintains 'Women are the sex which is constantly questioned, explained, defined.'[41] However, as Paul Julian Smith points out, 'For Coward it is no easy matter to transcend the imposed definition: to do so, she agrees, may be to abandon cherished pleasures.'[42] So how are the sexual relations between the two women presented here and are they mediated in traditionally pleasurable ways?

The orchestration of the look within the diegesis is telling. Each charac-

Assumpta Serna and Dominique Sanda in *Yo, la peor de todas*

ter is afforded two point of view shots of the other, but they are not equally weighted in either duration or content. Firstly, both of the vicereine's and only one of Juana's point of view shots are protracted. Furthermore, Juana's look here at the vicereine is almost erased for the spectator whose position is actually aligned, through the substance of her words, with the vicereine's sensual, though conjectural, visual appraisal of Sor Juana. She wonders, she says, what Sor Juana looks like when alone. To answer this, the camera cuts to a close-up of Sor Juana and remains poised there in the longest point of view take of the scene. The nun moves to the right of the frame, enabling the vicereine to move into the left of it behind her. The rest of the take is a two-shot in which the vicereine's dominance is similarly formally inscribed. The power of the latter's eloquent command, 'Take off your veil', is reinforced by the fact that she is behind and slightly above Sor Juana. To Sor Juana's hesitation she adds, 'It's an order.'[43] Sor Juana, face averted, slowly complies, removing the first layer of her veil. Neither looks back at the other, Sor Juana is being looked at by the vicereine whilst we the audience are watching the vicereine gaze at Sor Juana. When Sor Juana further hesitates she is instructed to take off all her veil. Still, there has been no cutting when the vicereine turns her around by the shoulders saying, 'This Juana is mine – only mine.'[44] She cups her face in her hands, and gives her a brief, even chaste, kiss on the lips.

Afterwards she gazes at Sor Juana (against the backdrop of shadows and silences still), finally saying *Para recordar* ('To remember'). *Para recordar* is a cue taken from an earlier scene in which the younger Juana, as lady-in-waiting, has flirtatiously kissed a courtier. They are thus two very loaded words, intimating that Sor Juana has already shared her life history with the vicereine, and also reinforcing that the keynote of this scene is strangely opposed to the one to which it refers: this is no mere flirtation, but erotically charged love. The scene is terminated by the shock cut to a close-up of a book attacked by a stamp suddenly coming down into the frame to the voice of the censor: *'Autorizado'* ('Authorised').

This love scene then is peculiarly charged, again framed by the ominous world of men and their threat to Sor Juana. Bemberg overdetermines audience interpretation here, for although she does not have them consummate their love, that they do love each other sexually is clear. I would nevertheless argue that she has not been able to transcend the imposed definitions of female sexuality. The power relations are clear with the vicereine controlling the actions and dominating the frame, and what lends the scene its eroticism is that the de-nuning of Sor Juana has denuded her indeed. The taking off of her veil has been the greatest exposure for her and the intimacy lies in the power of the vicereine. So that if the eroticism is uncomfortable, it is because it is enabled only within the context of unequal power relations whose construction is in the narrative content, the staging of the point of view shots and the domination within the frame.[45] And we, watching from the vantage point of the vicereine (in that for us, too, Sor Juana is lower in the frame) are the empowered voyeurs.

Not only is the kiss in her control but it is the realisation of her, rather than Juana's, earlier wishes. This fact is rendered clear with a close analysis of the first scene in which the two women, in a public and hence dangerous space, actually meet. It reveals that the vicereine and not Juana is the one – at least at first – to be touched by love.

It occurs early on in the film where the vicereine, newly arrived from Madrid, is introduced to Juana. It is at the performance, mentioned above, of one of Juana's lighthearted and, at moments, bawdy plays. The idea of theatre and of its attendant display are therefore rendered narratively explicit in this scene and also allows their introduction to be one of actor (Sor Juana) to director of the gaze (the vicereine). In short, their meeting is 'staged' and made explicitly so.

I begin with general observations on the entire scene of the play before moving into a closer analysis of this meeting of the two women. The second shot – after an establishment one of the play in performance – is of Juana in a mid-distance shot as she listens as prompt to the performance of her drama. After the final lines of the play have been delivered and during the rapturous applause, the camera's dolly from her to the left witnesses the diegetic audience in profile forming a fan around the *theatrical* space into which Juana will walk. Furthermore, the vicereine comes to occupy the same position in the right side of the frame as Juana had on the left side before the camera had moved left from her, and eventually leaving her outside the right edge of the frame. This mirror positioning picks out the two protagonists within the crowd and suggests their future identification. At the same time, their difference is underscored through striking colour oppositions – between the deep reds of the royal party and the greys and blues that frame Juana – connoting opulence and austerity respectively and these make up either side of the space that the camera moves across. These colour contrasts continue into the sequence that I analyse.

A closer framing starts with a cut of 90 degrees to a frontal three-shot of the vicereine, the viceroy and, behind them, the Bishop of Puebla. When we cut 180 degrees to behind them, and from their vantage point (although they are not looking) see Juana in the distance, just as she is about to move towards them we register the vivid colours of the players in the background. These remind us of this nun's true space. They remain imaginatively (and certainly audibly) present even when technically excluded by the tighter framing of close-ups on her.

The actual sequence of this meeting is one minute and ten seconds long and consists of 11 shots. It begins as Juana moves into the space of this narrower diegetic audience of vicereine, viceroy and Puebla and so can be staged as Juana's 'play' (and, as I suggest below, 'display') to the vicereine. It is also structured as a closing in, and as such suitably frames the star. Furthermore, in the orchestration of shots that move from a wider space of open quadrangle, to royal dias, to finally a series of close-ups, an intense and almost uncomfortable – because public – intimacy is displayed.

The framing of Juana, as she comes forward and to rest in the first shot of her, is most pointed. For she is not only framed by the two viceroys on a frontal plane of the screen but also, on a deeper background plane, by two arches of theatre in which she stands in the middle as a column. She is framed and displayed as theatre, once for the vicereine and twice for the spectator. Appropriately, once we move into the close-ups, it is Juana and not the vicereine, who is given the star treatment, evidenced not least in the lights shining in her black eyes. Also, the extremer close-ups of Juana not only signal the greater emotional weight attached to her image (witnessed significantly, through the point of view of the vicereine) but also they do allow nothing to distract from Juana's eyes. Because this is such an extreme close-up, Juana's wimple literally frames a halo around her head and at the edges of the screen, whereas the vicereine's more sensual opulence in a less extreme close-up is apparent in pearl earrings and necklace.

So there is here a 'fit' of saintliness to sensual Assumpta Serna.[46] It is a fit that holds in tension two opposing connotations – of asceticism and of physicality. These connotations are witnessed by the vicereine in the longest shot of the sequence, and is one which, as her point of view, also gives us the most extreme and therefore most intimate, close-up. It is clear that the one falling here is the vicereine.

The orchestration of the shots establishes this clearly. The first two shots establish Juana's position with relation to her audience. The second one confirms their configuration from her point of view: viceroy to the right, the Bishop of Puebla behind and the vicereine to the left, poised upright and in orange splendour. (In fact, the rich colours of the second shot, of Juana's intimate audience, form a composition of subtle juxtapositions in which the immediate backdrop for the sensual orange of the vicereine's dress is the red of Puebla's surplice. Furthermore, the viceroy's black defines the red, and the orange even more so, as brightly glowing.) The next four cuts are close-ups between vicereine and Juana with significantly more extreme close-ups on Juana.

In this scene we may therefore say that the looks of the vicereine frame Juana. The following four shots, however, deflect the intimacy somewhat in that they go from viceroy to Juana to viceroy and end on the vicereine, whose silent joy at her husband's suggestion that they adopt (i.e. protect) Juana, is evident. The eleventh shot is the framing one of the archbishop. So that in eight close-ups, two are accorded the viceroy and three each to Juana and the vicereine. Also, the rhythm of this sequence is such that the cutting slows down in the middle to give these six shots of the two women the greatest weight. In the longer close-up of the vicereine the silence (of her gazing at Juana) is most apparent.

The aural components of this scene work effectively with the imagery to suggest the dangers of a private space of love made integral with, and played out in, the public space of the theatre and of the convent. The exuberant noises of the players' laughter and chatting in the background (together with a brief hint of baroque harpsichord music that reinforces a sense of period) are loudest in the first shot and thereafter are continuous but muted. Such joyful sounds work against the sinister off-screen presence of the archbishop, but also with it, to suggest a sense of two opposed world views. (The spectator has always been aware of the archbishop beyond the right side of the frame, owing to one significant cut to him before Juana moved forward. In this he looked left to the space of the three-some's discussion of Juana's wit.) Otherwise, there is only one ambient sound and that is of the viceroy settling back into his chair as he turns from quoting to the archbishop (and looking out at us) to face Juana. This silence – and especially therefore of the women – is part of the emotional charge of the scene. In fact, in one close-up, when the viceroy (off-screen) is praising her intelligence and beauty, Juana's silence echoes that of the vicereine so that the visual rhymes across the shots of Juana and vicereine have their aural counterparts too. Finally, against their soft voices the quality of the archbishop's whispered voice rasps as it closes the scene.

But what shouts *loudest* in this sequence is the vicereine's silence. The fact that she initially took the reins from her husband by a confident quoting of Juana's poem underlines not only a predisposition towards Juana – she knows her poems well – but also, even more significantly, her falling in love (hence falling shy) as the scene unfolds.

The substance of the dialogue and of the quoted poem which introduces it – the viceroy has asked his wife, 'What's that poem that mocks men?' – is important too. It presents the introduction of the film's theme about the rarity of women intellectuals. The staging of its introduction is as significant as the staging of the meeting between nun and vicereine. (In fact, as already suggested above, both these themes of knowledge and of love, are linked. Here too Bemberg connects Sor Juana's intellectual with her emotional transgressions. It is therefore not just apposite but highly significant that she stages them together.)

On the whole, Juana maintains emotional as well as intellectual confidence in this scene. On the contrary, the vicereine's initial intellectual confidence – as evidenced in her quoting – is as soon erased as is her emotional poise. The viceroy's praise of Juana and of her poem, 'talented and lovely' shows the vicereine in a two-shot with him, nervously rubbing her hands. But while she may be silent in the next shot while she registers this praise, Juana does not look abashed. And when the vicereine then says that she has been wanting to meet her, we register its impact – accepted nonchalantly enough – on another cut back to Juana. She does proceed, however, to take exception to the vicereine's suggestion that there are few cultured women in Mexico, either to the slight on Mexico, or to the lack of opportunities for women to be cultured anywhere. She confidently suggests that it is true everywhere and continues her rebuffal with a pointed, '. . . en España' ('. . . in Spain') which is said on a cutback to the vicereine and which, judging by her shamed expression, the vicereine seems to take to heart. What proceeds is a lecture, with Juana using the example of St Teresa of Avila, the great Spanish intellectual who was called insane.

The viceroy sums up his impressions of Juana with 'Bella, apasionada, irónica' ('Beautiful, passionate, ironical') and the cutting around these words similarly sums up and sews the trio together. 'Beautiful' is off-screen to a shot on the vicereine who is assenting to this praise of Juana with a silent gaze towards her. 'Passionate' is on the happily smiling viceroy and, on 'ironical', there is a cut to Juana whose slight smile suggests absolute confidence and knowingness. Again, confident woman fits constructively with sanctified nun.

It is impossible to disentangle analysis of this dialogue and its staging in cuts between its three participants from the relay of looks between them. This is a scene in which the vicereine falls in love with Juana, but of Juana and herself, it is only the vicereine's point of view with which we are aligned. Point of view is obviously linked to display of the loved one, of Sor Juana. But this exposure is precisely to the feeling gaze of the vicereine whose real power, as in the scene of the kiss, is thus inscribed formally.

In fact a close analysis does reveal something strange about Juana's point of view. The vicereine is always looking obliquely right to Juana so that all cuts back from her to Juana are held in the vicereine's point of view. But even when Juana answers the latter's 'there are few cultured women' most directly and confidently, with, 'Everywhere, Señora' and we feel it is a direct look back, she is in fact addressing, with a look to the left of screen, the viceroy with her look. This means that cuts back to the vicereine are not from Juana's point of view.

Such a misalignment and hence disorientation of her look is underlined by the fact that when she first moves towards and takes up her final position facing them, Juana has already looked – in a correct alignment – to the right of the screen (and shyly, or slyly?) to the vicereine. Of course the dislocation of Juana's look can be interpreted in many ways – such as that her real subservience must be to the viceroy, or that she recognises and is fearful of the vicereine's emotional power. But we cannot read such ambiguity into the vicereine's gaze.

For the vicereine, it is an emotionally charged scene and furthermore the vicereine, who holds the point of view, and the spectator witness the scene as theatrical. All of the explicit narrative and visual references to

Assumpta Serna as Sor Juana in *Yo, la peor de todas*

theatre are underlined by a formal recourse in this sequence to a tableau effect. There are qualities here of suspended movement and of stillness. Firstly, the only real sense of physical movement within its frames is in the play of expressions on the protagonists' faces. So that, secondly, emotion in this sequence is expressed through the long visual still as does the subtle play of expressions across the vicereine's shy but struggling face and Juana's more open and confident one.

According to Brewster and Jacobs in their study of theatrical influences on early cinema, tableaux provided, among other things, '. . . The suspension characteristic of the stage picture, where the action stops while its significance is presented.'[47] And this significance is often precisely that of 'intense psychological dilemmas.'[48] But a major difference between theatrical tableaux and their use in early cinema was that even if the characters remained still within the frame, cinematic movements could and usually did render the tableau dynamic. Bemberg actually keeps her camera still, rendering her tableau effect even more pronounced. This effect of an underlined emotional intensity is felt all the more strongly in a modern cinema where tableaux are rare.

What is being signalled is both the *theatricality* of the occasion and its psychological weight. Of course, the emotional weight of their meeting is rendered the heavier precisely because it must be held down in the public arena. But the emotional weight falls on the side of the vicereine and it is this that she has carried into the scene of the kiss.

So that in that scene of the kiss in which it would appear that the director would most want to accord autonomy, in that it is celebrating a transgression – that of the nun's sexuality – she has possibly disinvested Sor Juana of her autonomy. This is doubly ironic in that it is a transgression that, as we have seen, Paz simply is not interested in, other than that he wishes to accord her the experience of having loved.

KNOWLEDGE

For Paz, Sor Juana's transgression was the outburst of 'the other voice'; that voice that violates the code of what is utterable in every age and society.[49] As he explains in the Preface to his book (in which, it should be noted, her gender is so insignificant to him that he fails to mention it): 'That was the cause of the misfortunes she suffered in the last years of her life, for such transgressions were, and are, punished with severity.'[50]

Sor Juana herself bears out this interpretation of her transgression. For in her *Intellectual Autobiography* she talks of her almost criminal love of learning.[51] But Paz makes it clear that Sor Juana was never daring enough to be critical of the system, often noting her silence on the topics of Spanish imperialism and its conversion programmes. And although he argues that in the end it was a conspiracy against her, it is merely that advantage was taken of this other voice, not by men because they were men, but because they were powerful men, pitted against each other. He talks at length of the rivalry between the Bishop of Puebla in Sor Juana's parish and the archbishop, and how the former put her up to the criticism of the latter's favourite, Vieyra (the subject of her essay). This caused her downfall.[52]

Furthermore, Paz acknowledges her own motives here. He paints a detailed picture of the archbishop's misogyny, and his final judgement of her end is that 'Sor Juana intervened in the quarrel between two powerful princes of the Roman church and was destroyed in the process.'[53] She may not have known what she was doing, but what she did, she did willingly.

Bemberg's treatment sees Sor Juana more as victim: she is completely set up in the sequence that deals with the idea for her polemical essay against Vieyra. This begins with a scene between the new viceroy and two men, Sigüenza and Puebla, whose backs, to the left and right of the frame respectively, are flanking him. One of them is Puebla, Sor Juana's bishop, and they are at conference upon the archbishop's excesses. The editing forcibly constructs the sense of their relative power. Although most of the point of view shots are given to the viceroy (after all, he is vested with civic power), it is clear whenever there is a cut back to him from his point of view shot of Sigüenza that he has 'switched off' from the latter's complaints. The direction of the viceroy's eyes, obliquely to the right of the screen, suggest a look at and acknowledgement only of the more powerful, and as it turns out, more sinister, Puebla. This latter mutters that 'we can merely punish him . . .'[54] – there is a protracted close-up on him think-

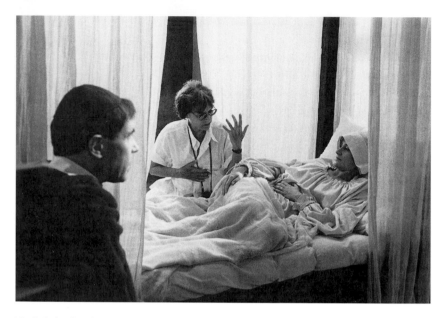

María Luisa Bemberg directs Assumpta Serna in *Yo, la peor de todas*

ing – until he continues, 'with a provocation'.[55] At this point there is a freeze whilst against the frame comes the external diegetic sound of Sor Juana reading in innocent tones the much later result of these ruminations: her critique of Vieyra. The cut to where we actually see her doing so, behind the grille, and shot over, and including, the menacing back, this time of Puebla himself, comes a few seconds later; the inference is clear: the tiger has seized the lamb. This is underlined in the rest of the sequence between them, composed of shot reverse shots in which, however, all cuts to extremer close-ups of him reveal the menace of sinister intrigue in his smile.

Next we see exactly how she has been manipulated. What Paz sees as personal motivation in Sor Juana has been relegated by the film to her mere *amusement*, 'I've enjoyed contradicting him',[56] whilst she remains innocent to the implication of Puebla's using of her, inherent in his 'And that it should be *you* exactly.'[57] (Our response as audience has of course been likewise 'manipulated': *our* privileged access to the text provides the dramatic irony: we have seen Puebla stroking his beard, Sor Juana has not.) Furthermore, Bemberg underlines Sor Juana's reluctance to intervene politically, 'Neither do I wish that the snake should bite me',[58] to which Puebla ingenuously replies, 'Please – no one's going to publish it.'[59] In this of course, Bemberg is true to Paz's contention that Sor Juana would never attack the system, but the context here of clear manipulation only serves to reinforce the entire 'innocence' of the nun, which Paz always disclaims.

In the next sequence, in which nun accounts to archbishop, Bemberg portrays, further to her innocence, her abandonment which is inflected, I argue, with a (problematic) martyrdom. She does this both in the visual treatment of Sor Juana and of Puebla (who has published against Juana's express will her diatribe against Vieyra) and through the presence of a third man, Miranda, her confessor. Moreover, Puebla's cruel deception is under-written by the progression of the narrative: the two sequences under discussion (that of her 'manipulation' and now the archbishop's response), are in fact separated by a third one, leaving us to absorb the implication that it was during this – her visit to her dying mother – that the conspiracy of publication took effect.[60] This is not part of Paz's argument.

So Sor Juana has to confront the archbishop's accusations alone. Such loneliness is made forceful by juxtaposition. Immediately prior to this scene is another image of two women in domestic harmony and fidelity; she is composing her defence to her amanuensis and the last image is a close-up of the two with their arms around each other. This is as preface to the overtones of masculine power in what is now a familiar motif: the camera moves with the backs of three men around a corner to – again, a familiar scene – the grille in long shot with Sor Juana behind it. As it moves forwards (with the men), to the sinister tapping of the archbishop's stick, the grille finally comes to take up yet again, the entire width of the frame, so that our visual access to the nun is once more through the bars of a 'prison'.

Sor Juana then presents her answer to her 'persecutors', to which the archbishop counters, 'Can you identify them?'[61] She will not, except to name one of them by his pseudonym of Sor Filotea. However, the camera accuses Puebla by twice cutting to and moving into close-ups on him while she presents her defence of having obeyed a man of the church who won't defend her and who remains silent. It is significant that these takes allow for his two long, slow and obliquely sideways looks, which in contrast to the one of Miranda looking to the floor, suggest slyness and lack of shame. But it is the silence of both of them, flanking as they do the ravings of the archbishop (the camera constantly reverts to their three heads at 90 degrees, with Puebla assuming the foreground of the frame) that is eloquent of utter betrayal. The archbishop is mad but they are wicked.

Sor Juana assumes centre frame, frontally and in extreme close-up, when she seizes upon the archbishop's castigation of Miranda for having trusted to the judgement of a woman. 'Ah, finally you've said it . . . if I weren't a woman, it wouldn't matter',[62] the end result of which is that she grabs his hand and makes him smell her own. Her parting shot to the archbishop is that he bears the devil in his heart. Following hard on the heels of the manifestation of his physical disgust of woman, the implication is a universal one, that Sor Juana is the victim of misogyny, rather than of what for Paz is more local: three particular men in a power struggle. Also, Bemberg's implication is that Sor Juana is abandoned by him as well by Miranda as he was also present at the above interviews, as we have seen. Paz does not ever argue this, although he reserves strong criticism for her confessor, whom he denounces early on in the book as a sinister 'fisher of souls', and who actually abandoned her much later than in the events filmed and described above.[63] Nevertheless, even here, he confesses that we cannot know Sor Juana's reaction, 'How did Sor Juana feel about Nuñez de Miranda's defection? We know nothing at all.'[64] Furthermore, Paz does not deny but is at pains to delineate the archbishop's misogyny (in an attempt to understand his motivations and also the motivations of those who dislike him, including of course those of Sor Juana). He does not see in it however a direct argument for her abandonment.

Again Bemberg is condensing separate arguments to reinforce a feminist theme which is that the nun's betrayal is a conspiracy of misogynist men. Aptly, Miranda closes the scene by telling her to find another confessor and its final image is haunting. The camera moves away with him, leaving us to the receding image of Juana holding the grille and with an expression of surprised disbelief. The composition – her arm, holding on to the bars, is outstretched along the frame – suggests abandonment. This works with the lighting – which picks out a saintly halo on her forehead and runs along her arm – to suggest, most problematically to a feminist reading of this film, her martyrdom.

In its treatments of Juana's transgressions of love and of knowledge, it is arguable that the film, more than the book, inadvertently inscribes Sor Juana as a victim so that her final abdication to her confessor is all of a piece.

CONFESSION

In the last chapter of *Sor Juana* Paz returns to a discussion of Sor Juana's *villancicos* written in honour of St Catherine of Alexandria and sung in the Cathedral of Oaxaca on 25 November 1691. These 'include some of Sor Juana's most beautiful verses, many resonant with autobiographical references and several promoting a defiant feminism'.[65] Here he finds and quotes 'a prophecy of what awaited her':

> Now all her learned arguments
> Are lost to us (how great the grief)
> But with her blood, if not with ink
> She wrote the lesson of her life.[66]

It is this image, of nun signing her confession in her own blood, towards which the entire film has moved.

Paz and Bemberg agree that her 'confession' was made because she was entirely helpless, but for Paz she is rendered so by empirical events, both of plague and of politics.[67] He talks of her confession as an abdication and a denial rather than as a surrender and as one that is orchestrated by her confessor to whom she capitulates. Paz further maintains that the substance of this abdication was an intellectual one,[68] and therefore that what she was abdicating from was the pursuit of her very argument that 'Gender is not of the essence in matters of intelligence.'[69] Although Bemberg is faithful to these ideas she also – I think inadvertently – suggests a surrender to God which Paz denies. Narratively, the prelude to the confession, as well as the scene itself, details Sor Juana's surrender to her confessor, but underlines thereby the iconography (most especially suggested in the lighting) of a spiritual renunciation.[70]

The sequence of her confession begins with an establishing long shot of the 'courtroom', the nuns' assembly, the first image of which includes Sor Juana's back, centre-frame. (This aptly rhymes with the establishing shots of just this 'courtroom' in the opening sequence of the film.) After a cut to an extreme close-up of her reading her confession is another to what is by now a familiar and sinister motif: a middle distance frontal view of two representatives of enthroned power; but now it is the enthroned power not of state and of church but of the latter only and entirely, in the persons of

A scene from *Yo, la peor de todas*

the mother abbess and confessor. So that with the subsequent cut and return to Sor Juana's face (she is intoning that her crimes deserve everlasting hell) we can understand from whom, when she states this and looks up, she is looking for guidance: her confessor. Bemberg clearly insinuates therefore that they are his and not her words.

The camera cuts back to Sor Juana for the final images: 'In support of what I say', and now she takes off her glasses, 'I wish to spill my blood.'[71] It is only with the words *la sangre* that she looks to her confessor: now we're no longer sure. Is this his idea or is this intended to contravene him? Her hand comes through and down the right side of the frame and we understand that she has cut her hand with that which has helped her to see. This is Paz's abdication: that of the intelligence and of the light.

The three final images of this particular scene are eloquent: the first freezes three constituents of her final humiliation: the broken glasses in the bottom centre of the frame, against the backdrop of the parchment of her confession, and in the left side of the frame her damaged and shaking hand which she turns over in order to write. The second, a cut to an extreme close-up of her bowed head – an articulate image of her humiliation – but now without cutting, she moves out of the frame. The sincerity of her supplication to God is again rendered doubtful by this abdication from the frame before the final cut to the substance of that confession, the blood-red signature: '*Yo, la peor de todas.*'

Finally, just as the scenes with the confessor have preluded this scene, so the framing of her confession is made complete by the thirteenth and final sequence in her cell. The first image of this world speaks of its reductiveness; the shelves no longer have books on them, and the camera pans around the entire cell, showing its new emptiness. It finally moves across the study table, bare but for crucifix and candle, to the disconsolate figure in long shot of Sor Juana, alone with her dreams. Behind her the window is now blank and devoid of stars. Without her books and instruments she has no way of seeing them.

But Paz still accords her some remnants of defiance. He cites the strangeness of a penitent wishing to keep as many possessions as possible and suggests that the one act that might corroborate her change – the surrender of

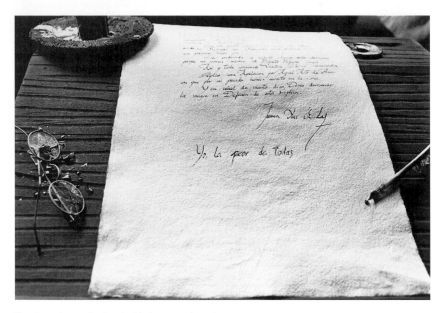

Sor Juana's confession in *Yo, la peor de todas*

her library – was more likely intended to placate the archbishop.[72] Accordingly, in the prelude to the final sequence, Bemberg's Sor Juana refuses her assistance in the dismantling of her library. Instead, she constitutes the forlorn background, holding Moctezuma's gorgeous feathers against her chest, thereby demonstrating that she is still wedded to the secular.

Thus in spirit and in argument too, we may say that Bemberg's final scenes are the greatest and most faithful tribute to the contentions of Paz: that her surrender was not a surrender of a supplicant to God but that of an unwilling captive to a 'fisher of souls'.[73] However, the symbolic weight of lighting and music works to suggest otherwise. For when Juana is most abject, in the scenes of her confession and of the subsequent emptying of her cell, she is most 'sanctified' by the light. The arched window of the latter scene, blank as it is, does suggest the only source of diegetic light and as such forms a framing halo around the almost silhouetted figure of

Sor Juana. The 'heavenly' non-diegetic soprano voice which enters from another space and on which the image fades to the credits, reinforces and gives a final impression of beatitude. Similarly the extremity of the close-ups in the scene of her confession render her framed by her wimple which works therefore as a halo around her head. The chiaroscuro effect of the lighting whitens this halo to an intense brightness and renders her — and with her dark eyes which are the only other items to catch the light on the two occasions when briefly she looks up and into the camera — 'enchanting' as an angel.

So it is also possible to argue that the final images of the film which, given its title, would appear to be central to its import, do communicate a more thorough defeat than Paz accords Sor Juana. Moreover, although the film portrays an ambiguity in that Sor Juana 'abdicates' from the 'frame' of her confession, it does not underline what is so vital to Paz, that 'she was simply using a common formula of vilification'.[74] And, that, of those self-negating words from which the film takes its title and therefore its colour, he says, 'More than once she wrote in the margins of her books, "I, the least worthy of all" and "It is true that this phrase was often used by both monks and nuns".'[75]

Self-hatred is only the flip side of the coin of narcissism whose other side of course is self-love. That she had enough of this left to her is clear to Paz who has no doubt, 'That she defended herself to the last and refused to sign an abdication and nullification of her entire life.'[76] Furthermore in the first (with which the film deals) and the two further documents signed there is, 'Not a single declaration in which Sor Juana formally and expressly renounces letters.'[77] He underlines the importance of this statement typographically with the use of italics. Finally, of the fact that at her death there was haggling over ownership of her estate, Paz asks, 'How can we interpret the evidence to the contrary except as a sign that some part of her remained unvanquished?'[78] Bemberg's final images in their communication of utter desolation do not suggest this.

It is my argument therefore that Paz's Sor Juana contains more hope, even unto the end. It is apposite to compare the ending of this film with the earlier *Miss Mary*, dealing in those Argentine 'Señoras with their painted faces'. Miss Mary, as lonely governess, is meant to be counterpointing their seemingly more fortunate, but actually unfortunate, situation and by doing so the implication of the film's momentum is that it is heading towards her own freedom. Certainly, Perón is released at the end of the film (it too is dealing in more 'universal' questions of liberty) and Miss Mary is by now an independent teacher working in Buenos Aires, but the final images – she closes the shutters on the celebrants in the streets – are again those of a woman who cannot face up to the implications of her liberty.[79]

Clearly, this is all part of Bemberg's intention, but in this case it is arguable that the film risks reinscription into a culture it is trying to transcend; in other words, that her defiant and transgressing woman is less free than Paz's. In terms of its spirit it is a loving tribute, not only to Paz's erudite and grave treatment of his subject, but also to that subject herself. Perhaps, however, it is too much of a tribute, for in the final images the nun is indeed 'almost arrestingly saintly' in those quiet tones, the opposite of Bemberg's earlier sensuous productions.

While Paz ends his book on the image of Phaethon, 'flight and fall, transgression and punishment',[80] and leaves Sor Juana with some human vestiges of herself, for Bemberg, the most eloquent image from this world is that of those words signed in blood: 'Yo, la peor de todas'. As textual overlay they are rendered stark in their jagged outlines and they are stark in meaning to any feminist, and bleak: 'I, the worst *woman* of all.'

The visual and audible symbolism of the film suggests Sor Juana's defeat. In consolation, it places her where, according to Paz, her honest uncompromising modernism could not allow her to be – in heaven.

NOTES

The quotations are in the original Spanish and the translations into English within the text are my own.

1 Stephanie Merrim, 'Toward a Feminist Reading of Sor Juana Inés de la Cruz', in S. Merrim (ed.) *Feminist Perspectives on Sor Juana Inés de la Cruz*, Wayne State University Press, 1991, p. 11.

2 In so doing, Octavio Paz, *Sor Juana: Her Life and Her World* (trans from *Sor Juana Inés de la Cruz, o, Las trampas de la fé*, Margaret Sayers Peden), Harvard University Press, Boston, 1988, p. 476, paints her particular circumstances, 'History was the misogyny of Aguiar y Seijas and his rivalry with Fernández de Santa Cruz; the obsessions of Nuñez de Miranda, intent on making a saint of a woman who had no religious vocation; the politics of the Society of Jesus in China and Mexico'; and so on. 'Without the riots of 1692 or the death of the Marquis de la Laguna . . . she might never have been disturbed. Her personal history was made of the same perpetually fluctuating substance as the history of the world.'

3 This is the contention of Electa Arenal in her play based upon the lives of Sor Juana and of Anne Bradstreet, in *This Life Within Me Won't Keep Still*; in B. Chevigny and G. Laguardia (eds), *Reinventing the Americas*, Cambridge University Press, Cambridge, 1986, pp. 160.

4 Octavio Paz, 1988, op. cit., see final chapter.

5 Ibid., p. 469.

6 To cite just two examples, Serna plays the role of a lesbian in *El jardin secreto* (dir: Carlos Suarez, Spain, 1984) and Sanda plays Hélène, who can be interpreted as lesbian, in *La voyage en douce* (dir: Michel Deville, France, 1979).

7 Octavio Paz too has his own agenda; according to Stephanie Merrim, op. cit., p. 14, it is that of the Mexican essayist tradition which tries to come to terms with the nation's past. It is also one in which his favourite theme of solitude obtrudes.

8 Quoted in Luis Trelles Plazaola, *Cine y mujer en America Latina*, Universidad de Puerto Rico, San Juan, 1991, p. 91.

9 John King, 'Assailing the heights of macho pictures', in Susan Bassnett, ed., *Knives and Angels: Women Writers in Latin America*, Zed, London, 1990, p. 164.

10 'Otro desafío gue me gusta es hacer histories universales. Tolstoy dice "habla de tu pueblo y hablarás del universo, si hablas con una dimensión universal".' Quoted in Luis Trelles Plazaola, op. cit., p. 123.

11 Octavio Paz, 1988, op. cit., p. 447.

12 I have viewed many North American and European 'convent' films, ranging in date from 1943 – *The Song of Bernadette* (dir: Henry King, prod: CBS Fox, USA) to 1992 – *Sister Act* (dir: Emile Ardolino, prod: Touchstone Pictures, USA) and also from semi-porn – *The Devils* (dir. Ken Russell, prod: Warner

Brothers, UK) – to the surreal *Viridiana* (dir: Buñuel, Spain, 1961). With the exception of Russell's film, they are all filmed on location.

13 Ibid., p. 386.

14 Heinrich Wölfflin, *The Art of Albrecht Dürer*, Phaidon, London, 1971, p. 201.

15 Ibid., p. 201.

16 Ibid., p. 201.

17 Octavio Paz, 1988, op. cit., p. 245.

18 'Octavio Paz habla de que la celda de Sor Juana es como una enorme matriz y los bocetos la diseñan como celda redonda – como la mente de Sor Juana, como el mundo.' Quoted in Luis Trelles Plazaola, op. cit., p. 122.

19 'No soporto los barrotes de su locutorio.'

20 'Se dice que tienes la mas grande librería en las Américas, pero son libros peligrosos.'

21 'Mi espejo de obsidiana, en que leo el pasado y el futuro . . . mi autometa . . . mi astrolabio . . . mi lira.'

22 'Mis plumas, mis escritos . . . estos son mis niños.' Octavio Paz, 1998, op. cit., p. 247.

23 Octavio Paz, *The Labyrinth of Solitude*, Penguin, London, 1985, p. 105.

24 Octavio Paz, 1988, op. cit., p. 367.

25 Ibid., p. 377.

26 Feminist critics have argued the reverse, pointing out that the last line of the poem, *Yo, despierta*, specifically genders the author as a woman. (See G. Sabat Rivers, 'A feminist rereading of Sor Juana's dream' in Merrim 1991, pp. 142–61.) Furthermore, Jean Franco, 1989, p. 31, argues that *First Dream* is the nearest that Sor Juana comes to 'autonomy' in that she was not working to a commission here and so wilfully she was transgressing into male space.

27 Octavio Paz, 1988, op. cit., p. 378.

28 'Lo es.'

29 'Asi lo ha ordenado Dios/y César.'

30 The window is an important symbol of her connection to a 'wider world', even to the cosmos.

31 'No es un convento, es un bordello.'

32 'Nada mas aburrido que un convento y una monja a la que se le ve tan poco, no se le ve el pelo ni el cuerpo ni casi las manos. Llegué a la conclusíon de que lo que había que hacer era "desmonjizar" esta película.' Quoted in Luis Trelles Plazaola, op. cit., p. 122.

33 'Se trata de Assumpta Serna, la catalana, intérprete de *Matador*. Me parece perfecta.' Ibid., p. 123.

34 Ibid., p. 123.

35 Octavio Paz, 1988, op. cit., p. 98.

36 'Tenemos las vidas parecidas.'

37 Ibid., p. 216.

38 That feminist critics again dispute this is not the brief of this chapter, although important and interesting.

39 Octavio Paz, 1988, op. cit., p. 281.

40 Ibid., p. 216.

41 Rosalind Coward, *Female Desire: Women's Sexuality Today*, Paladin, London, 1984, p. 82.

42 Paul Julian Smith, 'Writing women in the golden age', in P. J. Smith, *The Body Hispanic*, Clarendon Press, Oxford, 1989, p. 12.

43 'Quita tu velo/Es un orden.'

44 'Esta Juana es mía, solamente mía.'

45 It is difficult to argue what else Bemberg might have done here for the Vicereine did have political power over Sor Juana. 'The women Sor Juana describes and to whom she dedicates much of her secular poetry were in fact in positions of real power; they were her patrons.' Emilie Bergmann, 'Sor Juana Inés de la Cruz: dreaming in a double voice', 1990, p. 164. Nevertheless Bemberg has elected to point up such unequal power relations, and in so doing, the audience sees Sor Juana from its own position of power.

46 I refer to chapter seven of *Stars* by Richard Dyer, *Stars*, British Film Institute, 1979, where he discusses the 'perfect' and 'problematic' fit between a star's image and the character that he or she is playing.

47 B. Brewster and L. Jacobs (eds.), *Theatre to Cinema: Stage Pictorialism and the Early Feature Film*, Oxford, University Press, 1997, p. 76.

48 Ibid., p. 49.

49 Octavio Paz, 1988, op. cit., p. 6.

50 Ibid., p. 6.

51 Margaret Sayers Peden (trans.), *Sor Juana Inés de la Cruz: la respuesta a sor filotea (The Intellectual Autobiography)*, Lime Rock Press, 1982, p. 44.

52 Octavio Paz, 1988, op. cit., p. 402.

53 Ibid., p. 403.

54 'Solo podemos castigarlo . . .'

55 'Con una provocación.'

56 'Me ha divertido contradecirle.'

57 'Y se es *vos* exactamente.'

58 'Yo tampoco quiero que la serpiente me muerda.'

59 'Por favor – nadie va a publicarlo.'

60 We (but not Sor Juana) have earlier learned of the fact of publication through Sigüenza's accusation of the bishop who hides behind his office, 'I am the Bishop. You cannot arraign me.' He explains that it was merely a joke, and that he doesn't want further to sour his relations with the archbishop.

61 '¿Habéis podido identificarlos?'

62 'Ah, al fin ha dicho el señor . . . si non fuera mujer nada importaría.'

63 Octavio Paz, 1988, op. cit., p. 109.

64 Ibid., p. 427.

65 Ibid., p. 434.

66 Ibid., p. 434.

67 Ibid., p. 444.

68 Her argument, as Paz maintains, never was with the body politic. Jean Franco, *Plotting Women: Gender and Representation in Mexico*, Verso, London, 1989, p. 47, in different terms would bear this out: 'In Sor Juana's time exceptional women were not excluded from political power (at least as sovereigns) but women were excluded from truth activities.'

69 Octavio Paz, 1988, op. cit., p. 434.

70 Although her erstwhile feminist interpretations of the Mexican seventeenth century are perhaps most fully justified in this respect.

71 'En señal de cuanto digo/quisiera derramar la sangre.'

72 Octavio Paz, 1988, op. cit., p. 468.

73 Ibid., p. 109: 'Fishers of souls are awesome because thy are also seducers.' Furthermore, p. 449, 'Master of the keys to her existence, he had opened the doors of the convent to her to enable her to escape an inhospitable world, and now he was preparing to close the doors to her essential vocation, letters, irrevocably.'

74 Ibid., p. 468.

75 Ibid., p. 448.

76 Ibid., p. 463.

77 Ibid.

78 Ibid., p. 468.

79 In this sense, *Miss Mary* and *Yo, la peor de todas* imply fewer liberating possi-

bilities than those films of Bemberg's Argentinian contemporary, Fernando Solanas, whose returning internal 'exile' in *Sur* for example, finally makes it home through the barrier of the window to become more than just a reflection to his wife.

80 Octavio Paz, 1988, op. cit., p. 70.

SEVEN

MARÍA LUISA BEMBERG'S *DE ESO NO SE HABLA*: FROM FICTION TO FILM, SOME NOTES

Jason Wilson

Before briefly looking at how the late María Luisa Bemberg's film *De eso no se habla* (*We Don't Want to Talk About It*) (1992), which diverges from Julio Llinás's short story of the same title, I must outline a worry about precedence of text over film. María Luisa Bemberg's co-script writer, Jorge Goldenberg, remembers Julio Llinás's story arriving as a typescript by post.[1] When it was decided to base a film on this story both scriptwriters were faced with translating a baroque story into a film with dialogue and visual scenes. Jorge Goldenberg recalled all the bits that were added but was sure that the story they worked on was not the finished story published in 1993. What seems probable is that Julio Llinás altered passages and added names and scenes, after working with the film-makers. This later writing would explain both Llinás dedicating the story to María Luisa Bemberg and the book featuring a clip from the film on its cover. How much Llinás altered his story after María Luisa Bemberg and Jorge Goldenberg had transformed it into a script is an intriguing point.

Before characterising Llinás's story, first something about its author's aesthetics. Julio Llinás (1929–) was an active surrealist poet and promoter in the 1950s (he founded an art magazine *Boa* and set up art shows as the Buenos Aires correspondent for the *Phases* group of abstract and experimental artists). He published two slim volumes of prose poems – *Panta rhei* (1950) (the title alludes to Heraclitus's 'everything flows') and *La ciencia natural* (*Natural Science*) (1959) – and co-edited a surrealist magazine called *À partir de cero*, with the Argentine poet Enrique Molina (who later crossed swords with María Luisa Bemberg because she did not acknowledge his *Una sombra donde sueña Camila O'Gorman* (*A Shadow Where Camila O'Gorman Dreams*) (1973), an erotic novel researching Camila O'Gorman's life, with an appendix of *documentos inéditos* [unpublished documents]).[2] After a gap of 34 years Llinás published his first book of short stories, *De eso no se habla* (*We Don't Want to Talk About It*), in 1993.[3] The opening story of the same title transforms his earlier surrealist vision of purifying natural forces ('One morning I drank that transparency, I bit that fruit matured by dreams, and in that barbarous state I found a new prayer')[4] into black humour and baroque exaggeration, mocking Argentine small-town pretensions. Set in a sierra village near Córdoba we read about a Buñuelesque, or grotesque, marriage between the *enana* and the Tyrone Power look-alike Ludovico D'Andrea, while the crippled alcalde who gives her away dies in his wheelchair without anybody noticing. D'Andrea's dwarf wife runs off with the circus as Doña Leonor Bacigalupo, her mother, is no longer able to repress her guilty, secret affair with the circus dwarf ('The great lie of his life was bubbling and boiling in his inner boiler, like a witch's potion, second after second, minute by minute, day after day, for twenty years . . .'[5]), and ends with Ludovico D'Andrea staring forlornly 'towards the empty infinity of himself, with the loneliness of heart of a man who had loved until he had extinguised himself in the extremes of a love without hope'.[6] Dwarves, desperate love, black humour, grotesque and pretentious villagers do not allow for a reader's sympathy; the baroque style and tone set up a farce and ask the reader to join in the mockery of these provincial caricatures.

María Luisa Bemberg's film modifies this story in fascinating ways. First of all she humanised the ridiculous inhabitants of San José de los Altares; Ludovico d'Andrea (the late Marcello Mastroianni) remains dignified and enigmatic, a failed artist (able to enchant the *enana*, Carlota, with his traveller's lies) who fell for Carlota, recognising the misfit or artist in her; Leonor, the proud mother, is also seen as more human, a semi-rebel refusing to be trampled on by local gossip and the *qué dirán* (what people say), insisting on the first meaning of the film's title *De eso no se habla* where

María Luisa Bemberg on location for *De eso no se habla*

the *eso* refers to the unmentionable dwarfness or stature of her daughter. María Luisa Bemberg also makes the film more a parable about freedom which ends with visual analogies linking a sad, caged lion, a desperate caged Leonor behind her *rejas* (balcony's iron bars) and the dwarf daughter riding free, running off, released like her white horse that Ludovico had set free without explanation, and travelling the roads towards the hilly horizon in the circus, with her possible father the *cocoliche*-speaking fake count Vasilievich. The second level of meaning of the *eso* of *De eso no se habla* is that Carlota may be the daughter of the circus director (the Llinás story suggests this turn of events by making him an attractive world-travelling but phoney aristocratic dwarf, while the film plays down this possible parentage by showing him as a bald, leering, sensuous man). The circus dwarf was probably the one-night-stand lover of Doña Leonor.

I counted some 17 scenes that María Luisa Bemberg and Jorge Goldenberg had added to the laconic short story in its published version. Pointing some of these additions out is my tribute to María Luisa Bemberg's filmic thinking, her – in her own words – 'visual story telling'. At Leeds Castle in 1989 she talked about 'my way of understanding the world [as being] predominantly visual'.[5] Translating the verbal to the visual is akin to the problem of dream interpretation where the inner visual logic of the dream, or what could be called 'dream thinking', ensures that visual imagery does the thinking usually entrusted to words.

When Doña Leonor finally realises that her beloved two-year-old daughter is a dwarf she goes out at night and smashes some kitschy dwarf statues belonging to the priest's rich German mistress, buries them sinisterly in a wood and then burns all the fairy-tale books with dwarves in the title. This strange scene is not in the story. This is a visual way of conveying Leonor's *'humilación'* ('humiliation') in the village when gossipers add two and two together concerning the paternity of the dwarf. Several short brothel scenes are added to the film that mock the self-important men of the *pueblo* and differentiate d'Andrea's tepid brothel sexuality with his later consuming passion and suffering for the *enana*. It allows the viewer to enter into the enigma of d'Andrea's hopeless love, though we do not see any sexual scenes between the old man and his child dwarf bride. It is clear, however, that

Luisina Brando and
Alejandra Podestá as
mother and daughter in
De eso no se habla

d'Andrea's passion is sexual and possessive when he rapes a whore on a billiard table before he dares ask for Carlota's hand and face village ridicule.

The piano concert scene where Doña Leonor wins her way about how to run the charity show was also absent from the story. The scene gives us a visual insight into the *enana*'s artistic talents (as a pianist she is 'normal', as gifted as any artist her age; she doesn't care about her mother's panic of becoming ridiculous and bows to the public, not remaining on her stool as ordered to in order to hide her dwarfness). The confusion about who d'Andrea is to marry is also absent in the story – a comic scene that humanises the situation. The way Marcello Mastroianni acts d'Andrea's falling into a hopeless passion ('*el amor es raro*' ['love is odd']) is both mockingly and endearingly conveyed, a touch totally absent from the story.

But rather than further enumerate the variations noted between short story and film I want to focus on the central visual metaphor as revealing the way cinema thinks visually as opposed to verbal narration which concerns the white horse. In the story there is no white horse. The *enana* simply insists on having acrobacy lessons without anyone really questioning why (except that it obviously anticipates her joining the circus). When she does ride it's on an '*obeso caballo afeminado*' ('obese, effeminate horse'), keeping the horse in tone with the mocking spirit of the tale. María Luisa Bemberg and Jorge Goldenberg transformed this fat nag first into a white

Shetland pony, furiously dismissed by Leonor the mother as the dwarf pony mimicked her daughter's stature (where we laugh at her), then into a white horse that the *enana* rides indoors until she is a skilled rider, unknowingly preparing for her destiny of joining the circus at the end.

A white horse has a fairy-tale connotation, the kind of surreal associations found in the paintings of Leonor Fini or of Leonora Carrington, and in the latter's case seem to stand for the mystique of childhood.[8] The old married man d'Andrea suddenly realises what is at stake and during a storm liberates the white horse as he let his child bride go (in the story he is a *cincuentón* [50-year-old]). This beautiful white horse suddenly becomes an image of aesthetic and animal freedom (as the absent stallion had in Lorca's drama *La casa de Bernarda Alba*). But more importantly the freed white horse is an image of Carlota the *enana*. She might be an *enana* on the outside, but on the inside she is as spirited as the white horse. This double image of self suggests the destiny of the artist, especially the woman artist, unable to conform to a philistine and provincial society (also a patriarchal one, complicated by a domineering mother) and ostracised. The parable, only implicit sarcastically in the story, becomes central to an understanding of María Luisa Bemberg's least autobiographical film, for the whole film is about how to break out of the prison of the *pueblo* and its suffocating whisperings. Only at the level of this parable can we place this film alongside María Luisa Bemberg's comment to Sheila Whitaker that 'I can only write and film about what I know',[9] for she had to break out, break away from feeling an inferior, as she also said 'the first step towards being more autonomous was getting a divorce', and thus become an outsider, a misfit, a metaphorical *enana* who 'dared to be daring' as she said at Leeds Castle in 1989.

María Luisa Bemberg and Jorge Goldenberg creatively adapted Llinás's story, humanised it without entering into the psychology of the characters who remain closed, made it more accessible, and created a contradictory visual parable that retained a surrealist angle (a dreamy unfamiliarity, a distancing, even comic oddity), complicating it with a fairy-tale sense of the ugly duckling who made it, found herself and went off with the circus of artists – dwarves were beloved of the surrealists – with the white horse inside, breaking out. María Luisa Bemberg told Caleb Bach: 'We saw the story as a fable, a fairy-tale. If we got psychological, I knew we were dead.'[10] The verb 'to break' links film and autobiography as parables of artistic freedom; María Luisa Bemberg said at Leeds Castle in 1989: 'To live my ideas meant breaking the evil spell of female isolation and working in solidarity with other women.'

NOTES

1 Jorge Goldenberg told me about this sequence at the University of Warwick's one-day conference on María Luisa Bemberg on the 12 October 1996.
2 See Graciela de Solá, *Proyecciones del surrealismo en la literatura Argentina*, Ediiones Culturales Argentinas, 1967, pp. 221–5.
3 I have used the Mondadori, Barcelona edition.
4 'Una mañana bebí esa transparencia, mordí ese fruto que el sueño desarrolla, y hallé una nueva oración en la barbarie.'Quoted from *Poesía argentina*, selección del Instituto Torcuato Di Tella, Editorial del Instituto, Buenos Aires, 1963, p. 155.
5 'En su caldero interior hervía borboteando, como una pócima de bruja, la gran mentira de su vida, segundo tras segundo, minuto tras minuto, día tras día, durante veinte años . . .' *De eso no se habla*, p. 40.
6 '[H]acia el vacío infinito de si mismo, con la soledad de corazón de un hombre que había amado hasta extinguirse en el extremo sin retorno del amor.' Ibid., p. 43.
7 I had been invited to participate at a conference held at Leeds Castle, organised by the Latin American Arts Association, with speakers ranging from Octavio Paz, Mario Vargas Llosa to María Luisa Bemberg. I translated her talk 'Being an artist in Latin America' (see Chapter Ten) and quote from my typescript, with her many revisions.
8 'The source of Carrington's magical white horse lies not in Freud's use of the horse as a symbol of male power but in the Celtic legends that nourished her childhood . . . it is faster than the wind and can fly through the air', Whitney Chadwick, *Women Artists and the Surrealist Movement*, Thames and Hudson, London, 1985, p. 79.
9 In John King and Nissa Torrents (eds), *The Garden of Forking Paths: Argentine Cinema*, British Film Institute, London, 1958.
10 Caleb Bach, 'María Luisa Bemberg tells the untold', *Américas,* March/April 1994, p. 26.

EIGHT

'CONVOCAR TANTO MUNDO': NARRATIVISING AUTHORITARIANISM AND GLOBALISATION IN *DE ESO NO SE HABLA*

Kathleen Newman

In the early 1990s, Argentine cinema, like other national cinemas in Latin America, seemed to be approaching an industrial impasse, a moment in which the political, economic and social conditions did not permit the further development of a national film industry. To this perception of a crisis of national cinemas in the first years of the last decade of the century, those directors who had sufficient national and international renown were able to respond with international co-productions which contemplated social decay and the end of the nation, such as *Fresa y chocolate* (*Strawberry and Chocolate*) (1993) and subsequently *Guantanamera* (1995), both co-directed by Tomás Gutiérrez Alea and Juan Carlos Tabío in Cuba, or *Caídos del cielo* (*Fallen from Heaven*) (1990) directed by Francisco Lombardi in Peru, or *De eso no se habla* (*We Don't Want to Talk About It*) (1993), directed by María Luisa Bemberg, in Argentina. With respect to the specific case of Argentina, Gabriela Fabbro and Diana Palladino note that, between 1983 and 1993, a decade of redemocratisation, there were 57 co-productions, or an average of five per year, a number which serves as an indication of the difficulty of sustaining a nationally funded industry. Fabbro and Palladino demonstrate that this created a new category of *cine de auteur* with directors such as Fernando Solanas, Eliseo Subiela, María Luisa Bemberg and Lita Stantic creating, through co-productions, a singular and new form of national film text.[1] This reconfiguration of *lo nacional*, of course, has determinants other than the obvious economic ones – the historical conjuncture also produced an insistence on the presence of 'the wider world' in the filmic text. Indeed, Bemberg's last film can be seen as evidence of a shift in national cinematic concerns, a recognition that redemocratisation had taken place during a new phase of globalisation in which the circulation of capital, information and people produced a heightened sense of the permeability of national borders. *De eso no se habla* deals directly with questions of authoritarianism and of marginalisation along lines of gender, class and sexual orientation, but it also registers audiovisually an unvoiced anxiety regarding the relation of a people to their nation and of the nation to the global political economy.

Midway through the film, in a scene in which some of the towns-people of San José de los Altares, *un pueblo de provincia*, are listening to the worldly (well travelled and seemingly well educated) Don Ludovico

On location for *De eso no se habla*

d'Andrea (played by Marcello Mastroianni) narrate stories of exotic, tropical locals 'where suffering can be endless', the voice-over narrator, revealed in the end to be the character of the observant young man Mohamé, observes for the benefit of the film's viewers that it would come to pass that Padre Aurelio, the priest *'sostuvo que no se puede convocar tanto mundo a espaldas de Satanás'* ('one cannot narrate, or bring so vividly to life, so much of the world without satan's involvement (behind his back)'). This devil of the greater world in *De eso no se habla* appears not so much in the enchanting stories or person of Don Ludovico, but rather in the figuration in the text of authoritarianism, the widow Doña Leonor de Azumendi (played by Luisina Brando), mother of Carlota, owner of the local store, the town's power broker who controls the minuscule world of *la gente bien* – the doctor, mayor, police chief as well as their female auxiliary, the ladies of the local *sociedad de beneficencia*. Bemberg said of Doña Leonor: 'The film is really about Carlota's possessive mother, an arrogant, absolutely horrible woman, who is for me a metaphor of repression and intolerance. She could represent any one of the many South American dictators we have had.'[2]

Doña Leonor as a dictator genders authoritarianism and produces in the film a tangential political reading to the main plotline concerning Carlota (also called Charlotte), the dwarf (*enana*) about whose physical stature Doña Leonor will not allow the townspeople to speak, hence the title of the film. Following on *Yo, la peor de todas* (1990), *De eso no se habla* is often taken as a commentary on sexuality and sexual orientation. While there is textual evidence supporting such an interpretation – for example, the film is proceeded by an inter title statement 'This tale is dedicated to all the people who have the courage to be different to be themselves' – the character of Carlota, about whose nature one is not to speak, is not the principal character of the film. Rather, she is an icon, one of Argentina's literary history's famous *'señalados de Dios'* who, by their marked nature reveal the limits of Argentine society (one thinks of El Rengo or La Coja in Roberto Arlt's novels). As a character in the film, Carlota is so unruffled by the self-deceptions of her mother and her fellow townspeople as to be opaque. Carlota's interior world is hers alone and her intellect and emotions are not revealed until the end of the film, and even then they are known only by her action of leaving the town with a circus, a circus which includes other enanos. The finale, in a homage to every Gabriel García Márquez homage to Greek tragedy, leaves *la mamá grande* entombed, shutting herself up in her house, never to be seen again. But the entombed woman herself once dug a very specific grave. In the opening of the film, Doña Leonor goes out at night to destroy the ceramic dwarves which decorate the property of the widow Schmidt. This scene opens with Doña Leonor reflected in a tripartite dressing table mirror as she remembers and the audience hears the sounds of the birthday party for the toddler Carlota. The audience is invited to consider who this woman may be, what kind of person she is. Later in the film, at her daughter's wedding, when Doña Leonor laughs hysterically at the sight of the difference in height between the groom Don Ludovico and her daughter, as they leave the altar and walk down the aisle, Doña Leonor will be revealed to be the one person in the town who could not accept Carlota's difference – the one person to whom 'eso' ('it') mattered as a question of identity, not though of her daughter's identity but rather her own identity as a mother and a woman. Doña Leonor sees herself in her daughter as she stares in that mirror in the opening sequence and the scene anticipates thematically the conclusion in which Doña Leonor will, for the audience, disappear from sight having lost her reflected identity and, from her perspective, her rightful class position. She sees herself marked as the outcast rather than the sovereign (if dictators can stand in for sovereignty).

Yet, Doña Leonor is a very oddly gendered authoritarian figure. When she leaves the house to destroy the dwarves, she is wearing a black negligée, boots and an overcoat. Her attack on the dwarves on the low wall (observed from a window by both the widow Schmidt and the priest, her lover) is simultaneously an attack on prejudice and hypocrisy, whether individual or institutional. The decorative dwarves are, in fact, offensive; they are a concretisation of prejudice, and the widow Schmidt and the priest are part of the social set (to which Doña Leonor belongs) which, as it is said, has made of hypocrisy an art form. We have then a momentary image of Doña Leonor combating prejudice, but the scene closes with the

Marcello Mastroianni and Alejandra Podestá in the wedding scene in
De eso no se habla

image of the sweaty and dirty, silk-clad, jack-booted woman satisfied with
her night's work of burying the dwarves. At the level of the plot, the scene
is obvious with regard to the character's operation of denial, but at the level
of the Argentine social imaginary, it evokes a more complicated story,
whether intentional or not. The shot of the earth partially covering the
dwarves must evoke the image of a mass grave and all the horror of the
'dirty war', the disappearances during which were only able to be investi-
gated after the return to democracy. There is an image of a mass grave but
the bodies buried in it are the social distortions of prejudice. Doña Leonor
eradicates the prejudice by means of an authoritarian act – two, in fact,
because she burns books as well (*Tom Thumb*, etc.). This image of the half-
buried dwarves haunts the film. It is Doña Leonor's efforts alone – by
means of education and a denial of prejudice – which gain for Carlota the

skills of survival and advancement, emotional and intellectual, in a world of prejudice. *La mamá grande* (this ferocious mother) turns out to be the dreaded monstrous feminist who sets free, or perhaps lets loose, her more refined intellectual daughter upon the world.

By here gendering authoritarian terror as female, Bemberg has created for *la pequeña* Carlota a more complicated genealogy than Doña Leonor ever imagined – or feared. The necessarily diachronic genealogy of generation after generation of imposing women is extended synchronically into the time-space of the nation by a second image which also haunts the films: the empty corridor of the colonial house of the Azumendi family. After Doña Leonor puts on her boots in the bedroom, she walks into the corridor and then out of frame to retrieve her coat. The camera lingers on the empty corridor, allowing the viewer to contemplate the architecture, the patterns of dark and light, the tiled floor and to pay attention to the now foregrounded soundscape. Just previously, as Doña Leonor sat before her dressing table, seeing herself reflected in the three mirrors and seeing herself in her mind's eye at Carlota's second birthday party pitied by the townspeople she considers her social inferiors, the soundtrack consists of slight echoes of party sounds and children's voices, sound as the memory of recent events. In the corridor there is little sound and the duration of the shot emphasises the traces of the past in the present – the emptiness of the colonial gallery as the presence of history. From the recent past of Carlota's second birthday, now Doña Leonor's memory, to the distant past of colonial Argentina, to what must finally be our own historical memory activated by Doña Leonor's absence from the frame – this brief narrative sequence anticipates the over-arching theme of the presence of the past in the current moment. Doña Leonor's buried dwarves – her massacre of the distorted image – cannot eradicate the presence of prejudice and authoritarianism but it can and does give way to a reflection on the wider world – *convocar tanto mundo*.

What the textual devil film-makers and other storytellers encounter when they narrativise, as opposed to analyse, authoritarianism is the danger of the re-enactment rather than the representation of authoritarianism. Bemberg would have left us with a film about the radical nature of a women's (Leonor's and Carlota's) decisions enabled by authoritarian practices (Leonor's with the town's complicity) had she not made story-telling itself the principal focus of the film. Having detemporalised the film – placing it as a fable or fairy-tale outside of history, Bemberg ended the film with a completely empty horizon, with a horizon beyond which there is nothing. At the beginning of the final sequence, Bemberg shoots the circus camp from Carlota's point of view, shifting the narrative to emphasise the individual's agency. As the circus leaves, with the towns-people waving and smiling at Carlota on her white horse, Doña Leonor shuts herself away. The voiceover narrator tells of Don Ludovico's disap-pearance and presumed suicide, while expressing his preference to think of Don Ludovico still following the circus. The repressive structure of the town (read nation) has lost both its worldly man, condemned to idle in fiction in the sordid slums of the Europe from which he came, and its mad-woman, now locked up as the emblem of a colonial past. The present of the film is not the eternal present of the genre to which it would subscribe but rather the intense immediacy of what is over that hill – a world in which worldliness is not the counter position to authoritarianism and globalisation not the guarantee of egalitarian practices. Bemberg, at the back of the devil himself, however, does show us, her audience, that the only course is to go over the empty horizon, to transgress past and place and to create a completely different world from the one which we now inhabit.

As mentioned above, Bemberg's choice to detach her filmic narrative from the stability of a familiar time and place parallels the recognition by other prominent Latin American directors in the early 1990s that national cinemas must confront a redefinition of the nation. In *Fresa y chocolate*, the main character, Diego, socially marginalised because of his sexual orientation, is figured in the film as the nation lost to itself, as a future for the nation that can only survive in exile or in the diaspora, outside of the border of the nation itself. The film is a narrative of seduction into friendship and from friendship into knowledge, here specifically the knowledge which is considered by Diego and a number of Latin American intellectuals as 'universal culture'. In the second half

María Luisa Bemberg and Marcello Mastroianni share a joke between takes in
De eso no se habla

of the film, when David, a university student, accepts Diego's friendship,
he also accepts Diego as a tutor. In this seduction into friendship, it is
books and music as well as the splendours of Cuba past that create a
neutral space to house and defuse the danger of seduction in terms of
sexuality. Yet the cultural artefacts themselves, over which the camera
lingers in Diego's apartment, are figured as a cumulative wealth of views
– the *encuadre* as a formal element and a motif – and are indicated to be
that which is most dangerous to Cuban authoritarianism, whenever and
however it might manifest itself. The views of Havana are framed literally
and metaphorically as disarticulated knowledge, architecture in ruins, a
nation breaking down precisely because there has not been the circulation
of information and ideas from the outside. Diego, maligned as a counter-
revolutionary, is ultimately the only Cuban in the film capable of carrying

forward the revolution, of taking advantage of the permeability of national borders, to deploy knowledge in the service of social justice – and he must leave the country. The people, in *Fresa y chocolate*, are not in a position to save the nation.

Likewise, *Caídos del cielo* allegorises national disintegration. A dark comedy set in 1989, the film examines three parallel stories of destruction: firstly, that of two scarred bodies, Don Ventura, the radio host of the ever-optimistic advice show '*Tú eres tu destino*' and the nameless woman he saves from suicide, only to cause her ultimate destruction by rejecting her after encouraging a romance between them because she, like Don Ventura, is scarred; secondly, an elderly oligarchic couple, Don Ventura's landlords, who sell every last item of luxury to build a marble tomb which they plan to share for eternity with their deceased son; and, thirdly, the couple's impoverished former servant, now blind, who lives with two grandchildren whom she mistreats. The children, who survive as garbage-pickers, bring the three stories to closure. One of them allows the giant hog (a gift from the former employers which they originally received as rent payment from a destitute tenant), in what is a perverse fairy-tale ending, to destroy the cruel grandmother by eating her all up: a final, albeit grotesque form of justice. The film ends with three interments: the woman with no name (NN), the grandmother, and the grandson of the elderly couple who argue over which side of the tomb each will sleep for eternity. Lombardi said this film: 'concerns those years [the 1980s], that decade of loss, deterioration, hopelessness, desperation. People wandered looking for something to hold on to, to find some sense in a situation that was unfavourable for everyone.'[3]

While these film-makers each emphasise a different aspect of the permeability of the nation-state in this phase of globalisation, like Bemberg, they sought a horizon that would be the transformation of the nation. All these film-makers, Bemberg, Gutiérrez Alea, Tabío and Lombardi do not see the populace as equivalent to the nation – an attitude quite the opposite of what we were accustomed to seeing in New Latin American cinema. In fact, the films suggest that the *pueblo* as a whole cannot be trusted, a homogeneous ensemble can be deadly, crushing or expelling the marginalised. At the same time, the *pueblo* as a fragmented ensemble is seen as not capable of carrying forward a project of social transformation at the national level. There is in these films an emergent theory of the strength of a decentred community, one that cannot mobilise itself in concert with the demands of globalisation; these films of the early 1990s hint at a future in which we will all be to one another diasporic subjects and that this may be for the best because the end of injustice can only be achieved, the films suggest, over the horizon in the everywhere of the here and now. As examples of cinemas of national crisis, these films register a hope that globalisation will be the synonym for, rather than the antonym of, a profound democratisation.

María Luisa Bemberg and Alejandra Podestá on the set of *De eso no se habla*

It is now clear that the later half of the decade was to bring quite a different resolution to the problems with which Bemberg was concerned. In Argentina, a new generation of directors addressed themselves to the ethical questions of young adults for whom the dictatorship is a childhood memory. The permeability of national boundaries was not conceptualised as a problem and neither was the accountability of the citizenry and the military for authoritarianism a central issue. María Luisa Bemberg's last film, *De eso no se habla*, can be seen in this light as the closure of the period of redemocratisation with its inherently national project. Indeed, writing about the later half of Bemberg's career, Diana Palladino has observed:

> [. . .] she gives up the small bourgeois world of the present and turns to the past. She universalises, then, a female problematic, giving her heroines the benefit of our knowledge of the history and radicalising her criticism by creating ever more profound transgressions by women against the institutional pyramid of family, church, and state. [. . .] her basic motives remain the same: the abuse of patriarchy, taboos on education, social hypocrisy and the defence of individual liberty.[4]

The ethical stance of María Luisa Bemberg in *De eso no se habla* can be seen to have cleared a path for the next generation of Argentine film-makers. While the younger generation will still have to address 'the abuses of patriarchy, taboos on education, social hypocrisy and the defence of individual liberty', there is no doubt they will find they have in María Luisa Bemberg an example of how to speak clearly of new horizons.

NOTES

1 'Los sistemas alternativos de producción' in *Cine en democracia, 1983–1993* (ed. Claudio), Fondo Nacional de las Artes, Buenos Aires, 1994, pp. 285–7.
2 Liner notes: *We Don't Want to Talk About It*, Columbia Tristar, Laserdisc, 1995.
3 'Gira en torno a esos años [los ochenta], a esa década perdida, de deterioro, desesperanza, desesperación. Hay personajes que deambulan tratando de aferrarse de algo, de encontrar algín sentido en medio de un ambiente que es muy desfavorable en general.' *La gran ilusión: revista de cine*, Lima, no. 2. primer semestre de 1994.

4 '[. . .] se deshace del micromundo burgués contemporáneo y se proyecta hacia el pasado. Universaliza, entonces, la problemática femenina dándoles a sus heroínas la prespectiva del devenir histórico y radicaliza la crítica profundizando la transgresión de la mujer en confrontación con la pirámide institucional: Familia, Iglesia y Estado. [. . .] sus motivos básicos permanecen invariables: los abusos del patriarcado, los tabúes de la educación, la hipocresía social y la defensa de la libertad individual.' *Diccionario de realizadores: cine latinoamericano I*, Ediciones del Jilgüero, Buenos Aires, 1997, p. 27.

NINE

EL IMPOSTOR: FROM *CUENTO* TO FILMSCRIPT

Fiona J. Mackintosh

The script for *El impostor* was in progress at the time of María Luisa Bemberg's death in May 1995; she began it less than a year before being diagnosed with terminal cancer in September 1994.[1] Bemberg had been considering calling the film *Un extraño verano* (*A Strange Summer*),[2] but it was eventually released as *El impostor* (*The Impostor*),[3] maintaining the title of Silvina Ocampo's original short story from which it is adapted.[4] The element of strangeness remains, however, and analysing the creation of this 'strange' atmosphere in text and filmscript provides insights into the differing visions of the two artists, Ocampo and Bemberg. Sadly, Bemberg was not able to take the project to completion although she had got to the stage of thinking about the setting, wardrobe and possible leading actors. For the purposes of this homage to Bemberg, therefore, analysis will be limited to the filmscript, since the eventual film version 'is not exactly the film that María Luisa Bemberg would have made, but rather a revision of the unfinished script'.[5] Although the script involved an initial draft with the novelist Ricardo Piglia and subsequent alterations with Alejandro Maci, it appears that Bemberg was up to this point in artistic control.[6]

Both Silvina Ocampo and María Luisa Bemberg belonged to significant and wealthy upper class families, moving in circles where *estancias*, governesses and the possibility of a leisured existence were the norm. The eponymous character of Bemberg's fourth feature film, *Miss Mary*, could be seen as the cinematic equivalent of the governesses Miss Harrington or Miss Hilton in Ocampo's short stories *El caballo muerto* (*The Dead Horse*) and *El vestido verde aceituna* (*The Olive Green Dress*) respectively, both published in 1937; indeed, *Miss Mary* portrays the 1930s of Bemberg's early girlhood, contemporary with the Ocampo volume *Viaje olvidado* (*Forgotten Journey*) in which these two governesses appear.

Apart from this similarity of background, the paths of the two artists were quite distinct, a fact which is partly explained by the generation gap; Silvina Ocampo was born in 1903, Bemberg in 1922. The most significant difference between the two women is in their approach to their art. Silvina Ocampo was initially devoted to painting, not publishing her first book until she was 34, but she then continued to write daily throughout her life. Publication of her work was sporadic since Ocampo abhorred publicity; she wrote bearing her husband Adolfo Bioy Casares's constructive criticisms in mind. Bioy Casares was also a prominent writer in the fantastic vein and both were close friends with Argentina's most celebrated writer of the twentieth century, Jorge Luis Borges. Ocampo even went so far as to declare herself not at all a feminist writer, in that she was more interested in knowing the sex of a dog or a plant than of a writer. Such comments not only sum up her indifference towards feminism as such but also give a fair impression of her quirky sense of humour, something which may well have endeared her to Bemberg,[7] although it is not a significant feature of *El impostor*.

María Luisa Bemberg, on the other hand, was overtly feminist in her approach, taking a sensitive and searching look at struggles and concerns specific to women[8]. She came to film-making late in life at the age of 58, and her artistic career was something of a bid for freedom and self-fulfilment in contrast to the lifelong but idiosyncratic literary partnership of Ocampo and Bioy Casares. In response to the kind of text she was dealing with, *El impostor* is the least feminist of Bemberg's filmscripts. Indeed, it signalled a new departure; as García Guevara remarks, 'she was entering a new stage in her career; she wanted to make a film that was different from her six previous ones.'[9]

El impostor was not Bemberg's first book adaptation; she had based *Yo, la peor de todas* (*I, the Worst of All*) on an essay by Octavio Paz and *De eso no se habla* (*We Don't Want to Talk About It*) was based on a literary text, the short story of that name by Julio Llinás. In both of these adaptations, her focus is on the emotional side of her characters and this emphasis is also present in *El impostor*. In the process of cutting and re-ordering the written text, Bemberg makes an obsessive relationship the focal point of the narrative, omitting Ocampo's sometimes rather wandering passages of speculation on re-incarnation and metempsychosis.[10]

It is interesting that Bemberg should adapt this particular story, in that it is in many ways atypical within Ocampo's oeuvre. This project was suggested to Bemberg by Rosita Zemborain[11] although Bemberg may already have had an interest in Ocampo. Bemberg was involved in a literary workshop with Ocampo's husband, Bioy Casares, at which she asked him about his interests in writing filmscripts; it is therefore possible that she had also come to Silvina Ocampo's work previously through this connection.[12] Silvina Ocampo herself expresses an interest in cinema: 'Cinema attracts me very very much. I think I could be capable of doing films'[13] and in fact there is a suggestion that Ocampo did indeed make a screenplay version of *El impostor*. In an interview Raúl Gálvez did with Ocampo, he asks her: 'What about the screenplay *The Impostor* that you wrote?' (Gálvez, page 153). The original interview was conducted in Spanish but it was only published in English. Assuming that the translation is accurate, we have therefore to believe that Ocampo herself had also referred to *El impostor* as a screenplay, at least in one version. Several of Silvina's short stories had already been adapted for television, for example *El enigma* (*The Enigma*) and *La casa de azúcar* (*The House of Sugar*) (Gálvez, page 131). Although Bemberg may have desired to make this publicity-shy Argentinian woman writer more widely known, it is equally likely that Bemberg simply found attractive the cinematic potential of a story which has elements of the fantastic, the detective story and the gothic, and empathised with Ocampo's tendency to put young characters centre stage.

The somewhat collage-like style of the narrative lends itself to filmic techniques; on page 40, for example, one paragraph ends with Armando asking Luis to recount some of his dreams. Luis replies that he would have to invent them, as he cannot remember any. The paragraph immediately following cuts to a hermetic scene of Luis wandering alone, which could be either dream or reality. In the next paragraph we are back to Luis's musings on Heredia's character. Intuitively, Bemberg found the essence of Ocampo's story in the elements of fantasy, detective fiction and ghost story, and in the ambiguous overlap between dreaming and waking states, madness and sanity.

OCAMPO'S ORIGINAL TEXT

El impostor comes from what is, as a whole, Silvina's least typical book; it is her most fantastic, and most under the influence of Borges and of Bioy Casares in terms of its blending of dream and reality and its ambiguities of time sequence. Ocampo's original story is extremely long compared to all of her other short stories; it comprises more than half of the book *Autobiografía de Irene*, which only contains four other stories. It is worth noting that *El impostor* was originally published in serial form in three consecutive issues of the influential cultural magazine, *Sur*; John King comments on its appearance: 'Silvina Ocampo's best story of the period [the years of Peronism, 1946–55], *El impostor*, was serialised between June and September 1948 (nos 164 and 167), and took up the by now familiar themes of premonitions in dreams, the cruelty and possible madness of adolescents and the narrative device of an unreliable narrator whose account is corrected and contradicted by another observer.'[14] The phrase 'by now familiar' refers to themes familiar not only to readers of Ocampo's work, but also to readers of the magazine in general. The magazine included similar stories by Ocampo's husband, Adolfo Bioy Casares, and by Borges. Indeed, Borges's *Emma Zunz*, the final sentences of which shed doubt on the foregoing narrative, shares the pages of *Sur* with the third and last episode of *El impostor*. Cruelty of adolescents and children becomes very much an Ocampo hallmark, but the themes of premonitions in dreams and the device of unreliable narrators are as much – or more – associated with Bioy and Borges. These latter traits are picked up by Bemberg and employed to dramatic effect in her structuring of the filmscript.

GENRE 1: THE FANTASTIC

I mentioned above the elements of the fantastic, the detective story and the gothic in Ocampo's *El impostor*. Reference to these three genres is clearly made in the text, though since the first was very much undergoing development as a group practice at the time *El impostor* was written it is not referred to explicitly as an established genre, but implicitly through the use of dreams and uncertainty.[15] A fascination with dreams and the crossover between dreaming and reality had always been of interest to Ocampo; her first published work *Enumeración de la patria* (*Enumeration of the Fatherland*) for example, includes a poem, *A una persona dormida* (*To Someone Asleep*), which contains germs of the ideas worked out in *El impostor*.[16] The play between dreams and reality in *El impostor* thus fits clearly into a literary context. This story in which a man apparently invents another man in dreams reminds us both of Silvina Ocampo's own poem and of Borges's *Las ruinas circulares* (*The Circular Ruins*).[17]

El impostor is set in the vast Argentinian *pampas*, at the *estancia* 'Los cisnes' ('The Swans') in Cacharí.[18] Armando Heredia, son of a wealthy landowning family, has buried himself in a solitary *estancia*; Luis Maidana is sent by the boy's family to investigate the possible reasons for his self-exile. It is the solitariness of the *pampas* landscape which first creates in the narrator the sensation of being in a dream. In what is now recognised as 'classic' fantastic style, a possible naturalistic explanation is hinted at near the opening of the story; the narrator is accustomed to suffering from disturbed sleep patterns when preparing for exams. But mere insomnia cannot account for the recurrent sensation of unreality he experiences in his dealings with Armando Heredia and in all aspects of his stay on the *estancia*, where he feels like a ghost among ghosts. The distinction between dreams and reality becomes less and less clear, and Luis fears plagiarising his dreams, unconsciously. Armando Heredia, the solitary boy whom Luis goes to keep company, had apparently also suffered from insomnia. This parallel between the two young men is only the beginning of a series of similarities which begin to influence the reader's perception of them, making them appear to be doubles in some sense.

Dreams play a major part in the narrative; the pyschoanalyst to whom

Armando's father sends him asks Armando to write down his dreams. He wishes to, but cannot, since he has no dreams, and is envious of Luis for this reason. 'I would like to have dreams, even if they were incompatible with reality. Not dreaming is like being dead. Reality loses its importance. [. . .] I would commit a crime if that crime would allow me to dream.'[19]

GENRE 2: THE DETECTIVE NOVEL

Armando's rather dramatic threat about committing a crime provides the link to the second genre which underlies *El impostor*, that of the detective or crime story. This was also a genre in vogue with the *Sur* writers at the time. Only two years before *El impostor* was serialised, Silvina Ocampo had published jointly with her husband the literary detective novel, *Los que aman, odian* (*Those Who Love, Hate*).[20] Throughout *El impostor* there are allusions to the conventions of crime novels, for example the narrator's mistaken belief that he has seen a dead body being carried into the estancia and the accumulation of motives for a possible crime in Armando's veiled and threatening remarks about how he would not tolerate intruders. Armando even goes so far as to refer to a crime, which he associates in his mind with the arrival of his father's friend, and one evening he is carried back to the *estancia* with a mysterious wound. Yet with all these references to a crime, it is precisely the eventual 'crime' which is most shrouded in ambiguity, not brought into wonderful clarity by a master detective. *El impostor*, as if deliberately playing with the formulas of conventional detective stories, presents various undecided alternatives, making Ocampo's engagement with the detective story genre most explicit at the very end of the *cuento*: 'And if this were a detective story, I would, perhaps, have had an argument with Armando; he (as happened in reality) would have committed suicide and I would accuse myself of being criminally responsible for his death. The consequences of any deed are, in some ways, infinite.'[21]

This very Borgesian phrase leaves the story open-ended, which is not so much the case with the January 1995 script. The filmscript version has two parallel scenes, each taking place in a town house in Buenos Aires. On both occasions, Señor Heredia and his wife are meeting with a doctor to discuss their problematic son and the mystery of his capricious self-exile in the *campo*. This frame associates the filmscript with those of the detective genre and this association is strengthened by the police chief's extended investigation of the crime. However, there are clues inserted into the script which facilitate a rational explanation of the mysterious crime: Serafina fills Juan in on the tragic story (January 1995, page 48), Señor Heredia admits to knowing the reason for his son's behaviour (January 1995, page 55) and Flores spells out the situation for the police chief: 'A village drama, officer [. . .] They made her marry someone else . . . and she died in an accident. [. . .] Since then, he's shut himself up in the *estancia* and won't go out.'[22]

Such explanations seem to run counter to Ocampo's attempt at undermining the detective genre and Bemberg may well have decided to omit them in her alteration of weak points after the first reading of the script, since they do not appear in the final film version. There is a crime, but its most satisfactory solution from an artistic point of view is to be found in the blurring of reality and dreams and in the possible madness of the main protagonist rather than in the careful collection of evidence.

GENRE 3: THE GOTHIC

The third genre to which Ocampo alludes is that of the gothic and of ghost stories. Both Ocampo and Bemberg use the legend of the terrible Indian chief, Cacharí (who was killed by the army) to establish the setting as a kind of *pampas* gothic. Talking to Luis on the train, Claudia and her aunt make moaning noises to mimic the dying Indian's cry which can be heard in the wind. Their repeated 'Cacharíiii, Cacharíiii' evokes the melodrama of a ghost story. This reference is made in a joky spirit but when the *estancia* 'Los cisnes' is mentioned, the aunt does not laugh. We realise that there is something sinister about this place, apparently more sinister and distasteful than the Cacharí legend.[23] A reading of Ocampo's text calls to mind the atmosphere created in Edgar Allan Poe's *The Fall of the House of*

Usher[24] and Ocampo refers specifically to the cinematic haunted house genre in her description of the *estancia* 'Los cisnes':

> It was an abandoned *estancia*. On the roof of the house grew a eucalyptus and a few wild flowers. Creepers devoured the doors, the gable-ends, the window-bars. He had seen something similar in a film. A house with cobwebs, doors off their hinges, and ghosts.[25]

The basic setting thus inherently lends itself to an already well established filmic and literary discourse, so it is interesting to observe to what extent Bemberg uses this discourse in her adaptation. Sebastián frightens Juan by appearing out of the gloom with a lamp (January 1995, page 10) and telling Juan not to be frightened, there are no ghosts. However, the very mention of fright and ghosts, though negated, raises their possibility in Juan and the viewer's mind. Luis's room in the *estancia* is similarly gothic in Ocampo's description, with furniture that has monsters carved on the legs, seen by the light of a flickering candle. Likewise, his tour of the estancia with Heredia also features blatantly gothic elements such as cobwebs and shrieking bats which cast huge shadows. The farmworker, Eladio, reminds us of Poe's 'valet of stealthy step' (*The Fall of the House of Usher*, page 141) and the 'many dark and intricate passages' of the Usher mansion are paralleled by the gloomy corridors of the 'Los cisnes' *estancia*. Ocampo's heavy gothic aspect (very much in keeping with the style of Poe) is echoed by Bemberg's directions for the *mise-en-scène* (January 1995, page 10): 'It all has the look of an abandoned house which is gradually rotting away with huge patches of damp. [. . .] It shows obvious decline.'[26]

SOCIAL CODES

In both *cuento* and filmscript, upper class Buenos Aires is embodied in the Heredia family, who are upset by their son Sebastián's strange behaviour; spurning a career, he has buried himself in the ruined family 'Los cisnes' *estancia* at Cacharí and is apparently involved with a girl. In Ocampo's story, this girl (María Gismondi) is the daughter of Valentín Gismondi, a man of a lower social class. This is quite typical of Ocampo's work; from childhood onwards she had been more fascinated by poverty and lower social classes than the élite to which she belonged. Ocampo also vaguely indicates some kind of estrangement between the Heredia and Maidana families in her story. Gismondi's equivalent in the script is called María Olsen, the name-change fitting in with an alteration of social situation; she is the daughter of a Danish immigrant family, whose father is a highly religious man. What both written text and script have in common is that this mysterious girl with whom the main character is in love, has apparently died four years earlier. Bemberg and Ocampo make this fantastic relationship significant in different ways: Ocampo uses it to weave an impossible and contradictory situation; Bemberg does this too, but also brings into play more contemporary social factors by inventing an immigrant colony.[27] This change is typical of the kind of changes made by Bemberg to Ocampo's text; cutting down on the philosophical aspects and grounding it more in a social and emotional reality. She had also elaborated the relationship between the doctor and his son (January 1995, pages 3–6) and made a social distinction between this family and the Heredias, the former more intellectual, the latter wealthy. With the Heredia family, all is suppressed and formal. By filling out the social situation, Bemberg domesticates Ocampo's text, making Sebastián's actions, and those of María Olsen, into a (doomed) rebellion of love against society and against tyrannical parents.

These social codes, together with the previously discussed literary and filmic genres, make up Bemberg's overall interpretation of the Ocampo text. This view is supported by the third page of Bemberg's synthesis which precedes the main body of the filmscript; here she lists four main plot points: spying and discovery (which relates to the detective novel genre), a hidden woman, either mad or a ghost (gothic novel genre), the love triangle (social codes), and dreams and the fantastic (fantastic literature genre).

CHARACTERS

Apart from changing María Gismondi to María Olsen, Bemberg also alters Armando to Sebastián and Luis Maidana to Juan Medina. At the risk of adding to the text's own deliberate confusion of characters,[28] I shall retain the distinct names when comparing the two versions. In Ocampo's text, the father's friend is coming to 'Los cisnes' on 28 February, announced by a telegram; Bemberg adds a further twist by making the telegram announce the arrival of Juan's father, the doctor; it later appears that the doctor never had a son, since Senor Heredia says to him, 'if you had children . . .' (January 1995, page 57).[29]

The characters as portrayed in the *cuento* have been fairly faithfully rendered in the script; Ocampo's Claudia is twice referred to as proud and Bemberg captures this proudness, though she also creates a more overtly flirtatious girl, whose behaviour is coquettish (see January 1995, page 29). Armando is occasionally somewhat cruel or scornful towards Luis in Ocampo's text, an aspect of Heredia's character which is also apparent in the filmscript. Indeed, Bemberg develops this maliciousness into an aspect of Sebastián's jealousy, as he keeps questioning Juan about his amorous success with Claudia. Señor Heredia and his wife are given more prominence and agency in the filmscript; this has the effect of shifting the tone of the film to one of parental intolerance and interference in a doomed passion (a thematic echo of *Camila*), whereas Ocampo's text had focused primarily on Luis and Armando's mental state.

THE ECLIPSE

Aside from these alterations of character, the most noticeable additions in the filmscript version are the episodes which elaborate Sebastián and María's relationship. These include dream sequences, flashbacks to their meeting at a rural fair and a total eclipse. I shall discuss the latter in more detail, since it also features prominently in the eventual film realisation. In a dream-like moment, Juan watches Sebastián and María making love. 'Everything is motionless, as if time had stood still [. . .] In the supernatural darkness of the eclipse, the two naked bodies are seen as if reflected in a mirror' (January 1995, page 52).[30] The eclipse acts as a focal point for all the main strands of Bemberg's story: the play of light and dark, bright sun and shadow, the theme of spying and watching, and the mysterious dreamlike relationship between Sebastián Heredia and María Olsen. The eclipse does not feature in Ocampo's story, and Bemberg may have been making an extra-textual reference to the total eclipse which happened in Chile at about the time the script was being finished.[31] Although the eclipse was an addition on the part of the scriptwriters, Ocampo does mention the unbearable brightness of the sun. The opposition between this unbearable brightness and the evening darkness of the *estancia* is taken up by the filmscript's repeated directions for extremes of light and dark. Linked to light and darkness is the theme of sight and blindness, which appears in Ocampo's text as part of Luis's interior monologue, and which becomes a crucial symbolic element of the filmscript: 'I had the sensation of being blind: at night, the darkness, and in the daytime the intense light, prevented me from seeing.'[32]

What might be the significance of adding an eclipse to the filmscript? Perhaps Bemberg uses its rarity and awesome power as a symbol for the fleeting but breathtakingly special nature of love. It is as if Sebastián's moment of happiness with María Olsen is contained within the brief duration of the eclipse, like a perfect but ephemeral experience. It also reinforces the supernatural aura which Ocampo had done through rather heavy-handed intellectual musings on reincarnation, wisely cut by Bemberg. Along with the gypsy-like figure of the *curandera*, the eclipse recalls atavistic beliefs.

ORNITHOLOGY . . .

The second most notable addition in the filmscript is Juan's assumed dedication to ornithology which Bemberg makes his alibi for being at the *estancia* and links it to spying. In Ocampo's text, Luis's pretext for being on the *estancia* is revision for exams. He does, however, have a single dream which involves birds; this passage may have provided the cue for Bemberg's idea of ornithology, since this dream sequence becomes in Bemberg's version one of a series of waking events in which Juan is birdwatching. Instead of spotting a mysterious long-haired man, as Luis does, he catches sight of Sebastián among the rushes, in a boat and apparently talking to someone, although he is alone (January 1995, page 17: 'Juan's point of view'). Thus what in the original text was merely further evidence of Juan's fertile dreamworld, apparently unconnected to the main action, becomes in the filmscript another crucial piece of evidence in Juan's dossier on the mysterious behaviour of Sebastián. Bemberg in this way draws the main threads of the plot more tightly together, giving the filmscript a greater sense of unity and cohesion (though not necessarily coherence) which is sometimes lacking in the *cuento*.

Juan's pretext of studying the local birdlife is a clever choice on Bemberg's part. Juan's activity is regarded highly suspiciously by Sebastián, who asks pointedly 'who would think of going climbing trees to spy on people?' (January 1995, page 19).[33] The implication is, of course, that Juan is the impostor of the title, pretending to be a genuine ornithologist when he is in fact a spy. Ocampo's original text explicitly mentions the theme of spying, and Bemberg's script – by making birdwatching Juan's pastime, rather than revision of history and algebra (see Ocampo, page 26 and page 53) – naturally creates even greater potential for camera shots emphasising watching, looking and spying.

. . . OR ESPIONAGE?

The theme of spying is emphasised in Bemberg's version most effectively by the interpolation of different points of view at certain moments which are designed to draw the spectator's attention to the act of observing, making the spectator feel like a spy, voyeur or even a non-human observer. We are, for example, made to look from the perspective of a frog under Juan's bed; Alejandro Maci has obviously incorporated Bemberg's last comment about wanting to see and hear frogs in the film. After one very brief frame of the frog leaping away, which is almost too quick to see, there is a cut to the frog's point of view seeing Juan's huge eyes through the lamp in black and white. We also have to adopt the point of view of a bird of prey circling above Juan as he watches through his binoculars, and that of an owl sitting above him on a tree-branch. We see an overhead shot of Sebastián sitting reading a telegram beneath a eucalyptus tree. Precisely this angle is later used to show us Juan birdwatching; the watcher is being watched. Shots showing the act of looking abound: we see through Juan's binoculars, through a kind of black and white kaleidoscope, and at the country fête we see Sebastián's point of view from the top of a tall pole which he has shinned up to win a competition. Here again the spy is being spied upon; Juan has coaxed his girl behind a stack of crates, believing that they can kiss unseen and undisturbed, but Sebastián's vantage point allows him to see over the wall of crates. Also at the fair we are suddenly given an inverted view of Sebastián and Juan, which turns out to be the photographer's view of them through the lens of an old-fashioned camera as they pose for a photograph. This is another shot detail taken from Bemberg's script (see January 1995, page 42). So whereas Ocampo's text obsessively questions memory, dreams and reality, Bemberg focuses on more direct visual questioning of seeing and perception; despite his spying activities, what Juan sees does not necessarily bring understanding. What he finds most difficult to grasp is the nature of the relationship between Sebastián and María Olsen, and how this relates to himself and Claudia.

DOUBLES

Of the pairings which form this awkward love triangle, the most mysterious is that of Juan and Sebastián (or Luis and Armando in the original), since at the dénouement it appears that Juan/Luis never existed, except in the mind of Sebastián/Armando. The two characters are possibly two aspects of the same character. In Ocampo this hypothesis is suggested by the final narrator's memory of Armando as a boy, his character and his imaginative games: 'Did Armando Heredia, by committing suicide, believe that he had killed Luis Maidana, the way as a child he thought he had killed an imaginary person? Instead of red ink, did he use his own blood to play with his enemy?'[34]

Ocampo was always fascinated with the behaviour and games of children, and particularly in their more cruel and unpredictable aspects, hence her using such a flashback as a possible explanation for Armando's adult state of mind. Although double characters are a Borgesian device, attempting to account for them by way of imaginative and cruel childhood games is very much Ocampo's trait. Bemberg's version does suggest using a flashback technique, but rather than using it to portray Sebastián's disturbed mental state, she shows us Sebastián as a boy of 12 (January 1995, page 43) in order to illustrate the development of his passionate clandestine relationship with María Olsen. So, as before, where Ocampo focuses on the double nature of the two boys and theories of re-incarnation, Bemberg concentrates more on the love relationship of Sebastián and María.

TEMPORAL UNCERTAINTY AND CIRCULARITY

Luis's confusion at his sensation of having already seen or dreamt all of the people and objects he encounters on the *estancia* leads him to experience time as essentially circular.[35] Bemberg's version makes repetition a deliberate structural device, in that the tense scene (between los Heredias and their doctor) in Buenos Aires returns after the dramatic shooting by Sebastián. But such circularity creates confusion; if Heredia's comment about doctor Medina having no son is true, how can we explain Juan's presence in the first such scene? Having initially based our cognitive process of piecing together the story on that scene in Buenos Aires, we have to reconsider; it might be a product of Sebastián's paranoid imaginings. Serafina's statement that Sebastián has not left his room since receiving the telegram from Buenos Aires would support this theory, yet as viewers we would be reluctant to explain away the majority of the film as simply belonging to the realms of an overwrought imagination. Our urge towards resolution and catharsis resists this rather lame let-out clause, and is frustrated by the futile attempts of the police chief who comes to investigate. Serafina's behaviour appears somewhat suspicious to him: Bemberg notes that 'he is convinced the woman is hiding something from him' (January 95, page 64).[36] We are thus not entirely convinced at Serafina's protestations of never having heard of Juan; her behaviour, and that of Eladio, is sufficient to leave doubts hanging in the air. This creates the 'strangeness' which surrounded the conclusion of Ocampo's text and which Bemberg sought to capture in the idea of 'a strange summer'.

'AT TIMES, AGAIN, I WAS OBLIGED TO RESOLVE ALL INTO THE MERE INEXPLICABLE VAGARIES OF MADNESS'[37]

The most logical explanation, since the overwhelming urge of the reader or viewer is to account for the story's curious turn of events, is that of Sebastián/Armando's madness, a possibility offered by both Bemberg and Ocampo. In the filmscript, the focal point of this madness is Sebastián's impossible love for a dead woman, but its source is traceable to a family history of madness; Sebastián admits that his family is full of mad people (January 1995, page 9) but tries to imply that his father is the mad one, rather than himself. Bemberg also introduces the concept of madness as social stigma, since at the opening, Sebastián's parents are paranoid about what people might say if they hear of Sebastián's odd behaviour. Ocampo, too, had worked in suggestions that Heredia might be mad. The first reports Luis hears of him on the train are not promising; rumour has it that he is 'a bit mad' (*medio loco*, page 28) and Heredia's own grandfather had superstitions and manias (page 34) which Luis begins to attribute also to the grandson, Armando. A family history of madness is further revealed in the disturbing account of Heredia's aunt Celina; after her tragic death, the *estancia*'s very name, *Los cisnes*, is connected with violence and madness. The suggestion in Ocampo's story, however, is not so much that Heredia's madness derives from paranoid jealousy after a disastrous love affair or indeed from his family, but from his desperation at not dreaming and from an extension of childhood games where he would invent a fictitious double (page 86). Ocampo's text posits Luis Maidana as a figment of Armando's deranged imagination, even as part of himself. 'Did he pretend or did he really dream that he was someone else, and see himself from outside? Was he obsessed by the idea of not dreaming [. . .]? Did he feel like a ghost, did he feel like a blank page? Was the obsession so strong that Armando ended up inventing his own dreams?'[38] Bemberg's adaptation gives a more tragic, romantic slant to the madness, anchoring it in a specific social situation of lovers faced with the prejudices of their families, whereas Ocampo's text preferred to show the severe emotional tests of childhood.

Even the hypothesis of Heredia's madness is not sufficient, however, to tie up all the loose ends, were this a good detective novel. In Ocampo's next narrative twist we are presented with a new narrator, Rómulo Sagasta, who claims to have interrogated María Gismondi (Ocampo, page 89). How can this narrator have interrogated a woman who has been dead four years? (see Ocampo, page 72). Doubt is inevitably cast on Sagasta's reliability as a narrator by this, and by his own comments that perhaps Heredia's madness has also affected him. Our expectations of fully solving the mysterious situation are once again frustrated.

What both versions bring out is the disturbing potentiality of contagion between the 'mad' person and the narrating voice. As Ocampo puts it, 'We end up by believing that we ourselves are mad when we suspect madness in another person.'[39]

Ocampo again echoes Poe's *The Fall of the House of Usher* in which the narrator fears the influence of Roderick Usher: 'It was no wonder that his condition terrified – that it infected me. I felt creeping upon me, by slow yet certain degrees, the wild influences of his own fantastic yet impressive superstitions.' (Poe, page 151) In Ocampo's text, Sagasta's fears are also a reflection of those of Luis Maidana in his letter to Señor Heredia. The idea of contagion is adopted by Bemberg in a scene in which Juan behaves uncharacteristically; immediately after having been discovered 'spying' by Sebastián, he goes into the stable in a violent mood, 'one would almost say contaminated by the spirit of Sebastián' (January 1995, page 26).[40] How can we be certain who is mad and who is sane?

QUESTIONING OF PERCEPTION – ¿VIDA O SUEÑO?

Ocampo's original story has many instances of uncertainty between dream and reality, culminating in a philosophical questioning of the nature of experience. Bemberg obviously concurs with Ocampo in seeing this blurring as crucial to the atmosphere of the narrative since she quotes Ocampo verbatim in her script, as part of Sebastián's writings (January 1995, page 68). Ocampo's text fits into a literary context which includes the experiments of her contemporaries, Borges and Bioy Casares, in the genres of the detective story and fantastic fiction.[41] Through the undermining of Luis, who had appeared to be a straightforward first-person narrator, Ocampo makes a point about readers' assumptions when faced with a fictional text. In what has elements of a detective story, we are prepared for conflicting evidence within the fictional frame, but we automatically count upon the existence and reliability of the main narrative voice.[42] Consequently, the abrupt ending of Juan's notebooks (Ocampo, page 84) and the continuation of the narrative through a previously unknown character (Rómulo Sagasta) undermines the reader's cognitive strategies. This sudden rip in narrative fabric, jolting us into a different frame, takes away from us what would have been the dramatic climax of a conventional detective story – the murder of Juan by an enraged Sebastián.[43] The narrative twists away from the detective story towards the fantastic.

This unexpected disruption to the basic narrative structure is echoed with visual alterations in Bemberg's *mise-en-scène*. The view through the *estancia* window as seen by Heredia's parents has changed from the wild *matorral* to a neatly tended garden. The *estancia* itself is now resplendent in daylight, without any of its former ruined appearance (see January 1995, page 57). Maci's film version echoes these changes with an even more theatrical gesture; we see a shot of Sebastián from behind, sitting slumped at his typewriter facing the window through which there is a view of the pampas. Suddenly, this view appears to crumple and fall like a sheet; we realise that it was a painted backcloth, a *trompe l'œil* which drops to reveal the 'real' view of closer eucalyptus trees. As spectators and interpreters of the film, we had assumed that what we could see through the window of Sebastián's room, and indeed what the dead boy was looking at, was simply reality, but then it crumples and falls, revealing itself to be a false reality, a mere backdrop. In the same way, the existence of Juan (or Luis) upon whom we had depended as central character/narrator is abruptly called into question. As a reader or spectator, one gets absorbed by the opening point of view. Particularly with cinematic viewing, where all senses are focused on the screen, surrounded by darkness, suspending disbelief and getting drawn into the story is easy. To then be presented with a deliberately

'stagey' effect destroys the storytelling illusion (although the earlier emphasis on unusual points of view was constantly drawing our attention to the
film's artifice).

The implication with both fictions, text and filmscript, is that the narrative could be undermined on many levels and that ultimately as readers
we cannot determine the boundary between dream and reality or madness
and sanity. At this point it is worth returning to the title; an impostor is
'one who assumes a false character or who passes himself off for someone
else.'[44] Who is the impostor, and according to whose terms? Not only do
we have an impostor within the narrative, who ostensibly comes to study
but in reality spies on Heredia; we also have an impostor narrator.[45]
Bemberg's tightening of the plot to make it more social and emotional than
intellectual, perhaps reduces something of the philosophical and literary
impact of the title. But both versions share the aim of questioning our
habitual perception whether at the level of sight, memory and interpretation, or dreams.

A strange summer indeed and a strange story. Perhaps the Curandera
speaks for Bemberg's vision: *No sólo hay que creer en lo que se ve* (January
1995, page 67); we should not only believe in what we see. What
emerges from Ocampo's text is that what we see may be dream or may
be reality, but is necessarily fragmentary and often terrible. What
Bemberg takes from Ocampo's text is that 'our life depends on a certain
number of people who see us as living beings. If these people imagine
us to be dead, we die'.[46] Perhaps we can imitate Sebastián in not imagining Bemberg dead, but alive through her films.

NOTES

1 Information taken from Leila Guerriero: 'María Luisa Bemberg' in *Mujeres
   argentinas: el lado femenino de nuestra historia*, prol: María Esther de Miguel,
   Alfaguara, Buenos Aires, 1998, pp. 157–90, and from Mercedes García
   Guevara's testimony to María Luisa Bemberg, who was her mother-in-law. The
   testimony, which can be found in this book, is dated December 1996 and will
   henceforth be referred to as MGG with an inserted page reference.

2 It is announced as such in *Sight and Sound*, 5 December 1995, Cybernotes,

p. 12: 'Readers who [. . .] regret the passing of Argentinian director María Luisa Bemberg in May will be pleased to know that the script she was working on at the time of her death is going to be made into a film after all. Bemberg apparently completed the screenplay for *Un extraño verano* (*A Strange Summer*) just two days before she died.'

3 The director (at Bemberg's request) was Alejandro Maci, producer Oscar Kramer (99 minutes, Mojamé SA, Argentina, 1997) with photography by Ricardo Aronovich. Bemberg, Maci and Jorge Goldenberg collaborated on the screenplay. The haunting soundtrack is by Nicola Piovani (published by Emergency Music, Italy). The film stars Antonio Birabent as Sebastián Heredia, Walter Quiroz as Juan Medina, and Belén Blanco as Teresita. Other characters included Norman Briski as Doctor Medina, Mónica Galán as Clotilde, Marilú Marini as Señora Heredia, Beatriz Malar as Serafina, Erasmo Olivera as Eladio and Eduardo Pavlovsky as Señor Heredia.

4 *El impostor* in *Autobiografía de Irene,* Sur, Buenos Aires, 1948. I shall take Spanish references from the 1975 edition in Sudamericana (pp. 25–90); all English versions are my own. No translation into English of Silvina Ocampo's complete works exists to date, but there are various collections and anthologies such as *Leopoldina's Dream: Stories of Silvina Ocampo* translated by Daniel Balderston, Penguin Books, Ontario, 1987, *Contemporary Women Authors of Latin America: New Translations* (ed.) Doris Meyer and Margarite Fernández Olmos, Brooklyn College Press, New York, 1983, and *The Secret Weavers: Stories of the Fantastic by Women of Argentina and Chile* (ed.) Marjorie Agosín, White Wine Press, 1991.

5 See *El impostor* in *Ambito financiero*, Buenos Aires, 16 May 1997, 2nd part, p. 6. 'No es exactamente la película que habría hecho María Luisa Bemberg, sino que una revisión del inconcluso libro.'

6 The copy of the filmscript from which I have worked is dated October 1994, but according to Alejandro Maci's covering letter of 30 January 1995 to María Luisa Bemberg it appears that this was still the most up-to-date written version. I shall therefore refer to this script as January 1995, followed by a page number. I would like to thank Sheila Whitaker for providing me with a copy of the script. We know, however, that Bemberg made more changes after the first reading of the script in April 1995. García Guevara's testimony and Guerriero's article (p. 188) mention her desire to include frogs (both seen and heard) in the film. These do not figure in the January 1995 script, but do feature in the film, evidently at Bemberg's wish. Occasional comments on filmic details will therefore be appropriate.

7 Bemberg is described as possessing 'an engaging humour and irony', see Sheila Whitaker, Polly Pattullo and Julie Christie's obituary of Bemberg: 'Breaking the Silence' in *The Guardian*, 16 May 1995, p. 16.

8 For explorations of Bemberg's feminism see Barbara Morris 'La mujer vista por la mujer: el discurso fílmico de María Luisa Bemberg' in *Discurso femenino actual* (ed.) Adelaida López de Martínez, University of Puerto Rico, Puerto Rico, 1995, pp. 253–67; Caleb Bach: 'María Luisa Bemberg tells the untold' in *Américas*, vol. 46, no. 2, 1994, pp. 20–7 and Jane A. Burke, *Mujeres directoras en el cine latinoamericano: hacia una representación feminista*, MA thesis, Arizona State University, 1995.

9 'Entraba en una nueva etapa de su carrera; quería hacer un cine diferente a sus seis films anteriores.' MGG.

10 Such passages, incidentally, call to mind the opening of Proust's *À la recherche du temps perdu* where Marcel describes the sensation of slipping between dreaming and waking states: 'I had gone on thinking while I was asleep about what I had just been reading, but these thoughts had taken a rather peculiar turn; it seemed to me that I myself was the immediate subject of my book [. . .] This impression would persist for some moments after I woke [. . .] Then it would begin to seem unintelligible, as the thoughts of a former existence must be to a reincarnate spirit.' English translation by Terence Kilmartin, Penguin, 1981. Ocampo's character Luis Maidana frequently wonders whether he is continuing a dream or fears plagiarising his dreams, and tries to account for the strangeness of coincidences with theories of metempyschosis. Ocampo had read Proust and admired him, see Noemí Ulla, *Encuentros con Silvina Ocampo*, Belgrano, Buenos Aires, 1982, p. 66.

11 *El impostor* in *Ambito financiero,* 2nd part, Buenos Aires, 16 May 1997, pp. 6–7.

12 See *Bioy Casares a la hora de escribir* (ed.) Esther Cross and Félix della Paolera, Tusquets, Barcelona, 1988, p. 104, '¿Tuvo usted alguna vez ganas de escribir guiones para cine?'

13 This interview was conducted in 1989 and published the same year in Raúl Gálvez: *From the Ashen Land of the Virgin*, Mosaic, Ontario, 1989, pp. 130–58.

14 John King, *Sur: A Study of the Argentine Literary Journal and its Role in the Development of a Culture, 1931–1970,* CUP, Cambridge, 1986, p. 152.

15 John King, op. cit., 'Borges, Bioy Casares, Silvina Ocampo and José Bianco begin to experiment with what can loosely be called "fantastic literature" in the late 1930s' (p. 59). 'Borges is the best-known writer of this period

[1935–40], but it will be argued that the development of these theories was very much a group practice, and that the contribution of Adolfo Bioy Casares, Silvina Ocampo and to a lesser extent José Bianco should not be underrated' (p. 90).

16 'You cannot make your brow blind:/in your closed eyes will persist/the world that you have seen.' ('No lograrás que ciega sea tu frente:/en tus cerrados ojos persistente/será el mundo que has visto.') *Enumeración de la patria*, Sur, Buenos Aires, 1937, pp. 133–4.

17 'Las ruinas circulares' is to be found in *El jardín de senderos que se bifurcan* (*The Garden of Forking Paths*), Buenos Aires, 1941. In this story, however, the emphasis is very different; the protagonist's specific aim is to dream a man: 'Quería soñar un hombre: quería soñarlo con integridad minuciosa e imponerlo a la realidad', *Ficciones*, Emecé, Buenos Aires, 1990, p. 62. 'He wanted to dream a man. He wanted to dream him completely, in painstaking detail, and impose him upon reality.' Jorge Luis Borges, *Collected Fictions*, translated by Andrew Hurley, Allen Lane, London, 1999, p. 97.

18 According to the film credits, the film version was made on the estancias 'El payé', 'El recuerdo', 'La dulce' and 'La rica' and in the *pueblo* of Chivilcoy.

19 'Yo quisiera tener sueños, aunque fueran inconciliables con la realidad. No soñar es como estar muerto. La realidad pierde importancia. [. . .] Cometería un crimen si ese crimen me permitiera soñar' (*El impostor*, Silvina Ocampo, p. 39).

20 *Los que aman, odian*, Emecé, Buenos Aires, 1946.

21 'Y si esto fuera una historia policial, yo habría sostenido, tal vez, una disputa con Armando; éste (como en la realidad) se habría suicidado y me acusaría criminalmente de su muerte. Las consecuencias de cualquier hecho son, en cierto modo, infinitas' (p. 90).

22 'Un drama de pueblo, comisario [. . .] La obligaron a casarse con otro . . . y ella murió en un accidente. [. . .] Desde entonces, él se encerró en la estancia y no quiso salir.'

23 Equivalent generic typing occurs in the edgy four-note ostinato on the film soundtrack, which has its roots in the kind of film music which plays on the nerves of the spectator. This ostinato, sometimes predominating in the violins, sometimes on the clarinet, accompanies all the eerie and mysterious aspects of the narrative.

24 Edgar Allan Poe: *The Fall of the House of Usher* and other writings (ed.) David Galloway, Penguin Books, Harmondsworth, Essex, 1986, pp. 138–57.

25 'Era aquella una estancia abandonada. Sobre el techo de la casa crecía un eucalipto y algunas flores silvestres. Las enredaderas devoraban las puertas, los aleros de los corredores, las rejas de las ventanas. En una película cinematográfica había visto algo parecido. Una casa con telarañas, con puertas desquiciadas, con fantasmas.' Silvina Ocampo, op. cit., p. 33.

26 'Todo tiene el aspecto abandonado de una casa que se va pudriendo con grandes manchas de humedad. [. . .] revela una ostensible decadencia.' This atmosphere was preserved in the film with sustained use of very shadowy lighting for many scenes inside the *estancia*, and gloomy corridors punctuated by water dripping from leaks in the roof.

27 Indeed, Bemberg inserts extended passages illustrating Pastor Olsen's religious fervour juxtaposed with his daughter's 'transgression'; it is likely that the over-explanation generated by these passages about the Olsen family was one of the weak points that Bemberg would wish to change after the first reading, since Maci was taking that passage to rework it. 'Yo me llevo el fragmento "relato de María Olsen" para trabajarlo.' Covering letter to script, dated 30 January 1995.

28 In both versions, some kind of parallel is suggested between the living girl, Claudia, and the dead girl, María Gismondi/Olsen. This is supported by the fact that Claudia wears a necklace saying 'María'.

29 'Si tuvieras chicos . . .' (January 1995).

30 'Todo está inmóvil, como si el tiempo se hubiera detenido. [. . .] En la oscuridad sobrenatural del eclipse, los dos cuerpos desnudos se ven como reflejados en un espejo' (January 1995).

31 My thanks to Catherine Grant for this observation.

32 'Tuve la sensación de estar ciego: de noche, la oscuridad; de día, la intensa luz, no me permitían ver.' Silvina Ocampo, op. cit., p. 33.

33 'A quién se le ocurre andar trepado a los árboles espiando a todo el mundo?' (January 1995).

34 'Armando Heredia, al suicidarse, ¿creyó matar a Luis Maidana, como creyó matar en su infancia a un personaje imaginario?¿En vez de tinta roja empleó su propia sangre para jugar con su enemigo?' Silvina Ocampo, op. cit., p. 89.

35 There is also a confusion of dates in Ocampo's text, which is entirely in keeping with the fantastic trait of obscuring narrative chronology. Armando Heredia expects the intrusion of his father's friend on 28 February (Silvina

Ocampo, op. cit., p. 50), but Rómulo Sagasta states twice in his narrative continuation (p. 85) that he arrived in Cacharí on 28 January 1930. However, he then contradicts this on the last page of the text, making it clear that he did in fact arrive on 28 February.

36 'Está convencido de que la mujer le oculta algo' (January 1995).

37 Edgar Allen Poe, *The Fall of the House of Usher*, p. 151.

38 '¿Fingía o realmente soñaba que era otro, y se veía desde afuera? ¿Lo obsesionaba la idea de no tener sueños [. . .]? ¿Se sentía como un fantasma, se sentía como una hoja en blanco? ¿La obsesión fue tan poderosa que Armando terminó por inventar sus sueños? [. . .] (Silvina Ocampo, op. cit., p. 89).

39 'Acabamos por creernos locos cuando sospechamos la locura en otra persona.' Silvina Ocampo, op. cit., p. 75.

40 'Casi se diría contagiado del ánimo de Sebastián.'

41 In a more general context, there is of course a long Hispanic tradition of meditating on life and dreams stemming from Pedro Calderón de la Barca's *La vida es sueño* (*Life is a Dream*), 1636.

42 We can contrast this to Ocampo and Bioy Casares's joint detective story of two years earlier, *Los que aman, odian*. In this, the narrator Dr Huberman rails against his embroilment in the mystery (thus creating a comic anti-hero or anti-detective figure) and playfully mocks the conventions of detective stories but does not undermine the narrative structure itself.

43 Though it would, of course, have been an unusual detective story, given that the detective himself seemed the most likely victim.

44 *The Concise Oxford Dictionary of Current English*, rev. H. W. Fowler, Oxford University Press, Oxford, 1931, p. 571.

45 'Rómulo Sagasta [. . .] semble se superposer à Luis Maidana, *prendre la place* du personnage-narrateur du texte no. 1 [. . .] Il y a là un effet de substitution, de superposition, de double, de jeu de masques, d'où naît le fantastique.' Annick Mangin, op. cit., p. 167.

46 'Nuestra vida depende de cierto número de personas que nos ven como seres vivos. Si esas personas nos imaginan muertos, morimos.' Silvina Ocampo, op. cit., p. 81.

TEN

BEING AN ARTIST IN LATIN AMERICA

María Luisa Bemberg

I would like to begin by saying how deeply grateful I am to have been chosen to represent Argentina when I was invited to participate in this symposium. Art and culture will help my country strengthen its long traditional ties with the English people, and thank you Jason Wilson for your – I believe – splendid translation.

When Silvia invited me to take part in this symposium my first impulse was to refuse, despite the honour and prestige of the invitation. What could I say as a visual story teller faced with so many eminent academics, painters, critics and poets? But Silvia insisted, so after my initial, emotional refusal, I came to the opposite conclusion; namely, that I could contribute something. So here I am with you today as an artisan of fantasies, cultivating that young but already aged art of the cinema.

Since the Lumière brothers first managed to reproduce movement on film, the influence of cinema, photography and television has continued to increase, to such an extent that it has been said that we live in 'the age of the image'.

Few can now doubt how incredibly popular the cinema has become. By juxtaposing different places and customs, by playing with labyrinths of time and the harshness of life, cinema allows disparate cultures to identify with each other through fantasy. Its popular message speaking to the heart of humanity reaches the remotest parts of the globe as never before.

Precisely because of the shrinking of distances, because of this planetary transmission of life-like and imaginary images, nations and individuals wish to escape the threat of uniformity and want to be known by what makes them unique. The diversified people of the world want to be identified idiosyncratically.

But what is this identity? A dictionary would define it as the relationships a person has with all his or her circumstances, 'Where we are and what surrounds us', to borrow a phrase from Ortega y Gasset.

In this sense to be a Latin American implies sharing circumstances ground together in an inherited culture that is not our own. It is arduous to find out who you are in this vast inter-breeding network of political regimes, customs and institutions, yet we have to accept them as Latin American.

To find your identity in Argentina, faced with other Latin American countries, is to inherit a double disadvantage. On the one hand we cannot depend on a rich, civilised, indigenous past with a refined technology that could build monuments like Macchu Picchu or Teotihuacán, or pick out the exact phases and orbits of planets in the sky, or develop a socialist empire like the Inca with their *ayllu*. We Argentines do not have a meaningful past (which in no way promises us a meaningful future!). On the other hand we were forced to become a country of immigrants as the traces left by the early, primitive inhabitants on Argentine soil blew away with the dust raised by the horses of the first conquistadors.

Our respected melting-pot of races has enriched us with elements from cultures spread all over the world. However, from the Conquest on, those who arrived brought with them the dilemma of a gap between image and reality, between what they sought and what they found, between dreams of the wealth and the hard work awaiting them. From the period of the greatest immigration in 1880 when the country doubled its population, this problematic gap became the way people embodied their country.

The first negative effect was the 1890 economic crisis, the first of many crises periodically shaking our country, up to the latest one from which we still have not emerged and I believe the worst. If the causes behind these crises have changed, in that earlier period the essential knot can be found in the duality of the immigrants. They arrived in harbours already victims of a nostalgia that set in the moment they left home. It was as if they were walking backwards in time towards the place that hunger or fantasy had forced them to abandon.

They arrived with their hieroglyphs of illusions and poverties, determined to remain faithful to their memories, rather than rooting themselves in Argentina. They were driven by a lasting yearning to return home. A popular expression summarises these polarities: they did not come to make America, but to 'make it in America'.

Some managed to return. But most stayed on forever in the city harbour where they first disembarked, their backs turned to the interior of the country. It had been the same in Europe, although there their hopes had been placed in a point beyond the horizon of sea. Most of them remained in the metropolis, the capital of the River Plate, which they had exaggeratedly transformed into something else.

Built up from imported models, our nation was torn into 'two countries', one belonging to 'civilisation', the other, the interior, condemned as Sarmiento said to 'barbarism'.

Buenos Aires, Goliath's head, developed so fast that by the 1920s it was the fifth commercial power in the world. But Buenos Aires grew at the expense of the provinces. Its growth gave it the same hegemony over its provinces as Europe had over Buenos Aires. The reason lay in the way that the cosmopolitan giant looked insistently and stubbornly towards Europe.

I was born in a traditional family of that capital city that Martínez Estrada called 'Madrid's legitimate daughter', a city decapitated from the body of the republic. The federal capital transformed its inhabitants into permanent exiles: they are *porteños* in Argentina, Europeans in Latin America and South Americans in Europe. Thanks to this the will and effort to find our identity has become particularly laborious, but ambivalence nourishes creative people.

My creative work arises from these hybrid origins. My drive to disentangle my identity would be reflected in this way in my cinematic work. Rather than complain, or vainly try to resist these circumstances, I decided to assume them and to try to universalise them. Also I had a particular angle from which to view these problems as I am a woman.

To be a woman in a patriarchal society is still to be considered inferior. In England you may not perhaps realise how extreme such conditioning can be in a land of fearless *gauchos* and *compadritos*, where brute strength is encouraged. These lands gave us a particular kind of man, a sad archetype called 'machismo', which is an attitude that blends boasting, indifference, misogyny and stupidity. It is true that the century-old mirror of oppression in which we were reflected has now broken. Yet, despite this fracturing, we still have not reconstructed an image of freedom from the splinters that would be valid for all of us.

For women of my generation to try to make art is a hard task. We lack social stimuli and a proper education, or are at best only partially educated, with nothing to fall back on. We are limited by a psychological conditioning that conspires against women: an absence of inner confidence and the authority to restrict sexist cultural models; an absence of the motivation needed to create art, like competitive spirit, the urge to differentiate yourself through what you do, and a liking for complex issues. On top, this man has cannibalised womanhood and tries to speak for both. What we assume as culture is a male, patriarchal culture.

However, some women have managed to get round these obstacles like the following writers from the southern tip of my continent: Alfonsina Storni and Juana de Ibarbourou from the River Plate and Gabriela Mistral from Chile. These women, like many others from all five continents, have achieved their goal of creating a well finished art, even if at times you can glimpse their Cheshire cat's smile of apology for having dared to be daring.

To write a poem or a short story is not the same as making a film. Even if the ultimate referent is the linguistic code – for language is at the source of our culture – cinematographic expression requires a different mode of understanding from that of other art forms whose gestation is solitary and secluded.

The relation of women to cinema has largely remained within traditional roles: from outside the art they are spectators and from inside they are designers, costumers, hairdressers, make-up assistants or mainly actresses. Cinema directed by women who think and analyse, who question themselves and take risks, continues to be rare; for every hundred film directors, only seven are women.

Having reached this far I must risk boring you with my own example as I can only turn to my own experience to illustrate the path taken by a film director searching for her own language. I will do this without embarrassment because as women we know how crucial our private lives are so that we can tear off the veil of ignorance and mystery that covers us. Silenced womanhood must not be seen as part of the masculine mainstream of life, but as a duality.

I used to question why women did not get involved in public life until I realised that I myself was a 'woman' and that if I wanted somehow to change patriarchal life I should take the plunge and do something to make myself anew. It was up to me 'to live my ideas' as Malraux demanded. To live my ideas meant breaking the evil spell of female isolation and working in solidarity with other women. I knew how difficult this decision would be, not only because feminine creation is always resisted, but especially because in such a moment of intense politicisation in my country, and coming from the upper class, I would only attract criticism and spite.

As a girl I entranced my audience of brothers and sisters by telling them stories. My stories, my puppet shows and improvisations held them in suspense. Imagination and fantasy helped me escape a stupid, repressive education. As an adult, I chose to make films because my way of understanding and expressing the world was predominantly visual.

Good luck and fortune ensured that certain things were made easier. However, this ease did not solve the real creative problems. I did not want to increase what Simone de Beauvoir rightly called a woman's 'mystified consciousness'. The point was to work, without complaining, from the specific situation in which I found myself: with my precarious, fragmented identity, living in a city without an artistic tradition that I could rely on, lacking in local colour because it had all the colours, in the midst of political and economic crises, and an almost permanent censorship, and angry at the way I, and all women, had been manipulated.

What I wanted to do with cinema was to suggest the possibility of a different and better reality. You could object to this by saying that art is not pedagogical, that to paraphrase Gide, worthy feelings do not make great art. I would partially agree but I think that some didactic elements contribute to the totality of art. This is my view, as women tend to write while men categorise and divide.

The best way to develop my aesthetic ideas was to listen to my own perceptions; they would also tell me what way to express them. I have never doubted that my gaze understands and synthesises reality. The continuous taking-into-consideration of the outer world would integrate with all my characters. The ages it took me in reaching this position would appear transformed into an absence of an omnipotent ego between my camera and what I shoot. A respect for others; letting my characters act according to their own truth. The lack of horizons imposed on me by my education would become a new way of organising inner and outer space.

And how could I ever forget the rhythm of the age we live in and that matures us?; the time spent waiting for love to happen, waiting for a child to be born, for death to reach us and also all the precious time I wasted . . .?

Then there are also the tough moral commitments: to avoid prolonging the moulds of sweet, corrupt and complacent female characters. I wanted to do away with all stereotypes. Using aspects of identity forged by male appropriation, I wanted to create more daring, imaginative, free and exemplary women.

To direct a film is not easy. Making films – the verb to 'make' reveals how this is a process of multiple production – means using diverse resources. Getting large groups of people to collaborate demands particular psychological talents, like those of a captain on the bridge and nothing is more remote from a girl's education than giving orders on a captain's bridge!

In contrast to literature or painting, making films is a schizophrenic experience in many ways. Given that it is based on team work, it is not accompanied by that 'sweet silence' referred to by Sor Juana.

One has to have talent for working within union timetables. There is no pause for inspiration, nor for those basic doubts that all artists have. There is no way to control your own internal *tempo*.

Nothing can be left to the creative freedom of the moment. Every detail has to be planned out in advance, calculated and ordered day by day. The only unpredictable aspect allowed during filming is whether it rains or not. Then, instead of filming outdoors, you film indoors, on the same schedule. Obviously, some people try to film at their own pace, changing the dialogues or situation but these few find it hard to get a producer for their next film. This leads to the worst kind of censorship, the kind a creator employs on him or herself.

Lastly, a film-maker is not judged as much for his or her talent as for his or her success. A classic American saying is 'you're as good as your last movie'.

For a *cinéma d'auteur*, the first filming of a film takes place on a typewriter. In this sense my first experience in cinema was scriptwriting. Once I had written the scripts, for those reasons that turn women into cowards when they try to reveal themselves, I handed them over to male directors.

Reinterpreted from a man's angle, my female characters were mutilated and my ideas about rebellion turned into political ideologies so I decided that I had to stand behind a camera in order to be true to my own script. If the task of the artist is to make his world credible, it is also true to say that life's values permeate fiction. As Virginia Woolf said, a novel that deals with an important theme like 'war' makes the work seem important, even if is poorly treated. Put another way, if a work deals with apparently trivial themes, the work is deemed trivial. War, sex, money, power, violence and certain pseudo-metaphysical conflicts seem to be more prestigious compared with themes that derive from a more intimate, less spectacular and usually feminine world.

There is a common thread to all my transgressing characters: they never give up, whatever the opposition, however seductive they are. There is an ethic of reconciliation and silent courage, of passive resistance, of care, another rhythm of breathing and loving. These qualities can be found above all other women in Sor Juana, a nun from Mexico, who I hope will be the central character in my next film.

I am very grateful to Octavio Paz for his wonderful book on Sor Juana for it allowed me to explore her complex personality. Sor Juana, beloved poet, critic of her times, a talented, perhaps genial, dissident. Anticipating Virginia Woolf by 300 years, she entered a convent in order to find a 'room of her own'.

The cinema and other media of mass communication have presented us with a new sensibility to capture reality and get to know ourselves and other women – the new women – no longer fixing their eyes on domestic issues but on all life, have brought for our times, a *'frisson nouveau'*.

As creative women we want an art that includes all existence, desire and dreams – an art that no longer excludes and marginalises, that leads us into the centre where difference is abolished to reveal a dazzling and new humanity.

This chapter was translated by Jason Wilson.

María Luisa Bemberg read her paper at a symposium held at Leeds Castle, May 1989, organised by Silvia de Condylis. Octavio Paz was among those participating.

CONTRIBUTORS

Rosa Bosch is a Spanish critic and film producer with widespread experience in Latin America. She produced the *Buena Vista Social Club* and is a founder member of the US-Mexican production company, The Tequila Gang.

Julie Christie is an Oscar-winning film actress who starred in such films as *Darling*, *Doctor Zhivago*, *Far From the Madding Crowd*, *McCabe and Mrs Miller*, *Don't Look Now* and *Shampoo* as well as many non-Hollywood films.

Jorge Goldenberg is one of Latin America's leading screenwriters. He worked on *Miss Mary* and *De eso no se habla*.

Mercedes García Guevara worked as an assistant on *De eso no se habla*. She directed her own first feature film, *Rio escondido*, in 1999.

Catherine Grant lectures in Film Studies at the University of Kent. She is currently researching the history of concepts and practices of film authorship, and questions of transnational cinema, particularly in Latin America and Europe. She has published widely on cinema, culture and feminist theory and was guest editor of a special Latin American issue of *Screen*.

Elia Geoffrey Kantaris is a lecturer in Latin American Culture at the University of Cambridge. His first book, *The Subversive Psyche* (Oxford University Press, 1996), was on women's narrative in the 'dirty war', and he is currently working on a book on urban cinema in Argentina, Colombia and Mexico. He has published several articles on Argentine and Colombian cinema.

John King is Professor of Latin American Cultural History at the University of Warwick. He is the author and editor of a number of books on twentieth-century Argentine and Latin American culture. A new expanded edition of his *Magical Reels: A History of Cinema in Latin America* was published by Verso in 2000.

Alejandro Maci worked as an assistant on *Yo, la peor de todas* and *De eso no se habla*. He also assisted with the script of *El impostor* which he directed after María Luisa Bemberg's death.

Gabriela Massuh is Cultural Director at the Goethe Institute in Buenos Aires. She is also a well known critic.

Félix Monti is one of Argentina's and Latin America's most distinguished cinematographers. He worked on *Yo, la peor de todas* and *De eso no se habla*.

Fiona J. Mackintosh teaches Spanish American Literature and Culture at Queen's University, Belfast. Her work focuses on contemporary Argentine women's writing, with particular reference to Luisa Valenzuela, Silvina Ocampo and Alejandra Pizarnik. She has published on Ocampo and other aspects of twentieth-century Argentine culture.

Denise Miller is currently completing a doctorate on the work of María Luisa Bemberg at the University of Warwick. She has taught literature and cultural studies in Britain, Spain and Mexico. She has a particular interest in the interrelationship between film and Spanish American and Italian literatures.

Kathleen Newman is Professor of Latin American and Spanish Film and Culture at the University of Iowa. Her work focuses on art and politics and interdisciplinary aesthetic and social theory. She is author of *La violencia del discurso: el estado autoritario y la novela política argentina*. Her current research involves Argentine silent films and early feminist movements.

Alan Pauls is an Argentine novelist, critic, and scriptwriter for film and television. His three novels have brought him international recognition and he has scripted some of the most innovative Argentine films to have appeared since the mid-1980s. He has published widely on Argentine film and popular culture and was editor of the film journal *Cine Libre*, from which his chapter in this book is taken.

Lita Stantic, an Argentine producer, set up GEA Cinematográfica, a production company, jointly with María Luisa Bemberg and produced her first five films. She directed her own first feature film, *Un muro de silencio*, in 1993.

Sheila Whitaker was for many years Head of Programming at the National Film Theatre in London and Director of the London Film Festival. She has published widely on contemporary world cinema and is co-editor of *Life and Art: The New Iranian Cinema* (1999).

Jason Wilson is Professor of Latin American Literature and Culture at University College London. He has published two books on the Mexican poet Octavio Paz and numerous articles on Spanish American poetry and fiction with a particular interest in surrealism. His most recently published books focus on the city of Buenos Aires and travel writers in Latin America.

INDEX

CRITICAL STUDIES IN LATIN AMERICAN AND IBERIAN CULTURES

SERIES EDITORS

James Dunkerley
John King